APOCALYPTIC TREMORS

Study the Revelation Like Never Before

C.R. CHAPMAN

WestBow
PRESS
A DIVISION OF THOMAS NELSON

ISBN: 978-1-4497-1960-9 (e)
ISBN: 978-1-4497-1961-6 (sc)

Library of Congress Control Number: 2011932415

WestBow Press books may be ordered through booksellers or by contacting:

WestBow Press
A Division of Thomas Nelson
1663 Liberty Drive
Bloomington, IN 47403
www.westbowpress.com
1-(866) 928-1240

Printed in the United States of America

WestBow Press rev. date: 7/27/2011

CONTENTS

Preface xi

Part A: The Introduction

1. Apocalypse of Jesus Christ   3
    A. Purposes of this Book..4
    B. My Basis of Interpretation...5
    Chart 1A: The Book of Revelation 8

2. Understanding Tribulation   9
    A. The Meaning of Tribulation 9
    B. Duration of the Tribulation 13
    C. Tribulation and Persecution 14
    D. Tribulation and the Wrath of God 16
    E. Sequence of Tribulation 16
    F. World-Wide Tribulation 17
            Events Comparison Table 19

Part B: Need for Justice

3. The Cry for Justice   23
    A. The Need for Vengeance 23
    B. The Martyr's Cry for Vengeance 24
    C. The Purposes of Justice 25
    D. Justice as Fulfillment of Prophecy 27
    E. Justice as Fulfillment of Promise... 28
    F. Justice and the Nature of God 28

4. Images of the Seal Period   31
    A. Justice and the Throne of Heaven 31
    B. Justice and the Rainbow... 33
    C. Justice and the Scroll... 34
    D. Images upon the Seals: 36

Chart 4B: Who Is Worthy to Open the Scroll? 39

Chart 4C: The Seals of the Scroll 40

Chart 4D: Scroll and Seven Seals 41

5. The Great Falling Away   43

A. The Seven Churches of the Apocalypse 43

B. The Church and the Great Falling Away 45

C. The Church of the Seven Seals 46

6. Four Horsemen of the Apocalypse   49

A. The First Seal: The Lion-like Beast and White Horse 49

B. The Second Seal: Calf-like Beast & Red Horse 53

C. The Third Seal: The Man-like Beast and Black Horse 56

D. The fourth Seal: The Eagle and Pale Horse 57

E. Summing up the Seal Period 58

Chart: Four Horsemen of the Apocalypse 60

Part C: Vengeance of Christ

7. Christ's Trumpet Vengeance   63

A. The Priestly Images of the Martyrs: 63

B. True And False Worshippers 65

C. Vengeance for the Persecuted Church 67

8. Christ's Trumpet Warnings   71

A. Warning Signs in the Heavens 71

B. Destruction in Thirds 73

C. Trumpets Warn and Announce 73

D. The Warning of the Two Witnesses: 74

E. Warnings of the Future Prophet John 78

Part D: Conflict of the Kingdoms Heavens are Purged

9. The Two Woes of Ironic Justice   81

A. Demonic Locusts: Trumpet 5, ... 82

B. Demonic Horses: Trumpet 6 83

Chart 9B: The Three Woes 88

Chart 9A: The Times of the Apocalypse 89

10. The Wrath of Satan   91

A. Antichrist and Mystery Babylon: 91

B. Antichrist and Israel 92

C. Antichrist and the Church 94

Chart 10A: Daniel's Seventieth Week 97

11. Reign of Antichrist   99
A. Who is The Antichrist? 99
B. Antiochus IV Ephiphanes 106
C. The Dan Connection 110
Chart 11A: Satan's Attempts to Overthrow the Kingdom 113
Chart 11B: Rise and Fall of Satan's Kingdom 114

12. Christ's Trumpet Protections   115
A. Purging of the Heavens 115
A. The Purging of Fire 116
C. Protection for the Saints 117
D. Protection for 144,000 118
E. Miracles and signs of Protection 118
F. The Wilderness Woman Protected 118
G. The Temple of God: Place of Safety 121
H. The Final Warning 121

13. The Harvest Rapture   125
A. The Time is Ripe 125
B. It's The Last Trump 126
C. There are Clouds 127
D. It's Harvest Time 127
E. Angels Are the Reapers 129
F. Jesus Appears 129
G. The Final Warning is Preached 129

Part E Kingdom's Fall And The Day of the Lord

14. The Prelude to the Day of the Lord   135
A. The Qol 135
B. Judgment.. 136
C. Wrath 137
D. Indignation 139

15. The Great Day of God Almighty   143
A. One Concluding Day of Darkness 143
B. The Battle of Armageddon 144
C. Army Tactics.. 149
D. The Army of God 150
E. The Fall of Mystery Babylon 151
F. Israel in that Day 155

    G. The Great Supper of Our God 156

Part F: All Things New: The Rewards of Justice

16. The Covenants of God are Fulfilled to Israel   **161**
    A. God's Promise 161
    B. The Land 163
    C. Jerusalem 163
    D. The People 165
    E. The Church 165
    F. The Nations 166
    G. Law and Order 166
    H. Time 167
    I. Shall Eden Be Restored? 167

17. The Covenants of God with the Church are Fulfilled   **171**

Part G: The Rapture

18. The Marriage Bonds   **177**

19. False Glimpses of a Rapture   **181**
    A. Come up Hither (pre-tribulation view) 181
    B. Tribulation Martyrs 183
    C. Two Witnesses Raised 184
    D. Rapture of 144,000 184
    E. The Spirit Departure 185

20. Day of the Lord or the Day of Christ   **187**
    A. Day of Christ 187
    B. Day of the Lord 189
    C. The Second Coming 194
    ChartA: 1 Thessalonians 2:3 196

21. Why the Church Must Go through Tribulation   **197**
    A. Persecution And Revenge 197
    B. Testimony to God's Righteousness 198
    C. The Purging of A Persecuted Church 199
    D. The Glory of Tribulation 201

Chapter 22: Further Evidence that the Church Will Go Through the Tribulation   **203**
    A. Evidence From Daniel 203

B. Evidence from Matthew...204

C. Evidence from Thessalonians...205

23. Why I Don't Believe in a Pre-wrath Rapture But the Harvest Rapture **209**

24. A Conclusion: What Must We Do? **211**

Appendix 1: The Early Church Fathers Speak..213

Appendix 2: Extra Charts...219

Endnotes..237

PREFACE

Eschatology should be examined and preached with great fervency, for the whole world is expecting a doom's day. I enjoy prophecy and I yearn for Christ's appearance and return.

His Word is our endowment to search out and to understand. Divine understanding is at our disposal that the eyes of our understanding would be enlightened and then the scriptures must be scrutinized and re-scrutinized for the truth with divine understanding. As we examine scripture, judge and discern for the truth.

For many years when I was homebound caring for my disabled mother and sister, I studied the book of Revelation and related passages for years seeking for the truth of the end-times. I put aside books by other authors and just studied the Word. As I studied the Word, two factors became important during my study. The scriptures clearly taught me that first, the Rapture is at the last trumpet or the seventh trumpet and second, while other scholars find escape from the tribulation, I find hope.

I also see that there is great hope and victory during the tribulation. The book of Revelation depicts gloom and doom for the world, but victory after victory for the believer and for righteousness as Christ prepares to set up His kingdom. A revelation of Jesus Christ is glorious for the believer, yet sorrowful for the unbeliever.

I write not with a purpose to destroy other views, but to clearly explain what I see when the scriptures only are opened before me. I do not claim to have all prophetic truth. I do not claim to be right and everyone else, wrong. What is not documented is usually my own opinion, deduction, and observations from scripture. We all need honest judging and discernment. No teaching is of private interpretation. However, what I say is important.

Scripture references should be read to understand clearly and better what I am saying. Yes, there are many scripture references. A book that does not refer to scripture is only supposition.

For colour graphics and charts for study and more ideas, and to ask questions and read more eschatology go to: **www. apocalyptictremors .com**

The Spirit said to John, *"Come and see."*

The Spirit today is summoning the church to *"Come and see."*

Study and teach the Revelation like never before.

I am a qualified school teacher and I have a master's degree from a theological seminary. I have studied the Word of God since a child, firstly with my father, secondly in five years of schooling, and now on my own. I have taught the Word of God to adults, children, and youth in a school, in a Bible school, in Sunday school, on my web page, and when preaching. For many years I studied the Revelation on my own apart from my schooling. I love prophecy and I love to teach it. Carolyn Ruth (Rumball) Chapman M.A.

PART A:

THE INTRODUCTION

Chapters 1 and 2

1. Apocalypse of Jesus Christ

Prophecy and the book of Revelation is the most intriguing study of the Bible; yet, it is the most controversial and mysterious study. Is it a mystery incomplete or is the mystery unfolding before our blinded eyes? The earth shakes and the seas rise. The tremors of our age cannot be ignored. Has the end-time tribulation made her entrance upon the stage of our sinful world?

This book was written to enable you to study the Revelation as never before with joy and not fear. Have you wondered what all the strange images of the Apocalypse represent? As we use scripture to unfold the meanings of biblical images, an enlightening story will be revealed, and you will realize that every vision of John was given with great purpose.

Have you wondered why God ends this age with such disaster? Is disaster a stepping- stone to millennial and eternal peace? The eschatological future is not only filled with destruction, but bursting with hope one miracle of God after another for the people of God, whether Jew or Gentile. Rejoice with the saints of the Revelation as each miracle occurs, for this revelation of Jesus Christ is truly a revelation of magnificent glory.

Are you puzzled as to when the rapture occurs? This book gives at least twenty reasons against a pre-tribulation rapture. The church will go through the tribulation of the seals and the trumpet but the church will be raptured when Jesus appears for the saints just before the vials of God's wrath are poured out.

Have you considered God as unjust? Just as injustice has prevailed at the hands of evil man, true justice shall be demonstrated in the apocalypse. Divine recompense of reward shall be measured out for evil and good, for faith or unbelief, just as God promised from the beginning of time.

Do you focus upon who is the Antichrist or upon the one who gives power to be an overcomer? The role of kings, political leaders, religious leaders, Christians, Jews, the evil man, demonic spirits, angels of heaven and hell, New Agers, the Arab nations, and the Antichrist himself are dynamic dimensions of eschatology. The greater dynamic of eschatology is the power of God manifested through every believer.

John had been exiled to the Island of Patmos when the prophetic visions appeared to him. This was surely no treatment for a prophet, but this was nothing new for a true prophet of the Lord. John considered himself a "brother and companion in tribulation" (Rev.1:9). He was a companion to many Christians of his day who were suffering severe persecution, most probably under the cruel Roman rule of Domitian at the close of the first century. He is a companion in tribulation to the millions of Christians of our generation who have been martyred for their faith, and a companion to those who shall be martyred during the final days of tribulation.

In addition to calling himself a brother and companion to other believers in tribulation, John also called himself a servant of the Lord God. Indeed he was faithful to bestow to the church all that the angel revealed to him. He revealed the end-time story of our age as it exists today. He revealed what will come to pass at the end of time. John was, therefore, both a servant, and a faithful prophet of the Lord.

In Revelation 1:1, John said that his writing was an apocalypse of Jesus Christ. "*Apocalypse*" was a common word in the Greek world. It meant to unveil, reveal, uncover, and disclose.[1] Within the religious world of Christianity, as well as in the Greek religions, --of mysticism, and Gnosticism, the word "*apocalypse*" included the idea of *revelation*[2] from a god or God. The book of Revelation is about Christ, the true God, and we shall see how the Revelation is a new Revelation of the Son.

In the first chapter of Revelation, Christ is described as the Faithful Witness, the First Begotten of the dead, and the Prince of the Kings of the earth. He is the saving one who has washed us from our sins. He is our High Priest who has made us kings and priests. His kingdom is everlasting. He is the Alpha and Omega, the beginning and the end. He's the eternal one. He is alive forever more. He is the Almighty. This was not a new revelation of the Christ; but to those who are in tribulation, these words are comforting. However, never before in the Bible is Jesus portrayed with such clarity as the judge of the whole earth as in Revelation.

Apocalyptic Tremors explains how the Apocalypse is also a revelation of triple wrath -- the wrath of man as seen in the terrors of the seal period, the wrath of Satan as seen in the woes of the trumpets, and the wrath of God as seen in the seven bowls of God's wrath.

While the Apocalypse is also a revelation of the justice and judgments of God, the need for justice calls Christ to be judge of all people. During this time, heaven shakes the earth with true justice. At the same time, heaven rewards the righteous believer.

A. Purposes of this Book

1. May you see and understand the Revelation of Christ as judge of all the earth. Justice and judgment becomes necessary to purge all evil and wickedness.

2. May you see and understand the glory of tribulation. God has a beautiful plan throughout end-time disasters. Not everything is gloom and doom. The process brings complete victory for the believer and the defeat of all that is evil. May you see and understand the glorious victory that Christ wins over Satan during the tribulation and wrath of God. God is on the throne of heaven.

3. May you see and understand that tribulation and the wrath of God establishes the throne of righteousness. Men and nations learn to worship the God of Heaven and Earth, the God of Abraham, the God of David, and the God of our Lord Jesus Christ.

4. May you see and understand the Harvest Rapture. Although the church goes through the tribulation of the seals and trumpets, victory awaits in eternity. I grew up with the belief of a pre-tribulation rapture but after intense study, I have changed. Don't be offended if you believe differently. I don't want church members to be deceived or fall away from the truth because they have found themselves in the tribulation when they were told differently.

B. My Basis of Interpretation

Some prophecy teachers base their eschatology upon historic events; others see in the Apocalypse political intrigue; and others focus upon earthly happenings whether signs in the heaven, wars, changes in nations, or changes in the church. For me, the spiritual battles of the Apocalypse are far more important than earthly wars. John's revelation has a deep spiritual purpose, rather than just political-war intrigues. God's justice brings hope, but war and demonic struggles bring horror. Focusing upon the justice of God is more important than understanding symbolism and war intrigues.

Time and events change too quickly to use events to interpret prophecy; therefore, I have used scripture to interpret eschatological scripture and the many images of the Revelation. I ask myself the following questions.

*   How has God dealt with this type of situation before?
*   How have these same images been used before in scripture?
*   What do I know about God from scripture that helps me interpret the book of Revelation?

The Old and New Testaments give us a clear understanding of what God is like. His immutable character is an unambiguous guide to interpreting the prophecy of John. He shall never act contrary to His character. A theology of God and Christ based upon scripture cannot be ignored.

John the apostle had excellent knowledge of Old Testament scriptures. Swete refers to the appendix of Westcott and Hort when he writes: "It appears that of the 404 verses of the Apocalypse there are 278 which contain references to the Jewish Scriptures."[3] The Old Testament is very important in interpreting the Apocalypse and its many symbols. The Apocalypse is the completion of every Old Testament prophecy and promise to the people of God.

I take every word as literally as I can and use logic to sort out the uncertain. God is not illogical and he provides us three great resources to interpret scripture – Scripture itself, the brains to use logic, and the Holy Spirit to guide us and teach us.

A fundamental theological exegetical approach is necessary to interpret the book of Revelation. The context, repetitious words, comparisons, parallel passages, grammar, and word exegesis are used as much as possible.

Foundational Biblical Truths

There are several biblical truths that lay a foundation for understanding this interpretation of the Apocalypse. I firmly believe in the inerrancy of God's Word. Every word of the Bible is divinely inspired by God and the Revelation was given to his prophet John. Satan is real and the Antichrist is a real person. The rapture and resurrection, which is a single event, is a pre-millennial belief. It happens at the seventh trumpet just before the literal reign of Christ during the millennium.

Dispensationalism is biblical truth applicable to the Apocalypse in that the age of grace continues until the Rapture. Then shortly after the millennial dispensation begins, the church age continues until the end of the seventh trumpet. The promises of God to Israel and the Jews are a reality for the Jews and no displacement theology can claim the Jewish inheritance and promise concerning the land, its people, and its kingship.

History follows biblical truth and evidence. History is examined and applied to Old Testament text to determine what has not come to pass and what prophecies can be merged with the Apocalypse. My interpretation of prophecy is not in the light of past or present-day history, but in the light of Old Testament and New Testament theology and facts.

The Apocalypse has yet to be fulfilled. However, we can question whether we have entered the seal period of John's Apocalypse.

Take a look at Old Testament prophecies that were fulfilled with Jesus Christ. They are clear to us now, but how many people actually understood the mission of Christ when He came into the world as a babe in a manger. Anna the prophetess who spent all her time in the temple praying and seeking God knew who Jesus was when He entered the temple. Simeon the priest knew that He would see the Christ before he died. John the Baptist knew that he was preparing the way for the Christ. The apostles themselves misunderstood His mission until after the resurrection. Not many interpreted the Old Testament prophecy accurately. They had it all wrong about Christ. If the Old Testament prophets had understood their own prophetic words, the message of Jesus would have been easier to understand for the people of Jesus' day. Prophecy remains a mystery. End-times shall be understood as truth by the "in Christ believer" when it happens.

I use scripture to interpret truth to the best of my ability. I examine every word carefully, but I still end up with an interpretation. Interpretation and examination of prophetic truth does not always equal truth. We must be discerning always.

What is John the prophet really saying? I believe that John did not have 100 percent understanding of what he wrote. He did not have a complete understanding of the visions he saw. Neither shall we have a complete understanding of future events until they actually come to pass.

Prophetic Symbolism

Prophetic symbolism makes it impossible to understand the Apocalypse in its entirety. John's Apocalypse is full of symbolism and the angel never told John the meaning of most symbols. In Revelation 1:20, the angel does explain the symbolism of the stars and the lamp stands. The seven stars are the angels of the seven churches, and the seven lampstands are the seven churches. We know by association that the Beast is the Antichrist, but there are many symbols used that are not identified in the prophecy itself.

When we compare the prophetic symbolism of Daniel and Zechariah to Revelation, we see an important difference. Gabriel came in Daniel 8 and explained that the ram with two horns was the Media and Persian empires, that the male goat was the Grecian empire, and that the vision referred to the time of the end. The angel of Zechariah's visions often explains the meaning of his visions. For example: The horses among the myrtle trees were those whom the Lord had sent to walk to and fro throughout the earth. Prophecy can be interpreted with much more accuracy when the angel explains the images. But that is not the case with much of John's visions. Until an angel comes and interprets the visions of John, we cannot interpret with total accuracy. Nevertheless, I have attempted to give the symbols of Revelation meaning and understanding by comparing the symbols with similar symbols throughout scripture, but prophecy can never be of private interpretation (2 Peter 1:20). No one person can claim the truth of scripture but there should be some consensus within the church.

It is time to study the Revelation as never before. Study the chart "Book of Revelation" on the next page to have a clear map in your mind of where we are heading. Notice what I call the "wrath of man", the "wrath of Satan", the "wrath of God", and the "vengeance of Christ". Please read the scripture to better understand.

Book of Revelation

Wrath of Man upon Man	S E A L S	1. Conquer 2. No peace, sword 3. Famine 4. Death 5. Persecution 6. Cosmic Eruptions 7. Silence	1st Throne Scene 4 beasts hurt the earth Sealing of 144,00 2nd Throne Scene
Vengeance of Christ	T R	1. Hail, fire 2. Sea to blood 3. Wormwood 4. Sun Smitten	Angels Hurt the Earth

Wrath of Satan Upon Man	U M P E T S	5. 1st woe: 5 months
		  plague of locust
		6. 2nd woe: 3 yrs. 1 month
		  Spirits in Euphrates
		  Seven Thunders
		  Little Book
		Two Witnesses killed
		      and resurrected
		
		7. Prophetic voices
		  3rd Woe
		  Dragon and Two beasts
		      144.000 raptured
		Abomination of Desolation
		Everlasting gospel
		Mark of the Best
		  Harvest Rapture
		Wheat Gathered
		Grapes cast into the Vials of God's Wrath
			3 1/2 Years — Battle in Euphrates
			3rd Throne Scene
			Battle in the City
			
			3/12 Years — War in Heaven
			Satan Cast down
			Abomination of Desolation
			
			4th Throne Scene
			
			5th to 7th Throne Scenes

Wrath of God upon Man	V I A L S	1. Grievous Sores 2. Sea to Blood 3. Rivers to blood 4. Sun Scorches men 5. Beast's Kingdom, Darkness & Pain 6. Wuphrates Drys up 7. Armageddon C. R. Chapman	**45 Days** — Wine Press Battle outside the City Second Coming & Day of the Lord End of 1st Resirrection

2. Understanding Tribulation

A. The Meaning of Tribulation

When a person uses the word *tribulation* referring to the last days, you are not sure what he has included in his definition; therefore, the meaning of tribulation must be defined from scripture. Various contemporary opinions define the tribulation differently. Some start the tribulation with the first seal and continue to the seventh vial. Some overlap the seals and the trumpets thus defining the tribulation differently. I see two periods of tribulation and define the wrath of God separately.

How we define tribulation determines our view of the rapture, Christ's purposes for the tribulation, and our understanding of the judgment and justice of God. According to the Bible, tribulation in scripture can mean oppression, affliction, pressure, distress, and persecution; therefore, what may be included in the term tribulation?

1. Tribulation: A Time of Joy

Tribulation is a time of joy and victory for the Christian. It is not a time of defeat. Our attitude in tribulation is to be one of joy. Paul wrote, "I am exceeding joyful in all our tribulation" (2 Corinthians 7:4). We are admonished to glory in tribulation (Romans. 5:3), not fear or fret. American society with its abundant affluence does not know the victories of tribulation. The God who gives in abundance is the same God who can bring victories and greater victories in the midst of tribulation.

2. Tribulation: Associated with the Church

Throughout the Old Testament and the New Testament, tribulation was the portion of the people of God. Is it wrong to associate the final tribulation of the apocalypse with the people of God and with the church? No! For the sake of the elect, these times will be shortened (Matthew 24:22). Therefore, this documentation on the Revelation follows the belief that the Rapture of the church will be at the last trumpet and that the church will go through the seal and trumpet periods of tribulation, but the victories during tribulation will receive attention showing that God is just.

In fact, only two times in the whole New Testament does tribulation not refer to the church. In Romans 2:9, tribulation accompanies the wrath of God upon the evil man and in 2 Thessalonians 1:6, God recompenses tribulation to them that trouble the church.

> *Tribulation and anguish, on every soul of man who does evil, of the Jew first and also of the Greek; … since it is a righteous thing with God to repay with tribulation those who trouble you (2 Thess.1:6).*

Tribulation can be ascribed to the saints because tribulation is the natural course of this life, and shall be for all peoples at the end of time. "Then shall they deliver you up to tribulation (thlipsis, Greek) and kill you, and you will be hated by all nations for my name's sake" (Matthew 24:9).

Although tribulation is the natural course of this life, Christ has given us the power to overcome. For Christ's sake we can endure persecution and tribulation, but for one's own sake, many view the rapture as an escape from all tribulation. It is the wrath of God that the believer shall escape, not tribulation. "God did not appoint us to wrath [orgé, Greek], but to obtain salvation through our Lord Jesus Christ" (Matthew. 24:9). Christ's alternative is: 'salvation or wrath', not 'salvation or no tribulation" (1Thessalonians. 5:9).

The Revelation assigns tribulation to the people of God. The word *tribulation (thlipsis)* is used five times in the book of Revelation. With all five occurrences there is reference to the people of God, the saints. Four times it refers to the churches of the Apocalypse. Never does *tribulation* in the book of Revelation refer to the punishment of the wicked.

3. Tribulation: A Time of Testing

Tribulation is a time of testing. In the parable of the sower, the circumstances that hindered the growth of the seeds symbolically represented forces of tribulation and persecution that could hinder the growth of faith in the heart of a man (Matthew 13:3). There was the dryness of the soil, the rocky soil, and the birds of the air that robbed the seed so that it could not mature. Only the well-nurtured seed survived. In the tribulation of the last days also, it will be the steadfast believer, the Word-believing Christian, and the man of faith and prayer who will be the overcomer. The Shepherd of Hermas explains a falling away from the faith during the tribulation as follows:

> *When tribulation cometh, they deny their Lord by reason of their riches and their business affairs.* [1] *… For as their grass was withered up when it saw the sun, so also the double-minded, when they hear of tribulation, through their cowardice worship idols and are ashamed of the name of their Lord.* [2]

How many believers in the end time tribulation shall slip from the faith for these same reasons?

4. Tribulation: Time of Persecution

Tribulation can imply persecution. As a result of Stephen's martyrdom, the church was scattered because of tribulation (in Greek, thlipsis) or persecution that occurred (Acts 11:19,20). Paul endured such tribulation (thlipsis) or persecution in Asia Minor so that he was "despaired even unto death. He was pressed out of measure above strength" (2 Corinthians. 1:8). In such tribulation, Paul learned to trust God to deliver Him by giving him strength to overcome, not by means of escape. The Latin root of tribulation is *tribalum*, meaning a threshing sledge. The action of the threshing sledge separated the wheat from the tares. The threshing sledge of end-time persecution will separate the righteous from the evil man, the believer from the unbeliever. God is just in His action of the threshing sledge.

The Old Testament is not silent about tribulation meaning persecution. One hundred and fourteen verses in the Old Testament Septuagint and Apocrypha use the word *thlipsis*, being translated as besieged, distress, straightness, trouble, enemy, calamity, or vexed. Often tribulation was the destiny of the Children of Israel as a natural outcome of sin.

It is apparent that tribulation in the Old Testament also has an association with an enemy or an adversary which was great tribulation. The enemy caused distress (Deuteronomy 28:53). Nehemiah wrote of distress or tribulation at the hands of the Persians (Nehemiah 9:37). David found that God would deliver him in the time of tribulation from the hand of the wicked (Psalms 37:39-40). David met with tribulation because of the oppression that the enemy was deliberating. The enemies' hatred brought forth wrath (Psalms 55:2, 3). David cried unto the Lord for mercy in the day of tribulation (trouble). "Cut off my enemies, and destroy all those who afflict my soul ... (Psalms 143:11,12). The word for *trouble* and *afflict my soul* used in these verses, comes from the same root (θλιψις, thlipsis). The Greek Septuagint text of the Old Testament also uses thlipsis (θλιψις) in each of the above verses. When God chose to bring judgment upon the children of Israel, it was often at the hand of the enemy - the Egyptians, the Syrians, or the Babylonians.

Is shall happen like this again. Great and powerful will be our adversaries at the end time. The believer's adversaries during the seal period will be the nations of the world. The believer shall be hated of all nations (Matthew 24:9). All testimonies for the Lord Jesus Christ will breed contemptuous adversaries from among our friends, relatives, and neighbors. Satan, our greatest adversary, shall be cast out of heaven and he shall destroy man with great wrath during the trumpets (Rev. 13:7). The False Prophet and the Antichrist shall join the devil as adversaries of the faithful in Christ Jesus because their allegiance is to Satan. Jews and Christians usually have the same adversary.

During the seals, tribulation is administered by the hands of wicked men who are pictured as riding upon horses. During the trumpets, Christ's judgment is administered by the adversary the devil: his host of demons, the False Prophet and the Antichrist. It is Satan who leads man into temptation, into deception, and into apostasy (Rev. 2:10). Although we may have many adversaries, it is essential to remember that God is not the adversary of the faithful. Those who endure end-time tribulation would be devastated without a strong faith in God and without the knowledge that God is not our adversary but our deliverer.

5. Tribulation: Time for Punishment

Tribulation is the result of a world or nation turning away from God. Tribulation is a natural result of sinfulness. God's people of the Old Testament faced bondage in Babylon because of their failure to worship God in obedience. Man asks for tribulation when he ignores the laws of God and ignores God. "Then when desire has conceived, it gives birth to sin; and sin, when it is full-grown, brings forth death" (James 1:15).

6. Tribulation: An Appointed Time

The prophets proclaimed that Christ would come at an appointed time in Christ's calendar. Daniel wrote: "Look I am making known to you what shall happen in the latter time of the indignation; for at the appointed time the end shall be" (Daniel 8:19). God's appointed time occurs when He can no longer ignore sin. Christ's calendar is closed when transgressors have reached their fullness, when sin has reached the deepest degradation, and when the wickedness of man has been wrenched to its limit.

Has not God also appointed the seventh millennium as a day of rest? God created the earth in six days and rested on the Sabbath; therefore, the seventh thousandth year of history is considered the millennium of Christ's rest. Four thousand years of history elapsed before the time of Christ's birth. Now we are soon to enter the seventh-thousandth year of history. Many early church fathers believed that the reign of Antichrist and the second coming of Christ would concur at the end of the sixth-thousandth year (see Appendix 1).

7. Tribulation and Then Time of Deliverance

God shall deliver his people from tribulation, but this deliverance is not as some saints expect it to be. In this life we shall have tribulation, but in our eternal home, Christ shall wipe away all tears from our eyes and there will be no more tribulation. There are numerous tribulation martyrs, but their victory songs are sung in the presence of God for eternity. Each overcomer inherits eternal life (Rev. 2:7).

Daniel was promised that in the time of great tribulation, his people would find deliverance. That deliverance is to be resurrection to everlasting life but not until after the tribulation.

> "At that time Michael shall stand up, The great prince who stands watch over the sons of your people; And there shall be a time of trouble, Such as never was since there was a nation, Even to that time. And at that time your people shall be delivered, Everyone who is found written in the book. And many of those who sleep in the dust of the earth shall awake, Some to everlasting life, Some to shame and everlasting contempt (Daniel 12:1, 2).

Daniel was also delivered from the lion's den but after he was cast into the den of lions. The Israelites were delivered from Egypt after four hundred years of bondage. We have been delivered from the power of Satan, but the struggle is rough. Christ's deliverance is not always immediate. Jeremiah was promised that his enemies would not overcome him. Jehovah promised him deliverance (Jeremiah 1:19), but when we examine Jeremiah's life, we see that he endured many tribulations and imprisonments. We must carefully examine the context of scripture to determine what God means by the word *deliverance*.

B. Duration of the Tribulation

There is no verse in scripture that defines the duration of end-time tribulation. It could be seven years or thirty years or more. The Bible does not declare that the tribulation of the end times is seven years long. The seventh week of Daniel is seven years but the abomination of desolation in only 3½ years. Many often equate the two and say the abomination of desolation *is* days of great tribulation, but tribulation is never defined as the seventh week of Daniel only. The abomination of desolation is a 3½ year period and is the last half of the seventh week of Daniel, but the abomination of desolation is never equated in the Bible as *the great tribulation* but as a time of great tribulation such as never before (Matthew 24:21). As you study this book you will understand how the seventh week of Daniel is only the duration of the seven trumpets.

TRIBULATION OF THE SEAL PERIOD

Read Rev. 6, 7

The length of the seal period tribulation is not stated. We do not know how long the seal period is. In the Apocalypse, the period of the seals is an indefinite time period and is clearly referred to as *great tribulation*. The martyrs at the close of the seal period are seen about the throne of God. These martyrs are those who have come out of great tribulation, referring to the time of the seals.

> ...So he said to me, "These are the ones who come out of great tribulation, and washed their robes and made them white in the blood of the Lamb" (Rev. 7:14).

These same martyrs cry out to the Lord after the unsealing of the fifth seal. "How long, O Lord, Holy and true, dost thou not judge and avenge our blood on them that dwell on the earth? (Rev. 6:10) John identifies the seal period as *great tribulation*; yet, the martyrs will have not as yet witnessed the revenge of God upon the unbeliever. Therefore, the church must go through the great tribulation of the seal period.

It is important to note that John does not employ the word *tribulation* after the seventh chapter of Revelation or after the sixth seal. Note that the word *judgment* seems to replace the word tribulation and God is not out to bring judgment to the saints. Could this infer that during the trumpets, God passes judgment and protects the saints? God is just.

Christ's Vengeance: Trumpets 1-4:

At the beginning of the first four trumpets, the Antichrist makes a treaty with Israel and therefore during this time there is relative peace for Israel for 3 ½ years. At the same time, Christ's vengeance is pronounced upon the earth and seas. Most tribulation during this period of time is upon the enemy of the Jews (see chapter 7).

Tribulation: Wrath of Satan: Trumpets 5 to 7

Rev. 9-13

During trumpet 7, the Antichrist rules with evil intent called the *third woe* and the *wrath of Satan*. Heaven warns the earth that Satan has fallen and to beware of the *woes*. Under the Antichrist, man suffers great persecution. This is the second period of tribulation for all men especially the saints because they are severely persecuted. In a later chapter we study the details of these three woes which Matthew 24 defines as the *abomination of desolation* and as a time of tribulation like never before (see chapters 9-11).

C. Tribulation and Persecution

The First Persecution

Tribulation can imply persecution. There are two distinct periods of persecution for the church in the book of Revelation. The first revolves around the martyrs during the fifth seal and who are seen before God's throne in the second throne scene. Matthew refers to this tribulation period during the seals as that which results from lawlessness and hatred (Matthew 24:4-9).

The Second Persecution

The second persecution is administered by the Antichrist during the 7th trumpet. Men are beheaded and persecuted for not receiving the mark of the Beast (Rev.20:4). The early church fathers saw persecution under the Antichrist as the most dreadful of all persecutions (See appendix I).

Matthew also speaks of a time of great tribulation in Matthew 20:15- 28, which he identifies with the abomination of desolation. "For then there will be great tribulation, such as has not been since the beginning of the world until this time, nor ever shall be" (Matthew 20:21).

Two Periods of Persecution		
Persecution by Apostate Forces	Matthew 24: 9-12 Hated by all nations	Revelation 6:9-11 Souls slain for the word of God and for the testimony they had
Under Antichrist	Matthew 24:15-28 Abomination of Desolation	Revelation 12:11 And they overcame him by the blood of the Lamb ...loved not their lives to the death.

The abomination of desolation always refers to the desecration of the temple and to the rule of the Antichrist in the land of Israel. The abomination of desolation is not until the seventh trumpet (Matthew 24:29).

Matthew also tells us that the tribulation of those days ends with great signs in the heavens. "The sun will be darkened, and the moon shall not give her light, and the stars shall fall from heaven, and the powers of the heavens shall be shaken" (Matt. 24:28). When shall this be?

WHEN ARE GREAT SIGNS IN THE HEAVENS?

At the close of the sixth seal, there is a great earthquake that shakes every mountain and island out of their place. The sun becomes black and the moon becomes as blood and the stars fall from heaven, but this is not the last of tribulation.

These signs in the heavens continue to occur during the trumpets. Great stars continue to fall during the time of the trumpets. The star Wormwood falls to the earth (Rev. 8:10). At the fourth trumpet one third of the sun is smitten; one third of the moon is darkened; and one-third part of the stars is darkened (Rev. 8:12). One star that is given the key to the bottomless pit falls to the earth (Rev.9:1). The smoke from the pit darkens the sun and air. The dragon is cast to the earth during the trumpets and with him one third of the stars of heaven are cast to the earth.

Matthew speaks of these similar signs in the heavens as preceding the Second Coming of the Lord. "Then the sign of the Son of Man will appear in heaven" (Matthew 24:30). This earthquake is greater than any preceding one. It shakes the cities of the world to destruction. Zion is split into three parts, every island disappears into the sea, and no mountain is found. So in the day of the Lord, we witness a greater earthquake, but John does not speak of any signs in the heavens (see chapter 15).

However, Zechariah does. Zechariah links the darkness of the earth with the day of the Lord just before Christ's return. In the day of the Lord there will be no light for a whole day. Then at night-time there is light as the heavens are lit with the coming of the King.

It shall come to pass in that day that there will be no light; the lights will diminish.

It shall be one day which is known to the Lord—Neither day nor night. But at evening time it shall happen That it will be light (Zechariah 14:6, 7).

In that day, *"it is finished"* and there is no more tribulation to the world as a whole. The tribulation of these days refers to the tribulation under the reign of the Antichrist that precedes the Second Coming.

D. Tribulation and the Wrath of God

Can we label the vials of Christ's wrath as part of the tribulation days also? Tribulation can be defined as a testing time; however, the church is raptured before the vials of Christ's wrath which are poured out upon only those who take the mark of the Beast. These men have no faith; therefore, how can their faith be tested? It is the faith of a righteous man that is tested. We also know that no man repents during the woes of the trumpets and during the vials of Christ's wrath (Rev. 9:21, 16:9, 11). The *vials of God's wrath are* a time of punishment for only those who take the mark of the Beast.

There is also no persecution of the saints during the wrath of God because they have been raptured. Therefore, it is not necessary to call the *wrath of God*, a time of tribulation when referring to the saints; but the wrath of God is a time of terrible punishment for the unrighteous sinner.

If we define the tribulation as a time of oppression, then the vials of Christ's wrath can be labeled as days of tribulation. To avoid confusion, I will define the seal period as days of tribulation under apostate forces; trumpets 5 and 6 as times of demonic oppression; trumpet 7 as days of great tribulation under the Antichrist; and define *the vials of God's wrath* as the wrath of God, and not days of tribulation. We shall also call *the wrath of God* the *wrath of Christ* because it is Christ who shall administer justice.

E. Sequence of Tribulation

Many scholars today overlap the period of the seals with the trumpet period. There are many reasons why I place the events of the trumpets sequentially after the seven seals.

1. First, there are four beasts that administer the first four seals, but angels administer the first four trumpet judgments. The administration of both is so completely different.

2. The heavenly scenes change progressively throughout the record of John. With each new heavenly scene, more classes of people are witnessed before the throne of God. Before the seal period, only twenty-four elders and four beasts sit about the throne. After the seals, the victorious martyrs who have endured great tribulation stand clothed in white garments before the throne. They are a multitude from every nation, tribe, people, and tongue (Rev. 7:9). In the sixth scene, the bride of Christ is seen preparing for the marriage supper of the Lamb. They are preparing for the Battle of Armageddon and their rule upon the earth. This gradual addition before the throne of heaven witnesses

to the fact that the new peoples before the throne have died and gone to heaven and does not convince me that there are many resurrections or raptures.

What happens at the sixth seal is different from what happens at the seventh trumpet which means that the seals do not overlap with the trumpets. At the end of the sixth seal, men are hiding in fear. They cry out, "Hide us from the face of him who sits on the throne and from the wrath of the Lamb for the great day of his wrath is come..." (Rev. 6:15-17). It is not the righteous man who would make such a cry, but the unrighteous man who fears the throne of God. The faithful Christians are the persecuted people of the seal tribulations, but are raptured people at the end of the trumpets.

3. Again we see a difference of events. At the end of the sixth trumpet; it is different. The unrighteous men are waging war against Israel and the elect are hiding. At the end of the sixth vial, the King of kings and the saints are waging spiritual warfare against the Beast. If you overlap the seals, trumpets, or the vials, the events do not interconnect.

4. The cosmic disturbances at the end of the seals differ from the cosmic disturbances at the end of the trumpets and the vials of Christ's wrath. After the seals, every island is moved out of its place. After the sixth trumpet the earthquake slays seven thousand and one tenth of the city of Jerusalem falls. But at the great day of the Lord and the Battle of Armageddon (16:20, 21) every island disappears and the mountains are not found. The final earthquake is much more severe therefore the seals, trumpets and vials occur in sequence.

5. The theme of the seals is different from the theme of the trumpets. The vision of the seals portrays many images of the church and the saints. The vision of the trumpets emphasizes the Jewish nation and the abomination of desolation under the rule of Antichrist. Therefore, the seals, trumpets, and vials occur in sequence and do not overlap.

6. The phrase *after these things* is used seven times in the book of Revelation. It is used twice after the sixth seal and before the seventh seal. *After these things*, the 144,000 are sealed (Rev.7:1). They are sealed for the period of the trumpets but not during the seal period; therefore, the seals and the trumpets could not possibly overlap in time.

F. World-Wide Tribulation

There is much proof that tribulation is worldwide. The book of Revelation continually speaks of the tribulation as worldwide. Christ says to the church of Philadelphia, "I will keep thee from the hour of temptation, which shall come upon the whole habitable world" (Rev. 3:10).

The earth is given much prominence in the book of Revelation. The word *earth* is mentioned in sixty-seven verses. A study of each verse would reinforce the belief that the tribulation of the later days is worldwide. Examine these verses.

1. The seven spirits of God were sent forth into all the earth. (Rev. 5:6).

2. Christ shall reign upon the whole earth not just a part of it (Rev. 5:10); therefore, when John speaks of the earth as the target of tribulation, he is speaking also of the same entire earth over which Christ shall reign.

3. The martyrs from the seal period were from all nations, kindred, people, and tongues (Rev. 7:9); therefore, we can come to the conclusion that the church world-wide will experience persecution.

4. John will again prophesy in those days about many nations not just Israel (Rev. 10:11). Before sending the trumpet judgments upon the earth, four angels are seen standing not in the center but on the four corners of the earth as restraining forces until the 144,000 are sealed (Rev. 7:1).

5. The whole earth wondered after the Beast (Rev.13:3).

6. Satan descends with great wrath upon the inhabitants of the whole earth (Rev. 12:12).

7. Power was given unto the Antichrist over all kindred, tongues and nations (Rev. 13:7).

8. All that dwell upon the earth shall worship the Antichrist (Rev. 13:8).

9. The last warning and preaching of the gospel is to every nation, kindred, tongue, and people (Rev. 14:6). Because the warnings are worldwide so shall the judgment be worldwide.

10. The rainbow given by God represented a covenant with all human inhabitants of the earth. The whole earth in Noah's day was covered with water, so shall the whole earth experience the fire of Christ's judgment.

11. God's promises throughout His word are accurate. He promised judgment upon the whole earth. None shall escape except the righteous.

Let all Ears Hear

There are several admonitions in the Apocalypse that place the church in the midst of tribulation. Each admonition is to the church or the believer in Christ. To the Ephesian church was the admonition to "Remember therefore from whence thou art fallen" (Rev. 2:5). To the church of Pergamos He warned: "Repent or else I will come unto thee quickly" (Rev. 2:16).

To the church of Thessalonica He said: "Hold fast till I come." The lukewarm Laodiceans were counseled to buy gold tried in the fire. To Sardis He prayed: Be watchful, and strengthen the things which remain. "Remember therefore how you received and heard the gospel" (Rev. 3:2). "Hold fast and repent. Watch or I will come as a thief" (Rev. 3:3). The Philadelphian church heard the admonition to: "Hold fast which thou hast, that no man takes thy crown" (Rev. 3:11). To the Laodiceans Christ admonished them to anoint their eyes with eye salve that they might see. Be zealous and repent. Those believers who associated with the wickedness of Babylon were warned to come out from among them. "Be not partakers of her sins" (Rev. 8:4).

Each admonition warns against an apostasy. Each admonition for repentance is directed to the church not the pagan. Each admonition casts an ugly shadow of warning before the coming tribulation and judgment. Steadfastness is encouraged that they may endure until the end. Lastly, each admonition recognizes sin that must be purged from the congregations of the churches.

An early church father, Shepherd of Hermas warned the church: "Blessed are ye, as many as endure patiently the great tribulation that cometh, and as many as shall not deny their life.[3]"

FURTHER QUESTIONS:

1. Find all references for deliverance in scripture from a Bible concordance.
2. What did deliverance mean for Shadrach, Meshach, and Abednego? (Daniel).
3. What did deliverance mean for Paul? (Romans 11:26, Philippians 1:19, Hebrews 11:35).

	Events Comparison Table		
	Seal Tribulations	**Trumpet Tribulations**	**Vials of God's Wrath**
1.	White Horse to conquer	1/3 trees & grass burn	Soars upon man
2.	Red horse takes peace away	1/3 sea turns to blood 1/3 fish die 1/3 ships destroyed	Sea becomes blood
3.	Black horse of famine	Waters become bitter	Rivers & springs become blood
4.	Pale horse of death	1/3 sun, moon is darkened	Sun scorches men
5.	Martyrs slain	1st woe: Demonic locust, 5 months	Darkness and pain
6.	Cosmic Disturbances Earthquake	2nd woe: Demonic horse plague	Three unclean spirits from Euphrates deceive kings for battle
7.	Censer from heaven filled with fire is cast down	Abomination of desolation Reign of Antichrist	Earthquake Battle of Armageddon

PART B:

NEED FOR JUSTICE

Chapters 3,4,5,6

3. The Cry for Justice

The Apocalypse is a profound revelation of Christ as judge of the whole earth. His feet were like fine brass, as if refined in a furnace, and His voice as the sound of many waters (Rev. 1:16). John fell as dead when he saw the image of the one like unto the Son of Man (Rev. 1:13-18). It was frightening to see a man with eyes as a flame of fire, with feet like burning brass, a sword proceeding from His mouth, and a countenance brighter than the brightest sun. These images alone prove that there is a need for Justice.

Don't fear, John, I am the one who lived and died. I am the one with whom you walked and talked. I am the one upon whose breast you laid your head, but now I have the keys of hell and of death. John had written in his gospel: "For God so loved the world that He gave His only begotten Son (1John 3:16)," but in Revelation, the world becomes the victim of the wrath of God by the hand of Christ. John the apostle had heard Christ speak of His first coming, when He said, "I came not to judge the world, but to save the world" (John 12:47). But in the Apocalypse, Christ's Second Coming is with fierce judgment, and everyone whose name is not written in the book of life is cast into eternal hell. John was the tender apostle who wrote: "Behold, what manner of love the Father has bestowed upon us, that we should be called the children of God (2 John 3:1); yet, in the Apocalypse, the angel of God with a sickle in his hand gathers the grapes of iniquity and they are thrust into the vials of Christ's wrath. Never before has the image of Jesus been so clearly portrayed with judgment and justice. Gentle and loving men, as was John, must now realize the character of Christ as the coming judge of the earth and of sinfulness. With this knowledge of the Word of God, we do not have to fear.

A. The Need for Vengeance

The Apocalypse depicts Christ as the Alpha. He was the one who not only created the universe in the beginning of time, but Christ is the only one who is worthy to loosen the seals allowing man to proceed with their own cruelties, wars, and murders, thus bringing this wicked world to a quick conclusion. The world gets out of control, but Christ is pictured as master of the apocalypse.

Revelation chapters 3 to 6 relate the happenings of the seal period and the wrath of man.

During the seal period of time, tribulation unveils the hearts of men as a great apostasy or falling away occurs. During the Apocalypse there is a purging and sifting of true worshippers and a disclosure of the true intents of the heart. During the Apocalypse sin becomes more sinful and righteousness becomes more righteous. Both evil and goodness blossom to maturity. Man's fruits are clearly manifested as poisonous or edible, acceptable or non-acceptable. This is the process of purging or casting out the dross. It is a time that no man shall escape. And the seal period ends with the cry of righteous men: "When oh Lord shall you judge the world?" (Rev. 6:10).

Mystical trends of religions today consider karma as a natural justice of the universal forces of nature but even the natural laws of nature are under divine authority. New Age trends spit upon the idea of judgment, considering it a negative and unnecessary ingredient of life but God will reveal in the last days that judgment is good and necessary for His judgment is just and righteous. In the last days the true church will be persecuted for claiming that Jesus is the only way. In the last days those who follow witchcraft shall avenge the Christian for their differences, for their condemnations, and for that which is against their own laws and wishes. Islam already is murdering Christians because they don't follow the laws of Islam, but Christ recompenses wrath for unrighteousness and for that which is against His law.

Vengeance and justice are necessary before the establishment of Christ's new kingdom. Sin must be punished.

Chapters three through six of *Apocalyptic Tremors* depict the need for justice upon the earth.

Chapter three examines Christ's purposes for judgment upon the world. The martyrs of the seal period cry out for the justice of God and justice is completed.

The symbols of chapter four depict the right for Christ to pour out His justice, --examining the throne scene, the rainbow about the throne, and the seven seals.

Chapter five explains the falling away in the end-times. Apostasy shall thrive. What greater reason for a need for justice in the church?

Chapter six recounts the wrath of man when the four horsemen come riding. Justice must be served to violent men. Chapter six also recounts the disasters of the four horsemen of the apocalypse. These horsemen go forth to take peace from the earth. Famine and death prevail. We shall see how these four horsemen enact the wrath of man, trampling one upon another. Then observe: Is terrorism not one of the four horsemen now riding in the earth? Is there not a need for justice?

B. The Martyr's Cry for Vengeance

Read Rev. 6

> *And they cried with a loud voice, saying: "Sovereign Lord, Holy and true, how long will it be before you judge and avenge our blood on the inhabitants of the earth? (Rev 6:10)*

The martyrs know the need for justice and vengeance. The martyrs under the fifth seal cry out to the Lord for vengeance. They seek the justice of God just as all righteous men have from the beginning of time. The righteous man seeks justice; but the unrighteous man only seeks his own justice and denies the justice of God.

The martyrs know they have a right to call for vengeance. To whom can man cry for true justice but to the God of the Bible for He is true holiness and true righteousness? He knows the heart of every man. The idea of vengeance and justice is rooted deeply within Judaism. It is a constant theme of the Old Testament. Josephus writes concerning the many times the Jews sought God to avenge them of their enemies. He writes concerning the times when God did avenge His people.

> And when the priests found they had been cheated, and that the agreements they had made were violated, they prayed God that he would avenge them on their countrymen. Nor did he delay their punishment, but sent a strong and vehement storm of wind that destroyed the fruits of the whole country.[1]

The martyrs' cry for vengeance is to their Sovereign Lord. *Lord*, in this verse means despot, not an evil, self-serving despot but a righteous, divine despot. The Jewish nation called for a despot ruler at Christ's first coming, and again in Revelation, the martyrs cry for the King of glory to reign. This time He shall be King. "Thy kingdom come," Your will be done to the unrighteous that righteous men might reign with Christ.

The martyr's cry is also to a holy and true God. Without righteousness there is no true vengeance and justice. To avenge means to redeem, to ransom, to recover, or to repay. Only Christ can redeem, ransom, or repay because he knows the hearts of all men.

Christ's vengeance is vindictiveness against the evil man for hurting the righteous and ignoring the righteousness of God. The church knows that she cannot seek vengeance for herself. "Beloved, never avenge yourselves, but leave it to the wrath of God; for it is written, "Vengeance is mine, I will repay, says the Lord" (Romans 12:19). In Revelation 6, we see the patience of the saints who wait for God to avenge them of their enemies. Vengeance brings justice when God is avenging.

Victory is for every believer who does not surrender hope in the promises of God. In the gospels we read "If even an evil judge can be worn down like that, don't you think that God will surely give justice to his people who plead with him day and night? Yes, He will answer them quickly!" (Luke 18:6-8, Living Bible). We shall see how quickly God answers the prayers of these Martyrs.

C. The Purposes of Justice

THAT MEN MIGHT KNOW THAT I AM GOD

God has a purpose in all things. Continually throughout the Old Testament, God declared His justice that men might know that He was God. The children of Israel were delivered from their enemies that they might know their God. They were delivered from Egypt and the cruel thumb of Pharaoh. "Then I will harden Pharaoh's heart, so that he will pursue them, and I will gain honor over Pharaoh and over all his army, that the Egyptians may know that I am the LORD" (Exodus 14:4).

King Ben-Hadad was delivered into the hands of Ahab that Israel might know the true God. Then a man of God came and spoke to the king of Israel, and said, "Thus says the Lord: Because the Syrians have said. "The LORD is God of the hills, but He is not God of the valleys," therefore, I will deliver all this great multitude into your hand, and you shall know that I am the Lord" (I Kings 29:29).

Hezekiah prayed and said, "Now therefore, O Lord our God, I pray, save us from (Sennacherib's) hand, that all the kingdoms of the earth may know that You are the Lord God, You alone (2 Kings 19:19).

God provided for Israel's needs even when they complained in order that they might know that He was God. He fed them manna and meat in the wilderness when there was nothing to eat (Exodus 16:12).

Judgment was also exercised against the nation that they might know that he was God. Israel was scattered among the nations of the world; they were carried captive into Babylon; and the people were slain by the sword, by famine, and by pestilence that they might know their God (Ezekiel 6:7-14). The land was desolate that they might know that He was the Lord (Ezekiel 12:20).

Judgment shall be executed in the last days for the same reason -- that man might know who God is. He is the God, who hates sin. Sin shall be cut off from the earth. Those who practice divination and commit idolatry in their heart shall be destroyed (Ezekiel 13:23, 14:7, 8). The loftiness of man that exalts the self shall bow low (Isaiah 2:15-22).

> *I will punish the world for its evil, and the wicked for their iniquity. I will halt the arrogance of the proud, and will lay low the haughtiness of the terrible. I will make a mortal more rare than fine gold, a man more than the golden wedge of Ophir (Isaiah 13:11-12).*

JUDGMENT & JUSTICE VERIFIES TRUTH

The judgment of Revelation is according to Christ's laws. Judgment will verify that there is right and wrong, in a world where man sees only his own will and his own laws, where there is no consideration of moral rights and wrongs, and where personal rights and rites replace moral rights. With a people who are mystically controlled by satanic voices, right has already become wrong (Isaiah 5:20) and both right and wrong have become a part of a "divine energy". Therefore, the judgment of God shall thunder forth to destroy man's empire of self-justifications.

1. For the atheist who believes there is no God, judgment proves that there is a God who rules and reigns from His heavenly throne.

2. For the agnostic, who believes God is unconcerned about his creation, God does not only intervene in man's affairs but He assumes control.

3. For innate godism, the belief that evil is more powerful than God, God will overcome evil.

4. For necessitarianism, the belief that evil is necessary for life, evil will be cast into hell for eternity.

5. The pantheist may deny that evil is real, but Christ's judgment will utterly destroy the wicked man.

6. For the New Age believer who sees hardships as merely the birth pains into a new era are sadly hallucinated to think that they are the survivors into a new age. God will shake the illusions of the New Ager and Christian Scientists.

7. For the belief that says God can not foresee evil, God fulfills the prophecies of Daniel and the apostle John to every minute detail. The final events of history are not mere political battles between nations but conflicts between the righteousness of God and the willfulness of man.

D. Justice as Fulfillment of Prophecy

> *"Behold, the days are coming," says the Lord, "That I will raise to David a Branch of righteousness; A King shall reign and prosper, and execute judgment and righteousness in the earth (Jeremiah 13:5).*

Prophecy will sound forth because of nations that forget the promises of God and fall into sin; yet, the apocalypse is also the fulfillment of prophecy. Messiah shall judge all the earth. God informed Jeremiah that just as a potter fashions a vessel, God is *"fashioning a disaster"* for the nations of the world" (Jeremiah 18:11). The bowls of Christ's wrath are real prophetic pictures of God *"fashioning disaster."*

In the days of the judges, Hannah knew the prophetic justice of God. In her thanksgiving prayer after receiving a son, she promised:

> *The adversaries of the Lord shall be broken to pieces; out of heaven shall he thunder upon them; the Lord shall judge the ends of the earth; and he shall give strength unto his king, and exalt the horn of his anointed (1 Samuel 2:10).*

Who is this king, but Jesus the Lamb? Who is this anointed, but the King of kings of the book of Revelation?

God promised to shake the earth. The whole heaven and earth shall be shaken so that every nation shall know that God dwells in Zion (Joel 3:16). Like a father who shakes his disobedient child, there is a violent shaking of the earth several times in the Apocalypse that says to the wayward sons of the earth: "I mean business. Awaken to the lateness of time. Awake, I'm coming. Stop sinning." Paul, writing to the Hebrews, prophesied of the final great shaking of the earth.

> *"See that you do not refuse Him who speaks. For if they did not escape who refused Him who spoke on earth, much more shall we not escape if we turn away from Him who speaks from heaven, whose voice then shook the earth; but now He has promised, saying,*

"Yet once more I shake not only the earth, but also heaven." Now this, "Yet once more," indicates the removal of those things that are being shaken, as of things that are made, that the things which cannot be shaken may remain" (Hebrews 12:25–27)

The kingdom of God cannot be shaken but shall remain and the church cannot be shaken; it is a house that is founded upon the rock Christ Jesus.

E. Justice as Fulfillment of Promise

Justice is the fulfillment of promise to the righteous just as justice concerning the evil man is a fulfillment of prophecy. Justice is witnessed in Christ's covenant with Isaac.

"Cursed be everyone that curses you, and blessed be those who bless you" (Genesis 27:29). David knew the justice of God in His promise to establish an eternal kingship from his seed. David the Psalmist wrote, "He shall have dominion also from sea to sea, and from the river to the ends of the earth" (Psalms 72:8).

Jesus himself promised a final day of reckoning. Just as God the Father brought the flood of judgment upon the earth in the time of Noah, God will bring judgment at His Second Coming. "But as the days of Noah were so shall also the coming of the Son of Man be" (Matthew 24:37).

God fulfills His promises and appropriates revenge upon injustices. The nation shall be gathered, their land shall be established in peace, and every nation that despises Israel shall be judged (Ezekiel 16).

> Then the trees of the field shall yield their fruit, and the earth shall yield her increase. They shall be safe in their land; and they shall know that I am the LORD when I have broken the bands of their yoke and delivered them from the hand of those who enslaved them. And they shall no longer be a prey for the nations, nor shall beasts of the land devour them, but they shall dwell safely, and no one shall make them afraid. I will raise up for them a garden of renown, and they shall no longer be consumed with hunger in the land, nor bear the shame of the Gentiles anymore. Thus they shall know that I, the Lord their God, am with them, and they the house of Israel, are My people, says the Lord God (Ezekiel 34: 27-31).

As graves open, so Israel shall resurrect into a land of safety, where God will be magnified.

F. Justice and the Nature of God

Justice is the declaration of Christ's righteousness and holiness. The judgment of God is the manifesto that the courts and governments of this world cannot procure. The Nature of God is the basis for all judgment. The judgment of the Revelation is not the result of man's corrupted karma. This judgment is not the result of a polluted ecology, but the inescapable result of sin -- sin not as man measures sin, but sin that does not align with the righteousness of God. Christ's Kingdom is established with judgment and with justice (Isaiah 9:7). Judgment is necessary to the establishment of His kingdom, for His kingdom is a kingdom of righteousness.

The vengeance of God is good and right according to the nature of Almighty God. Paul speaks of this to the church of Thessalonica which was quite concerned about the Second Coming and the judgment of God. "It is a righteous thing with God to recompense tribulation to them that trouble you" (2 Thessalonians 1:6).

Judgment is a declaration of His faithfulness and truthfulness. As Christ descends to make war in that great day of the Lord, He is called *"Faithful and True" (Rev. 19:11)*. Not until then does righteousness finally prevail.

Just before the destruction of Sodom, Abraham said, "Shall not the judge of all the earth do right? (Genesis 18:25). The Lord would have saved the city if he had found ten righteous, but He found not even ten. So in the end-time, will God find faith upon the earth?

Justice is a declaration of His word. God has spoken and He will perform His word. God speaks not with flattering divination, but "I will say the word and perform it." says the *Lord God* (Ezekiel 12:25). He has promised justice and He will administer justice.

In John's vision in the first chapter (Rev. 1:16), we see the Son of Man with a two-edged sword proceeding from His mouth. This could depict the double witness of the two covenants – the Old Testament and the New Testament. The twice-sharpened sword represents the message and promise of the Old Covenant delivered by Moses, and the message of grace and truth delivered by the man Christ Jesus of the New Covenant. Armed with the law and grace, Christ pronounces judgment. We also know that by the breath of His mouth, Christ shall consume the wicked, and by the breath of His lips, Christ shall slay the wicked (Isaiah 11:4). Here, we have the life and power of this two-edged sword issuing out of His mouth.

> *And then the lawless one will be revealed, whom the Lord will consume with the breath of His mouth and destroy with the brightness of His coming but with righteousness He shall judge the poor, and decide with equity for the meek of the earth; He shall strike the earth with the rod of His mouth, And with the breath of His lips He shall slay the wicked (2 Thessalonians 2:8).*

Some may fear the terror of His judgment; yet, judgment verifies the presence of a Holy God. Judgment is a dreadful peril to the evil man, but a comforting promise to the righteous man. Judgment finalizes man's ignorance of God, and establishes a new world order according to the loving kindness of God. So when we are invited to "come and see," what do we see? Instead of focusing upon the earthly terror that shall happen, we can envision the throne of God that declares His supremacy above all powers, rulers, and principalities.

FURTHER QUESTIONS:

1. What do you feel God needs to bring justice upon?

2. Do you feel God was just when he sent the flood in Noah's day or was God unjust?

3. Is it right for God to *fashion a disaster*?

4. IMAGES OF THE SEAL PERIOD

A. Justice and the Throne of Heaven

Read Rev. 4 and 5

There are seven distinctive throne scenes in the book of Revelation and the word *throne (thronos)* appears in thirty-one verses. The throne of God is the source of the judgments of God. God sits upon this throne and the Son at His right hand. "Justice and judgment are the habitation of thy throne:" expressed the psalmist (Psalms 89:14). All judgment has been given to the Son (John 5:22). This is symbolically depicted when John sees the Lamb accepting the book from Him who sat upon the throne. It is Christ's judgment that is true and just (John 8:16). Final judgment does not advance from a judge's throne in the courtrooms of this world, nor from the philosophies of man enthroned in the minds of man, nor from the thrones of earthy kings and queens, but from the throne room of God Almighty. The Revelation constantly reminds us that God is in control, even when the world is caving in. And when all is dissolved of this earth, the throne of God and of the Lamb shall remain in the New Jerusalem (Rev. 22:3-5).

PRIESTLY STONES

The personage upon the throne appeared as the color of jasper and sardine. In the writings of the early church fathers, Victorianus gave an interesting interpretation to these colors.

> *The jasper is of the color of water, the sardine of fire. These two are thence manifested to be placed as judgments upon Christ's tribunal until the consummation of the world, of which judgments one is already completed in the deluge of water, and the other shall be completed by fire. I place my bow in the clouds, that ye may now no longer fear water, but fire.*[1]

From the throne of God, the judgment of Revelation is not a flood of water but a flood of fire.

Before Victorianus, jasper and sardine were stones in the high priest's vesture, which was a breastplate of judgment (Exodus 28:15). When Jesus walked the earth, the high priest was head of the Jewish court, the Sanhedrin. They sat in judgment upon the people and they presided over the illegal trials of Jesus.

Christ, the Branch was prophesied in the Old Testament. Zechariah announced that the Branch would sit and rule as priest upon the throne of God to usher forth peace.

> *Behold, the Man whose name is the Branch. From His place He shall branch out....* *and shall sit and rule on His throne; so He shall be a priest on His throne, and the counsel* *of peace shall be between them both (Zechariah 6:13).*

Not only by His kingly power shall Christ bring forth justice, but by His priestly authority. "We have such a High Priest, who is seated at the right hand of the throne of the Majesty in the heavens" (Hebrews 8:1). Christ stands at the right hand of the throne of God as High Priest during the seals and the trumpets. His earthly kingdom is not established until after the Battle of Armageddon and His Second Coming.

The colors of jasper and sardine identify the judge of all the earth who establishes justice, and our High Priest who establishes peace. These two offices of priest and king unite in perfect oneness with Christ. During the tribulation, however, the Antichrist with world leaders shall attempt to unite political powers and ecclesiastical powers. The Antichrist will attempt this union of priest and king when he sits in the temple of God claiming to be God, but Christ shall ultimately reign forever and forever as High Priest and King.

Continue to notice, as you study, all the priestly symbols during the seal period.

The Throne

Read Rev. 4

In Homer, the Greek classic, a throne was an armchair covered with cushions, with a high back and footstool. A throne was a royal chair, a judge's bench, a bishop's seat, and it was also an oracular seat of the priestess of Apollo. In Eumenides of Aeshylus Apollo says: "Never, when I sat in the diviner's seat did I speak aught else than Zeus the father of the Olympians bade me."[2]

During the tribulation, Christ's priestly throne will be higher and more puissant than all the oracular seats of witches, channelers, and soothsayers of the New Age. During the tribulation, the powers of evil will appear to be winning, but the prophetical promises of scripture will be finally fulfilled. Babylon and the powers of sorcery shall be destroyed. Every priest and priestess of the witch's whoredom will find their doom.

> *But the cowardly, unbelieving, abominable, murderers, sexually immoral, sorcerers,* *idolaters, and all liars shall have their part in the lake which burns with fire and* *brimstone, which is the second death." (Rev. 21:8)*

Christ not only has the power and ability to consummate all existence, but the will to do so. The will of God shall have dominion over the will of man. By Christ's will were men created and by Christ's will do men exist, and by Christ's will the destiny of man shall be determined according to His laws. The will of visualizers and shameful shamans shall someday confront the will of God and be destroyed. "Thy will be done on earth as it is in heaven."

God gave man a free will, but that does not justify a man's sin and disobedience. All must bow down before the creator.

The throne of God is that divine abode that man approaches through prayer and to where man calls out for mercy and whoever calls upon the Lord for mercy during the tribulation shall be saved (Acts 2:21). Our High Priest will still be upon the throne. As Priest after the order of Melchizedek and as a judge appointed by the Father, the Lamb will be found worthy to open the seals and judge the nations. As the tribulation progresses we discover that by the time of the sixth trumpet that man does not repent of his idolatry, devil worship, murder, or sorceries (Rev. 9:20). Although there is still mercy offered at the throne of God, the unrighteous cry no longer for mercy because of the over-ripening of their sin. God has had enough.

We see Christ the Lamb, not sitting, but standing beside the throne of God. Why? God's command to Christ was, "Sit on my right hand, 'til I make your enemies your footstool" (Hebrews 1:13). Now Christ is standing because the tribulation establishes that footstool. It is now time for the judge of all the earth to arise and unleash the powers of darkness and put the enemy under His feet forever.

B. Justice and the Rainbow

There is a rainbow around the throne scene (Rev. 4:3). Christ's promise to Noah was sanctioned. "And it shall come to pass, when I bring a cloud over the earth, that the bow shall be seen in the cloud" (Genesis 9:14). Noah saw that bow in the sky and rejoiced in the promises of God. The rainbow was a token of Christ's covenant with Noah, with his descendants, with all living creatures of the earth, and with the earth itself (Genesis 9:9-13) that He would not send another flood.

In the last days, as in Noah's day, God will bring a cloud over the earth, a cloud of darkness and judgment. The rainbow of mercy and justice shall encircle the throne of God (Rev. 4:3). The rainbow is a promise not to send a flood but fire. The rainbow of Christ's fairness encircles the angel who steps upon the land and the sea (Rev. 10:1). "I saw still another mighty angel coming down from heaven, clothed with a cloud. And a rainbow was on his head, his face was like the sun, and his feet like pillars of fire" (Rev. 9:20, 21).

Justice shall fall not only upon man, but also upon the beasts, and upon the earth. Christ's promises will be realized. There will be a remnant of man who lives into the millennium. The beasts of the earth shall not be completely destroyed, but the earth shall be dissolved, and a new heaven and a new earth shall descend from God out of heaven after the millennium.

This rainbow, remember, reminds us of God's previous judgment in the day of Noah and the rainbow confirms the end-time judgment. The rainbow is a covenant to Christ's man. The rainbow is not a sign to the unbeliever. In Revelation the church is assured as Noah was assured that God was about to perform His word, not contradict His word. The verdict is a sentence of fire not water, but the righteous shall be delivered just as Noah was delivered from the flood. Just as God endorsed a promise with the appearance of the rainbow, so God has promised to send judgment.

The Old Testament word for rainbow is *bow*. It means also the bow of a hunter or warrior. Christ's bow is in the clouds awaiting the final judgment. I see that this rainbow is like a warrior-bow of Christ's justice. Christ's war-bow will bring a pot of judgment, not gold, to the unrighteous, but Christ's war-bow will bring justice to the righteous as it is transformed into a rainbow of beauty by the sunlight of his mercy and grace.

In the Greek language of early Christendom, the word for rainbow, *iris*, had reference also to the eye, to a bright halo about a body, or to the deity known as the messenger-goddess of Olympus.[3] The rainbow of the new age philosophy today symbolizes the eye, the third eye, and the female power of the goddess. The western world is quickly mirroring the Greek world in aspects of worship and devotion to the deities of Olympus and the female goddesses. For the New Age, the eye personifies the rainbow and reflects the religious concepts and experiences of mysticism that are believed by the occult world today. The rainbow for the New Age ends where their formidable expanse of the spirit world begins. The rainbow encircles their mystical, enchanted experiences into timeless mind visions of the subconscious. Their rainbow defies the judgment of God, for no judgment exists in the New Age mind.

Christ's bow in the sky glares in opposition to the bow that the white horseman was carrying as he went forth to conquer (Rev.6:1-3). The rainbow John saw in his revelation represents the authority of Christ's divine justice and mercy in opposition to a false religion, false authority, and false christs that attempt to overthrow the kingdom of righteousness in the day of tribulation.

C. Justice and the Scroll

> *Then He came and took the scroll out of the right hand of Him who sat on the throne (Revelation 5:7).*

The scroll would have been wound around a staff and fastened down to the staff with the seven seals. The scroll John saw was written within and without. Rarely were scrolls written on both sides. Rolls written on both sides were called *opistographi*.[4] Ezekiel's roll was also written within and without; full of lamentations, mourning, and woe.

A full and large scroll tells us that the judgments of God are not minute but important. A large scroll reflects upon Christ's complete creation from the beginning of time. Judgment is determined upon the whole earth and every nation or ethnic group. A large scroll represents the Gentile nations as opposed to the Jewish nation and the small scroll of the trumpets (Rev. 10:1).

A seal was a small object usually made of a brass, silver, gold, pottery or stone set in metal. On one side was a skillfully carved, negative image that made a positive impression on clay, wax, or papyrus. Some seals were worn around the neck and attached by a chord that looped through a bored hole in the seal. When Joseph was governor of Egypt, he wore a ring-seal of Pharaoh. The impression of that seal would be notably designed and signed as belonging to the Pharaoh and gave authority to a written decree. Those owning seals were usually rich citizens or high officials with governing authority.

The image of a seal may have included an inscription, an emblem, or a scene. The image on seals often depicted the gods and deities of the people. The Egyptian scarab seals resembled the sacred winged beetle. Seals often had a symbolic meaning. The dung beetle was associated with the creator god. The heart scarab represented the heart of man that was to be weighed against the feather of truth in the judgment.

Seals marked wine jars and mummy pits as signs of possession. The grave of Jesus was sealed with the king's authority that no man might steal His body.

The purposes of ancient seals enable us today to understand the prophetical vision of John. Each seal was a stamp of authority and seals identified the owner or the individual who was administrating the authority. This scroll which John saw was in the right hand of Him who sat upon the throne. The Almighty, who is the highest authority, wrote the scroll and no other seal or agreement made by man, beast, or demon could change or reverse the mind of God.

John's scroll made valid not only with one seal, but with seven seals. Under Roman law, wills and testaments were sealed with seven seals. John's scroll can be considered a covenant will. God finally fulfills His covenants with the saints and with the Jews. Time has come for God to keep his promise, punish the unjust, and reward the just. Finally God will exercise justice and establish the kingdom that He has promised.

The uniqueness of the seals is not the Lamb's ability to know the contents of the seals, but his capability to open the seals and administer them. The scripture says that no one in heaven or earth could open the scroll.

Time is important when considering the sealing and unsealing of the books of God. Daniel was commanded to leave his prophetical book sealed until the end-times (Daniel 12:4), but the sealed prophecies of Revelation are now opened because the time of the end has come (Rev.22:10). It is not so much the secrecy of prophecy that is sealed, but the time of fulfillment. There is a restraining order with the sealing of prophecy. The prophecy will not be fulfilled until God says. The seals will not be opened until the precise time has come. The judgment has been postponed until the end. The sheep and the goats are left to pasture together until the time of judgment.

Concerning the prophecies of the thunders, John was commanded to seal up the uttering of the seven thunders. These things were not to be prophesied as yet. But it was said to John, "Thou must prophesy again" (Rev. 10:11).

It was the Lamb who was found worthy to open the book and to lose the seals (Rev. 5:2).

Who would be worthier to open the seals than He who sealed the scroll?

Who would be worthier to open the seals than He who uttered the prophetic words?

Who would be worthier to open the seals than He who had the authority to fulfill the promises made?

He is worthy to open the seals because he alone has the word of prophecy; (Rev.19:10).

He alone has the authority to pronounce judgment;

He alone is the king who can establish an eternal kingdom; and

He alone has the authority to consummate all things. No prophetic document is valid without the seal of Christ Jesus our Lord.

D. Images upon the Seals:

Read Rev. 5

The revelation of John does not reveal the inscription or the design of the seven seals. I project my imagination as to the inscriptions and images upon the seals. Just as the many seals of ancient Egypt depicted the deities of idolatry, so I imagine the seven seals of John's revelation engraved with the names of the Lamb, the one who is worthy of all praise.

1. **Lion of Judah:** When no man was found worthy to open the scroll, the elders about the throne cried, "Behold, the Lion of the tribe of Judah, the Root of David" (Rev. 5:5). Christ was the promised seed of David. He is the promised King who shall establish the eternal kingdom. He has the key of David with the power to open that which man cannot close and with the power to shut that which men cannot shut (Rev. 3:7). This is the King who was found worthy to open the seals of judgment. Christ has the authority over the white horse of the first seal that represent leaders of nations that go forth to conquer (Rev. 6:1-3).

2. **Redeemer:** A new song was sung about the throne. Christ was worthy to open the book because it was He who redeemed man to God from every kindred, tongue, and nation (Rev. 5:9). The red horse of the second seal had power to take peace from the earth. What a comparison to Christ, who is the Prince of Peace!

   The scroll could be seen as a scroll of Redemption. He is our Kinsman Redeemer. Christ has the right and duty to avenge the death of those whom he redeems. He has the right of a kinsman to redeem His own from the power of an alien dominion that they might enjoy the rights of a new freedom, an eternal freedom. As Kinsman Redeemer, Christ, not the environmentalist, has the authority to bring redemption to the earth. It is Christ who is worthy to redeem man from the bonds of this earth. Our redeemer, the Lamb, holds the title deed to the earth by right of creation and redemption.

3. **Son of Man:** Upon the third seal I see the image of the Old Testament Christ. He is the Angel of the Lord who appeared and ministered to Abraham, Gideon, the Israelites as they escaped from Egypt, and other Old Covenant patriarchs. His Shekinah filled the tabernacle of the wilderness and filled the cloud that led the children of Israel into the Promised Land. Christ is the Son of Man who appeared as the fourth man in the fire to protect the three Hebrew children from Nebuchadnezzar's furnace.

   He is the LORD of the Old Testament and He is the Son of Man of the New Testament who "came to seek and to save that which was lost" (Luke 19:10). The faithful One has the authority to punish the unfaithful. Man was given the law and the Great Lawmaker has the right to punish the lawbreaker. As the Son of Man, he was the Bread of Life and stands in contrast to the rider of the black horse that brings famines upon the earth (Rev. 6:5).

4. **The Resurrection and the Life**: "I am the resurrection and the life. He who believes in Me, though he may die, he shall live. And whoever lives and believes in Me shall never die." Do you believe this? (John 11:25, 26). Yet the rider upon the fourth horse was named Death, and Hell followed him. What a contrast between the life giving power of Christ and the power of death that follows the fourth rider. Christ is worthy to open the scroll because He has the keys of hell and death. Has not the giver of life and death power over the fourth rider, and is He not therefore worthy to open the fourth seal and permit death and hell to follow?

5. **The Lamb of God Slain**: The fifth seal must have pictured the Lamb. John the Baptist cried out to the people in the wilderness, "Behold the Lamb of God that takes away the sin of the world" (John 1:29). Now in John's apocalypse we witness the Lamb as it had been slain (Rev. 5:6). Who could be worthier to open the seals than He who bore the sins of many? He is a Lamb slain, yet alive, for He is the first begotten of the dead. He who provided redemption for all of mankind will now stand in judgment of those who had refused the provisions of the Lamb. As the Lamb of God, Christ brought victory over sin. Those who flounder to appropriate the divine plan of salvation can expect the redeemer to reject and discard their life and soul.

   When the 5th seal is opened, many martyrs are slain for their faith in Christ; yet, they faithfully follow the example of the Lamb by sacrificing their lives.

   By His blood He has redeemed man from sin and the curse of sin. During the tribulation, the church must remember that they have not been appointed unto wrath. Christians can rejoice in the tribulation for the judgments of the Lord are righteous and fair. It is the judgments of man and Satan that are unfair during the tribulation. Great honor is given to every martyr by Christ who deserves all honor.

6. **Creator:** Upon the sixth seal, I see the image of our Creator. The Lamb is worthy to open the scroll because He is our creator (Rev. 4:11). He who is the Creator is worthy to bring judgment on all His creation, whether it be upon man, beast, or the earth. For the 6th seal the Heavens which God created are shaken. The Sun is darkened and the moon appears red like blood. The earth quakes; the stars fall from heaven.

   We are firstly His because He created us. He who is the Alpha of man has the right to be the Omega of man.

7. **High Priest and Judge:** As High Priest, Christ is worthy to open the seals because He is the One who has made us kings and priests unto Him. He is the one who has called us to reign with Him on this earth (Rev. 5:10). He is the church's intercessor for justice. Only Christ, our High Priest is worthy to usher in the New Kingdom upon this earth.

   In the Old Testament, the priests were judges. As High Priest, Christ is judge. Who could judge more righteously man's heart than Emmanuel? It is He who knows the hearts of man; who became man to wipe away sin; and who can fathom man's weakness and infirmities. But he who accepts the redeemer will not fear the face of the judge.

"And when I saw Him, I fell at His feet as dead. But He laid His right hand on me, saying to me, "Do not be afraid; I am the First and the Last. I am He who lives, and was dead, and behold, I am alive forevermore. Amen. And I have the keys of Hades and of Death" (Revelation 1:17–18).

FURTHER STUDY

1. Are you willing to give your will over to Christ? Why?
2. Make a list of all the priestly symbols in Revelation 5 and 6.
3. What do the different throne scenes from chart 4A teach you?
4. Design a seal with another name of Christ on it. Share.

THE SCROLL AND SEVEN SEALS OF TRIBULATION

Proposed images on seals	Rev 5:12 Worthy is the Lamb that was slain to receive	Rev. 7:12 ..worshipped God. saying: Amen	The Seal Disasters
Jesus 1. Lion of Judah	Power	Power	1. Lion-like beast announces the white horse. The rider had a bow and a crown and went forth to conquer. 6:1-
Jesus 2. Redeemer	Riches	Thanksgiving	2. The calf life beast announces the re horse. Power is given to the man upon the horse to take peace from the earth He had a great sword. 6:4
Jesus 3. Son of Man	Wisdom	Wisdom	3. The man-like beast announces the black horse. The rider balances. 6:5-6
Jesus 4. Resurrection	Strength	Might	4. the fourth seal and the pale hors The rider is called 'death' and Hell followed. Power was given to kill with sword, hunger and death 1/4 of the earth, man, and beast. Rev 6:6-8 copywrite Carolyn Chapman

THE SEALS OF THE SCROLL AND THE SEVEN SEALS OF TRIBULATION:

Lion of Judah
Breaks every chain
but
The Lion Beast
Binds

The Seals

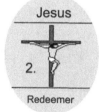

1. Lion-like beast announces the white horse. The rider had a bow and a crown and went forth to conquer. 6:1-3

Jesus Brought Peace
but
the Calf beast
Takes Peace
From the earth.

2. The calf life beast announces the red horse. Power is given to the man upon the horse to take peace from the earth. He had a great sword. 6:4

Son of Man
is the bread of life
but
the man-like beast
brings famine.

3. The man-like beast announces the black horse. The rider had a pair of balances. 6:5-6

The Seals

JESUS IS LIFE
BUT
4TH SEAL BRINGS
DEATH

4. The eagle-like beast introduces the fourth seal and the pale horse. The rider is called 'death' and Hell followed. Power was given to kill with sword, hunger and death 1/4 of the earth, man, and beast. Rev 6:6-8

JESUS GAVE HIS LIFE
BUT THE SIX SEAL
TAKES LIFE

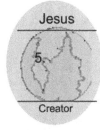

5. Martyrs are slain under the altars of the heathen. Given white robes and told to wait.
Rev 6:9-11 Jesus led the martyrs by giving his life.

JESUS IS CREATOR
BUT
5TH SEAL SHAKES
THE CREATION

6. Earthquakes, sun blackened, moon as blood, stars fall, heavens are shaken.
Kings, great, men, rich, chief captains, might men, bondman, free man hid in the dens and rocks. Rev 6:12-17
The heavens declare the glory of God.

JESUS AS PRIEST
INTERCESSOR
FOR SAINTS

chapter 7 introduction to trumpets

As Priest, casts the septer to the earth for the four vengeances of Christ.

5. The Great Falling Away

A. The Seven Churches of the Apocalypse

Read Rev. Ch. 2-3

The seven candlesticks epitomize the seven churches in the geographical area of Asia Minor where John had ministered. Some scholars also assign a different period in history to each of the seven churches. The church of Ephesus would thus correspond to the first century church and continue until the seventh church, the Laodicea church would represent the Church age just before Christ's return. The seven churches may also, in character and actions, represent the churches around the world during the tribulation period.

Each church is described with good words of commendation and words of disapproval. There is a negative and positive comment about each church.

The Ephesian church, although her works and labors were good, had left her first love. The Ephesian state of apostasy was serious because Christ, who stood amid the candlesticks, warned that the candle representing the Ephesian church would be removed unless they repented.

The church of Pergamos held the doctrine of Balaam and of the Nicolaitanes, which God hates. These needed to repent, and Christ said that He would fight against them with the sword of His mouth. This sword expresses the word of God but it also expresses judgment. John envisioned Christ standing with the seven candlesticks or churches, but He was dressed ready for judgment. His eyes were as a flame of fire. He carried in one hand the seven stars, but in the other hand he held a sharp two-edged sword. God does not overlook sin whether it is in the church or in the world.

Many in the Smyrna Church were living a lie. Many were really followers of the synagogue of Satan.

The church of Thyatira allowed woman like Jezebel to seduce the church into fornication.

The church of Sardis was dead and was warned to repent and watch or the coming of Christ would be "as a thief".

Many in the church of Laodicea were spewed out of Christ's mouth because of their lukewarmness. These were counseled to leave the gold of this world and find the gold tried in the fire of tribulation.

The church of Philadelphia was found faithful for they had kept His word; they did not deny His name; and they persevered. God promised to keep them safe from the 'hour of trial' (Rev. 3:10) that would engulf the whole world. "I also will keep thee from the hour of temptation which shall come upon the entire world, to try them that dwell upon the earth (Rev. 3:10). Praise God, there shall be a faithful remnant!

The church at the end of time will be no different than the churches throughout history, except worse. The church at the end of time will indeed be a church that will need to be purified and cleansed. The end time church will include those who are faithful and unfaithful, repentant and unrepentant, patient and impatient, and some of Christ and others of the synagogue of Satan (Rev. 2:9).

Tribulation was promised to many of the seven churches. Satan was allowed to cast many belonging to the church of Smyrna into the tribulation (thlipsis) ten days.

They were not to fear the trials but were admonished to be faithful unto death (Rev. 2:10,11). The church of Thyatira was given time to repent; but she would be cast into great tribulation (thlipsis) if she repented not. The church was to understand that Christ "searches the reins and hearts" (Rev. 2:23).

Judgment begins first at the house of the Lord. Christ's coming came as a thief in the night for many of the church of Sardis (Rev. 3:3).

We must also acknowledge that the word used to the Philadelphian church is the word *temptation* (peiravsou, πειραζου) not *tribulation* (thlipsis, θλιψις). "Because you have kept My command to persevere, I also will keep you from the 'hour of trial' which shall come upon the whole world, to test those who dwell on the earth" (Rev. 3:10). The word *trial* or *temptation*, however, alludes to great tribulation at which time God preserves the righteous believer from temptation or trial. We must understand that the tribulation is not only a time of judgment for the wicked but also a day of testing for the believer by the hand of the enemy.

Kept from the Hour of Temptation

Because you have kept My command to persevere, I also will keep you from the hour of trial which shall come upon the whole world, to test those who dwell on the earth (Rev. 3:10).

We must understand what is meant by *keeping one* from the hour of temptation (Rev. 3:10). Some people think that God will rapture the church out of the world before the time of testing. Others believe that God will keep the faithful true to Him throughout the hour of testing. A third view states that the unrighteous will be hurt during the tribulation and the righteous will be protected. God is able to perform all three possibilities.

The word *from* in this verse is *ek* in Greek. Zodhiates word study dictionary defines *ek* as follows:

If something is in something else, then the separation from it is expressed with the Greek word 'ek'-- meaning "out of". But if something is near it, on it, or with it, then apó is used. 'Ek' is used either in respect of place, time, source, or origin. It is the direct opposite of 'eis", meaning into or in.[1]

God cannot keep you from the hour of temptation if you have not been in that hour in the first place. He brings us *out of (ek)*, that terrible hour meaning the opposite of *eis* meaning into.

In deciding what the apostle means, we must recollect and consider the purpose of the tribulation and who administers the testing and tribulation. God tempts no man but "every man is tempted when he is drawn away of his own lust and enticed" (James 1:14). The word testing is *peiradzetai* (πειραζεται) from the root word *peiradzo* (πειραζω). "I will keep thee from the hour of temptation" (Rev 3:10).

It is interesting to note that the same word is used in verse 3. "Remember therefore how you have received and heard; *hold fast* and repent..." The word for *hold fast* is from the same root word as *keep*. Again in Rev.3:10 the same word is repeated. "Because you have *kept* My command to persevere, I also will *keep* you from the hour of trial which shall come upon the whole world, to test those who dwell on the earth." We cannot argue the truth that if we <u>hold fast</u> (keep) and repent, God shall <u>keep</u> us. The church of Philadelphia kept His commandments, while Christ kept them from the hour of trial. We can be confident; for, if we <u>keep</u> God's commandments and allow nothing to separate us from the love of God, then God will not allow anything to separate us from His love and a relationship with Him. Our relationship with the divine Father shall be preserved through every trial, and this truth is more important and victorious than being raptured before the hour of testing.

Did you know that Shadrach, Meshach, and Abednego were KEPT through the fiery furnace?

B. The Church and the Great Falling Away

The church and the apostate church are the two main themes symbolically portrayed by John's record of the seal tribulations. These themes I build with the image of the twenty-four elders and in the next chapter through the contrast of the symbols. A struggle arises between the bride of Christ and the bride of Satan. Many within the bride of Christ during the tribulation shall fall away and seek a bill of apostasy from their Husbandman and Redeemer. The pre-flood mentality prevails at the end of time for man's heart descends to the lowest pits of evil continually. Man scoffs at the ark of mercy; yet, thousands shall crown themselves with the glory of martyrdom. Who shall be able to stand and who shall fall?

THE TWENTY-FOUR ELDERS: SPIRITUAL PRIESTHOOD OF BELIEVERS

Read Rev. 4:1-5

Let us examine this passage. Who do the twenty-four elders represent? Some scholars say that the twenty-four elders represent the twelve patriarchs of the Old Testament and the twelve apostles of the New Testament. Jesus promised the disciples that they would sit with Him upon twelve thrones to judge the twelve tribes of Israel, but there is no evidence that this was their appointed time and Israel according to Matthew will not be judged until the Messianic Age which is not until after Armageddon.

God seals the twelve tribes of Israel later, at the beginning of the trumpets. This causes me to doubt whether the twelve elders represent the Old Testament patriarchs or the Jews. The saints are the central characters of the seal period and the saints are the victims of persecution during the seal period. The throne scene depicts many priestly images and believers have become kings and priests unto God.

> *And has made us kings and priests to His God and Father, to Him be glory and dominion forever and ever. Amen. (Rev.1:6) And have made us kings and priests to our God; and we shall reign on the earth"* (Rev. 5:10).

I believe that the twenty-four elders best represent the spiritual priesthood of believers. Why?

First, God portrays the colors of jasper and sardine as He sits upon the throne. Jasper and sardine were stones in the high priest's vesture. David appointed twenty-four thousand leaders to represent the entire Levitical priesthood (I Chronicles 23:4), so why could not twenty-four elders represent the churchly priesthood?

Second, John's twenty-four elders wear white robes. The Levites wore white; yet the church of Jesus Christ is depicted very strongly in the image of the twenty-four elders because they wore white. The elders are clothed with the beauty of the church -- in white raiment. Similarly, the undefiled of Sardis were promised white raiment. The Smyrna believers remind me of the saints martyred during the seal period. These also were given white robes (Rev.7:9).

Third, the twenty-four elders also wear crowns of gold. A crown was the reward to Smyrna believers who endured tribulation and were faithful unto death. For death they received a crown of life. A crown was the reward to the believers of Philadelphia who in the hour of temptation remained steadfast. The believers in Christ are often pictured with white robes and with crowns upon their heads especially in the Revelation of John. The Old Testament priests never wore crowns.

Also, during the tribulation of the seals, the prayers of the saints arise as incense before the throne of God. Just as priests offer sacrifices, so the saints of the seal period offer the sacrifice of their own lives that they may be found worthy. Not only the prayers but the song of the twenty-four elders was the song of the redeemed from every nation.

As priests unto God the saints sacrifice their lives for the truth. Truly the period of the seals is a time of great persecution. As the temperature of wickedness bubbles to its peak, the righteous men in earth's seething pot are cast out. However, our High Priest stands by the throne of God and above all powers during this terrible time of tribulation. A spiritual priesthood is then redeemed unto God and they serve in His temple night and day.

The images of the seal period render a negative and positive picture as we shall witness in the next chapter. Similarly, the two main themes of John's seal tribulations are the positive picture of the true church and the degraded image of the apostate church. A struggle arises between the bride of Christ and the bride of Satan. Many with the bride of Christ during the seal period shall fall away and seek a bill of apostasy from their Husbandman and Redeemer. The horsemen ride to kill and destroy. This is the negative picture of a fallen church. However, with a positive view of the church, thousands shall crown themselves with the glory of martyrdom (Rev. 7:9); therefore, Revelation 5 is full of worship and praise to the Lamb.

FURTHER STUDY

1. Check out the word kept in a Bible concordance and what does scripture teach you?

2. What was the pre-flood mentality that shall prevail at the end of time?

6. Four Horsemen of the Apocalypse

The Wrath of Man:

There are four beasts before the throne in Revelation chapter four and these four beasts release the four horsemen of Revelation chapter six. I take the beasts of Revelation chapter four in order, the lion, calf, the man-like beast, and the eagle and match them with the four horsemen of chapter six.

A. The First Seal: The Lion-like Beast and White Horse

> *Now I saw when the Lamb opened one of the seals; and I heard one of the four living creatures saying with a voice like thunder, "Come and see" And I looked, and behold, a white horse. He who sat on it had a bow; and a crown was given to him, and he went out conquering and to conquer (Rev. 6:1, 2).*

When the Lamb ruptures each seal, each beast in turn invites John to come and see. John then sees the four horsemen in turn (Rev. 6:1-7). There have been various interpretations as to the meaning of these four beasts. Strauss says, "They possess strength like the lion, they render service like the ox, they possess intelligence as does man, and they are swift like the eagle."[1] Others have said that the beasts represent all of Christ's creation.

Others have said that each beast represents the four gospels. Matthew recorded the genealogy of Christ as King representing the Lion. Mark presented Christ as Servant like the ox. Luke narrated the priesthood of Zacharias and taught Him as the Son of Man. John argued Christ was the Son of God just as an eagle soars to great heights.

Each beast is more relevant to the drama of the Apocalypse than what these previous ideas suggest. As each mysterious beast introduces a horse and rider, it is very interesting to see how these four horsemen could be riding the earth today.

Negative and Positive Images

Most images of scripture have a positive and negative representation. The lion can represent the Lion of the tribe of Judah or Satan the deceiver. These beasts of the seal period could also have a positive image and a negative image.

The four beasts of Revelation chapter four create a *positive image* when they worshipped at the throne of God. They cried *holy, holy, holy*. They gave honor, thanks, and glory to God (Rev. 4:9).

There is also a *negative image* portrayed by these four beasts when they are pictured having many eyes. Today, mystical creatures are pictured with eyes. The eye of Horus, the evil eye, the middle eye, and the inner eye are terms referring to the power of the inner energy force of man; that inner enlightening of the spirit of man that usurps the power of God. The eye pictures the knowledge of inner voices and the word of channelers.

The Lamb also is described as having seven eyes, and the beasts are described as having many eyes. This could speak of their wisdom and understanding, but the wisdom that proceeds from the throne of God is righteous and true. Do the eyes of the four beasts depict the wisdom of God or the spirit of apostasy?

For me, these eyes of the Revelation are saying that they are of one mind, purpose, and knowledge. Christ's purposes are of one mind, but the eyes of the evil one are of one purpose too. Twice the beasts are described as full of eyes. Their eyes are around and within (Rev. 4:8 εσωθεν) and they are described having eyes before and behind. (Rev. 4:6, οπισθεν). Each beast has a mission to fulfill as each seal is opened. Both these Greek words that describe the eyes of the beasts describe the scroll that is written within and on the backside. The scroll was so full that it was written inside and out. The knowledge and volume of the scroll is great.

The beasts in a negative context picture the apostate forces during the seal period. As each seal is unloosed, apostate forces, apostate religions, and the spirit of antichrist are unleashed to destroy, deceive, and kill. These beasts could represent the evil counterfeit church as well as the true church —both the positive and negative spiritual forces.

The many images of the seals portray the contrast between the holy and unholy during this time. The beasts sing holy, holy, holy in opposition to the sinfulness and hypocrisy of man. Man's voice during the seal period will be hypocritical and blasphemous. That is easy to believe when we see churches today sing holy, holy, holy; yet, they are full of incest, idolatry, mysticism, homosexuality, and adultery. The holiness of God demands justice first to the church that is not prepared for the Harvest Rapture (see chapter 13).

Seraphim appeared to Isaiah while singing *holy, holy, holy*. As a result, Isaiah realized his uncleanness and the seraphim proceeded to purge the lips of Isaiah with the hot coals from the altar.

> *And one cried to another and said: "Holy, holy, holy is the Lord of hosts; the whole earth is full of His glory!" And the posts of the door were shaken by the voice of him who cried out, and the house was filled with smoke. So I said: "Woe is me, for I am undone! Because I am a man of unclean lips, And I dwell in the midst of a people of unclean lips; For my eyes have seen the King, The Lord of hosts." Then one of the seraphim flew*

to me, having in his hand a live coal which he had taken with the tongs from the altar. And he touched my mouth with it, and said: "Behold, this has touched your lips; Your iniquity is taken away, And your sin purged (Isaiah 6:3–7).

The beasts of Revelation also cry *holy, holy, holy* to awaken man's lethargy to his own hypocrisy and uncleanness. Following this Old Testament example, the four beasts represent the spirit of purging that was to come upon man during the seal period.

There are three things in the book of Revelation that are called holy: he that has part in the first resurrection is called holy (Rev. 20:6); Jerusalem, the city of God is called Holy (Rev. 21:2, 22:19); and thirdly, the prophets of God are called Holy (Rev. 22:6). So we say: Holy, holy, holy, three times?

The First Beast: The Lion

The lion is the first living creature that ushers in the white horse. The lion creature is carrying a man with a bow and going forth to conquer. The lion has always characterized leaders of great strength.

In the Old Testament the lion represented the enemy nation of Babylon (Jeremiah 50:44, Daniel 7:4,3) and the lion destroyer of the north (Jeremiah 50:44). The lion represented the character of Dan, the conspiracy of evil prophets (Ezekiel 22:25), wicked rulers (Proverbs 28:15), a King's wrath (Proverbs 19:12) and as a destroyer of the nations (Jeremiah 4:7). False prophets lurked to deceive like lions and scatter the sheep (Jeremiah 50:17).

The Lion Dan (Antichrist) competes with the Lion of Judah (see chapter 11, the Dan connection).

In the New Testament, we see Satan as a roaring lion seeking whom he may devour (I Peter 5:8).

In the Revelation, the lion represents each of these above leaders as forces of evil and apostasy. This is the spirit of antichrist. This is the spirit of apostasy and rebellion that shall increase and increase as the seals are opened until the indignation is completed.

The apostate forces can truly be described as a lion. The Old Testament adjectives that describe the lion can also describe the forces of apostasy. The lion is described as, being strong and valiant, fierce, with great teeth, rendering in pieces, tearing, waiting in secret, greedy of prey, lurking in secret places, destroying, breaking all my bones, devouring men, drinking the blood of the slain, ravaging the prey, and devouring souls. What could better describe apostate forces in the latter days?

The White Horse: World Leaders

And I looked, and behold, a white horse. He who sat on it had a bow; and a crown was given to him, and he went out conquering and to conquer (Rev. 6:2).

His Crown

The rider is carrying a bow and is wearing one crown. The crown that the rider is wearing is a counter-image of the crown that the faithful martyrs receive. The rider wears a crown because he has the power to conquer, but the martyrs receive a crown because they give their lives, rather than identify with the apostate dream.

During this time, the apostate church develops; possibly as mystery Babylon (Rev. 17) who becomes the counterfeit bride of Christ, not cleansed and found faultless, but polluted with sin. The apostate church can never be truly the bride of Christ, but she can be misled into apostasy and be part of mystery Babylon.

Who might be this rider? He is not Christ because His coming is not to be in this fashion. Christ's coming is recorded in the nineteenth chapter of Revelation.

It is the lion-like beast that introduces the rider on the white horse. Both images represent many conquerors and destroyers. When you fit the puzzle together, all the facts and symbols around the narrative of the seals, you recognize the rider on the white horse as any apostate force, a false Christ, a political leader, or religion in the world at the end-time that has authority or may have no authority to ravage Christian principles and beliefs. Have you seen the logo of a man riding on a white horse upon magazines today? I have. Could these be apostate forces of society today?

Horses of Old Testament days usually spoke of a whole army of horses. Roman generals rode white horses and mythological stories included warriors who rode white horses. There was also the white unicorn. White horses were very common in those days. Conquerors and victorious leaders rode white horses. Homer pictures the horses of Rhesus as whiter than snow and as swifter than the winds. Herodotus, describing the battle of Plataea, says:

> *The fight went most against the Greeks were Mardonius, mounted on a white horse, and surrounded by the bravest of all the Persians, the thousand picked men, fought in person.*[2]

Since political leaders rode white horses in biblical days and after, then it is possible that the white horse not only represents false religious leaders but political leaders of the end-time who go forth into battle for reasons they justify as good and necessary. War is not a moral issue at the end of time. End-time leaders have only one selfish and destructive mind.

Stephen Gowans questions whether any country has the moral right to lead the world into war. He writes online in *"Truth behind white horse of Conquering"* the following:

> *It claims to be conducting a war on terrorism against a network (al-Qaeda) it helped create to fight proxy wars on its behalf (in Afghanistan and the Balkans.) The country's wars are always said to be fought for some high moral purpose: to stop ethnic cleansing, to prevent tyranny, to uphold international law, to defeat communist expansion, to root out terrorism, but somehow, while this is being done, the country always seems, as John Flynn once put it, to capture its enemies' markets while blundering into their oil wells.*[3]

The other three horsemen of the Revelation represent evil forces; therefore; we can conclude that the rider on the white horse is an evil force as well. But because it is a white horse, there appears to be deceptive and blasphemous forces at work here. These apostate forces appear to be good and holy; yet, they are evil and destructive. These forces may be different groups, ecumenical in nature, new age in philosophy, Catholic in authority, Babylonian and Islamic in spirituality, political forces, or environmental in policies. These forces are firstly, spirits of antichrist that are already going forth with great force to change the spirit of man and persecute the church.

Is the rider the Antichrist? Antichrist is described as a beast with seven heads and ten horns that arises from the sea and the Antichrist does not show his evil side until he breaks his treaty. One of my suppositions is that a great leader may arise and unite Syria, Libya, Egypt, and Ethiopia and then become known as the Antichrist. However, I can't ignore the possibility that the white horseman represents many apostate forces today.

This spirit is a spirit of rebellion against God. Rebellion is implied in the meaning of apostasy, especially from its Old Testament usage. The word apostasy or αποστασεις (Greek) is used in the Old Testament to mean: cause to change belief, a defection, and turning back. Is that not rebellion? The whole seal period is an age of growing apostasy. Paul prophesied that there would be a great falling away before the coming of Messiah (2 Thessalonians 2:2).

His Bow

The crown represents the authority of the man on the white horse but the bow, that the white horseman carries, contradicts the rainbow that was about the throne. Remember the Hebrew word for rainbow and bow is the same. Christ's rainbow represents a righteous and merciful judgment upon man. The bow of the first horseman shoots forth injustice without mercy upon the church, and the basics of evangelical Christianity, but God's bow shoots forth with mercy. The arrows of apostasy seek to kill all biblical morals and distinctions so that global allegiance might usurp authority in men's hearts. The apostasy of the last days will destroy true godly righteousness and replace it with a counterfeit human righteousness. Judgment from God shall then fall as a natural consequence of man's unrighteousness.

B. The Second Seal: Calf-like Beast & Red Horse

> When He opened the second seal, I heard the second living creature saying, "Come and see." Another horse, fiery red, went out. And it was granted to the one who sat on it to take peace from the earth, and that people should kill one another; and there was given to him a great sword (Revelation 6:3-4).

THE NEGATIVE AND POSITIVE IMAGE

The second living creature is the calf and introduces the red horse of Revelation 6. The calf represents a positive image when it is used as a sin offering. With a sin offering there is bloodshed; yet there is also forgiveness which is symbolic of the grace of our Lord and Savior Jesus who shed His blood.

The negative image of the calf in the Old Testament, characterizes the immensity of sin and the abomination of idolatry. The children of Israel shaped a molten calf and proclaimed that this was the god that had led them out of Egypt. They fell away in rebellion. Continual reference is made to this dreadful event of the molten calf which clearly represents the immorality of idolatry.

Today, apostate worship is setting up gods of the imagination in the hearts of men. Idolatry is the accepted way of worship today as men set themselves up as gods. Idolatry rages in many nations today as men unite pagan altars with idols of the Catholic Church. Idols are established as witchcraft increases in strength and the goddess receives new reverence in the hearts of millions. During the seal period, idolatry will increase in every nation of the globe and men's hearts will fall away from the truth.

As the seals are unloosed, idolatry increases. At that time God will repeat the cry He uttered during the reign of the judges: "You have forsaken Me and served other gods? Therefore I will deliver you no more. Go and cry out to the gods which you have chosen; let them deliver you in your time of tribulation" (Judges 10:13, 14).

The Calf-like Beast

The calf-like beast introduced the red horse. The two images again have something in common. Blood issues forth from both images. The calf in biblical times was the sacrifice for sin. And without the shedding of blood there is no remission of sins. The red horseman, however, has the power to take peace from the earth (Rev. 6:4) causing men everywhere to shed blood and kill one another. Terrorism and murder destroys peace and spills blood.

What a comparison of images! Because man has refused the blood of Christ for remission of sins, man is given over to evil deeds and to shedding blood.

Moses, after descending Mt. Horeb, witnessed the people of God worshipping a molten calf; so he broke the tablets of stone as a symbol of the breaking of God's commandments. In the latter days when wickedness and sinfulness is unrestrained, man will give no heed to the commandments of God. Man shall be just like the children of Israel who worshipped the golden calf and the tablets of Christ's law shall be trampled under the feet of mad men. Sin shall bring forth-natural consequences of judgment. These judgments of the seal period are those natural consequences of man's sin, and man's wickedness toward one another. Killings, terrorism, and murders beyond anything the world has ever seen shall be witnessed because man refuses to listen to Christ's laws.

The color red is not only associated with blood, but fire. The Greek word for red originates from the Greek word fire (purros, πυρρος). Fire always speaks of judgment. Because of the promise of the rainbow, the judgment at the end time will not be by water, but by fire

The Great Sword of Islam

Another horse, fiery red, went out. And it was granted to the one who sat on it to take peace from the earth, and that people should kill one another; and there was given to him a great sword (Revelation 6:4).

And there was given unto him a great sword. The rider personifies the man who has the power or has been given authority to kill, conceivably with a purpose that appears good to himself.

Is this great sword, *the sword of Islam?* There are over fifteen million Goggle search results with reference to the *sword of Islam.* The sword of Islam is jihad. There is a song called, "The Sword of Islam" used for ring tones on cell phones. The song tells of the sword that kills infidels, and that will invade the temple mount. Find for yourself on the web.

There is one search result *for 'the great sword of Islam'* that concerns Alija Izetbegovic who was an Islamic fundamentalist.

> *It is difficult to categorically state now that if Izetbegovic's book [The Islamic Declaration] had been read more closely on time numerous young Moslems wouldn't be losing their lives now, but it is sure that our wonder over events in Bosnia would be less. First of all, the careful analyst would realize that Izetbegovic did not see himself and his ideas as a European factor of small importance, tucked away in the mountains of Bosnia whence he had no desire to stir. This careful analyst would also see that the author saw himself (and his project and people) as the diamond tip on* **the great sword of Islam,** *which is now penetrating the belly and heart of Europe, but could turn tomorrow against Africa, Asia, America... as it surely will.*[4]

Alija said in His Islamic Declaration:

> *If he wishes to live and survive as a Muslim, he must create an environment, a community, an order. He must change the world or be changed himself." There can be no peace or coexistence between the "Islamic faith" and non-Islamic societies and political institutions. ... Islam clearly excludes the right and possibility of activity of any strange ideology on its own turf....."BOSNIAN MUSLIM BATTALIONS in Croatia comprising some twenty thousand men! These MUSLIM VOLUNTEER units, called Hanjar (***Sword***), were put in WAFFEN-SS, fought Yugoslav partisans in Bosnia, and carried out police and security duties in Hungary..... In the struggle for an Islamic order all methods are permitted, except one - except crime. No-one has the right to smear the beautiful name of Islam and this struggle by uncontrolled and excessive use of violence. ... In one of the thesis for an Islamic order today we have stated that it is a natural function of the Islamic order to gather all Muslims and Muslim communities throughout the world into one. Under present conditions, this desire means a struggle for creating a great Islamic federation from Morocco to Indonesia, from the tropical Africa to the Central Asia. ..*[5]

A large section of the Moslem population eagerly joined with the Germany Nazis and the Ustashe in World War II. This 20,000 strong force was called the *Hanjar*[6] which means sword. Their icon is the sword. Be aware of the Great Sword of Islam.

The sword that proceeded out of Christ's mouth (Rev. 1:16) is the word *rhomphaia* (ρομθαια) not the word *machaira* (μαχαιρα) which applies to the killing sword of the rider. The sword of Christ is the word of God that is able to discern and judge the intents of the heart. Christ's sword, (*rhomphaia*), is referenced six times in the revelation and each refers to the judgment of God. Christ sword proceeded from his mouth. The word of God is truth and with truth does Christ use his sword.

But the rider on the red horse used a sword (*machaira*) not for the purpose to discern by the power of the Spirit, but to kill by the sword of wickedness and terror. If these horses represent apostate forces, then their sword would counterfeit the Word of God which is the "sword of the spirit" (Ephesians 6:17). Lies from the mouth of this rider are believed by many --lies that deceive and kill. Man kills with this sword often with a purpose that appears good according to the reprobate minds of men who have not heeded the word of God.

Just as the white horse shows the need for justice, the red horse also shows the need for justice in the world.

C. The Third Seal: The Man-like Beast and Black Horse

> When He opened the third seal, I heard the third living creature say, "Come and see." So I looked, and behold, a black horse, and he who sat on it had a pair of scales in his hand. And I heard a voice in the midst of the four living creatures saying, "A quart of wheat for a denarius, and three quarts of barley for a denarius; and do not harm the oil and the wine" (Rev. 6:5,6).

The third living creature of Revelation chapter four has the appearance of a man, for humanism leads men into apostasy. This man-like creature announced the black horse of Revelation six. As knowledge continues to increase at the end time, man shall worship more fervently the works of his own hands. God promised judgment against man's vanity.

> I will utter My judgments against them concerning all their wickedness, because they have forsaken Me, burned incense to other gods, and worshipped the works of their own hands (Jeremiah 1:16).

The negative side of man is evil. Man will achieve greatly, yet God will destroy every achievement that denies holiness and His will. The will of man will usurp the will of God. Man will vainly attempt to establish a kingdom of peace that only Christ can establish. Although mighty in his own eyes, man's evil endeavour shall only lead to death and destruction.

The positive image of *man* is only found in the Son of Man who is also the Bread of life. The Son of Man is able to deliver from the fiery furnace, and no matter how powerful man becomes, he will not be able to deliver himself from God's fiery tribulations.

The rider on the black horse is carrying a pair of balances in his hands representing a shortage of food. We have already witnessed enough famines to realize that man today carries the balances in his own hands. Man today has the ability to tip the balances and meet the need of starving peoples. Instead, many men are tipping the balances and causing famines because of their own greed. Perhaps this horse is black with reference to the Lamentation of Jeremiah. "Our skin was black like an oven because of the terrible famine (Lamentations 5:10).

Jeremiah also uses the color black in reference to mourning. "For this shall the earth mourn, and the heavens above are black..." (Jeremiah 4:28). Is it possible that the seal of famines has already been loosed upon the earth?

D. The fourth Seal: The Eagle and Pale Horse

The fourth living creature of Revelation chapter four is the eagle that introduced the pale horse. There is a positive image of an eagle in scripture of a bird that gives safety to her young when she spreads abroad her great wings. She can bear her little ones upon her wings (Deuteronomy 28:49). The woman of Revelation chapter twelve, who represents Israel, is given two wings of a great eagle to enable her to fly into the wilderness during the abomination of desolation.

The greater image of the eagle is negative. She is an unclean beast not to be eaten according to the Levitical law (Leviticus 11:13, 21). They are an abomination. The eagle is a vulture with great strength and swiftness. It makes haste to destroy its prey. Their young suck blood (Job 39:30). Wicked Babylon is pictured as a lion with the feathers and wings of an eagle because she ravaged with great speed and tore apart the nations as an eagle eats its prey.

The high flight of an eagle is symbolic of man's pride and his arrogant exaltation of the self. Just as swiftly as an eagle mounts into the clouds, God will swiftly bring down the proud heart. The image of the man-like beast represents humanism and the image of man's pride, is represented by the ascent of the eagle. United, these images show destruction.

THE PALE HORSE: PLAGUES AND PESTILENCES

The eagle-like beast summons the man riding upon the pale green horse. Thucydides uses the color "pale green" to describe the people stricken with the plague.[7] Homer uses the color greenish yellow to describe the paleness of a face struck with fear.[8] It is also from the greenish-yellow color of the horse that men associate this horse with plagues and pestilence.

Green has always represented the vegetative kingdom. Why rule out the possibility that death here may have reference to the grass, herbs, and trees of the earth? Even as the earth is destroyed the earth shall be exalted and worshipped as God in the end-times. The earth that men worship will be destroyed, but will men realize that God is Creator and that He demands worship? God will destroy this false exaltation of the earth with the brightness of His coming.

> And they say to him, the God of the Hebrews has called us to him, we will go therefore a three days journey into the wilderness, that we may sacrifice to the Lord our God, lest at any time death (pestilence) or slaughter happen to us (Exodus 5:3, The Septuagint Version of the Old Testament Translated into English).

Notice the Hebrew word for pestilence is rendered *death* in the Septuagint. This rider's name of the Pale horse is death. Plagues, like AIDS, shall magnify the death toll. Similarly, man's vanity summons death. Spiritual death as well as physical death is implied here because hell followed the pale (chloros, χλωρος) horse. In the Old Testament, God often fashioned tribulation by this threesome -- the sword, the famine, and the pestilence or death. These parallel the three disasters of the second, third, and fourth horsemen

E. Summing up the Seal Period

THEIR IMAGE

The four beasts in a positive sense represent the chosen church when they call out holy, holy, holy. It is because of His holiness that He must judge sin. The holiness of God determines true justice. God has winked at sin long enough and it will be punished. The host magnifies his holiness before the throne at the time sin is unleashed in the hearts of evil men, and when the seven seals are broken.

Conversely, the four beasts negatively represent the apostate church, and the spirit of the Babylonian whore who shall develop quickly during the time of the seals. Apostasy of the last days will seemingly destroy true worship. Apostasy rings a clear note of hypocrisy today. The apostasy in the church today hypocritically glorifies God and sings *Holy, Holy, Holy*; yet, she is deluded and defiled with sin.

The seal period can be described by these picturesque and symbolic contrasts. The earthly altar slays the righteous (Rev. 6:9), while the heavenly altar intercedes in the presence of God (Rev. 8:3). False prophets ride white horses, while the martyrs wear white robes. Evil destroys while holiness is mocked. The bow of the general's kill, but the rainbow about the throne arches the promises of God. The sword of man destroys, but the sword of Christ raises justice.

THEIR CHARACTER OF EVIL

During the seals the world witnesses the greatest apostasy of all times, innumerable deaths, unbelievable killings, unforgivable murders, terrorism, and disastrous plagues. Matthew describes the great apostasy as a lawlessness that abounds, as hatred that increases, and as betrayals and coldness that subverts love (Matthew 24:9–13).

These are the judgments that God permits at the hands of sinful and depraved men. Even persecution shall be allowed at the hands of those who hate God and his righteousness. Man shall fall into the pathway of Cain the murderer; man shall run greedily in the error of Balaam; and man shall be consumed with the rebellion of Korah (Jude 11).

During these end-times, we shall witness more than a political tug of war. We shall witness spiritual battles between the forces of darkness and the forces of light. Even the occult world prophesies such a conflict, but confusion shall exist because sinful man will accept darkness as the truth and the light of the gospel as darkness. The forces of darkness wager against the forces of light and the power struggle consumes the affairs of man. The power struggle consumes the bride of Christ in the form of persecution. Sadly, a falling away warrants a bill of divorcement for many who are rebellious and unfaithful.

CHARACTER OF APOSTASY

The falling away that we have been discussing is during the seal period and precedes the evil of the trumpets and wrath periods. The seven seals are a countdown to Satan's wrath. As each seal is opened the dreadfulness of sin becomes more atrocious, and sin ripens for the gathering of the grapes that shall be tossed into the vials of Christ's wrath. It is very possible that we have entered the seal period because every disaster of the seal period is happening now and shall worsen over a period of many years. During the seal-tribulation man's wrath is seen -- one nation against another, one person against another, and one leader against another.

A falling away must occur before the Antichrist appears (1 Thessalonians 2:3). I believe that the falling away happens during the seal period. The seal-tribulation brings to light the abominations and rebellion of men's hearts, and the irrefutable, destructive power of Satan. The falling away steers reprobate men into the control of Satan. The Antichrist would not have sufficient power to rule with terror at the end of time if men's thoughts and ways were not continually corrupt (1 Thessalonians 2:3).

Have we already entered the seal Period? I believe so.

FURTHER STUDY

1. How do the four horsemen show the need for justice?

2. What are the signs today of apostasy?

3. What could future signs of apostasy be?

4. Make a list of verses in Revelation using the word mouth? What do you learn from them?

Four Horsemen of the Apocalypse

Lion Beast Introduces the White Horse
World Leaders

Lion of Judah   Vs.   Satan as a Roaring Lion

_____

Calf-Like Beast Introduces the Red Horse
Terrorism, Islam

Blood Shed for Forgiveness   Vs.   Blood Shed, Killing

_____

The Man-Like Beast Introduces the Black Horse
Famine

Son of Man   Vs .   Humanism & Pride

_____

The Eagle Beast Introduces the Pale Horse
Plagues, Pestilences

Safety Under His Wings   Vs.   Unclean Bird

PART C:

VENGEANCE OF CHRIST

Chapters 7, 8

7. Christ's Trumpet Vengeance

Read Rev. 8:1-13

When threatened by wild beasts Polycarp said:

> *"Call for them; for the repentance from better to worse is a change not permitted to us; but it is a noble thing to change from untowardness to righteousness."*

When threatened by fire Polycarp said:

> *"Thou threatenest that fire which burneth for a season and after a little while is quenched; for thou art ignorant of the fire of the future judgment and eternal punishment, which is reserved for the ungodly. But why delayest thou? Come, do what thou wilt."*[1]

Polycarp was considered an "illustrious teacher" and a "preeminent martyr." "He was not merely an illustrious teacher, but also a pre-eminent martyr, whose martyrdom all desire to imitate, as having been altogether consistent with the Gospel of Christ."[2] In the midst of the fires, God framed a wall of protection around him. The realization of Christ's presence and power in the midst of tribulation is essential if the church is about to encounter the greatest persecution of history without fear.

A. The Priestly Images of the Martyrs:

The throne scenes of the Apocalypse gloriously portray priestly images. The throne scenes are a figure of the temple of God in the heavens, and the access that believers have beyond the veil. The priestly ministry of Jesus is manifested as He stands at the right hand of the Father having been slain as a lamb for the sins of mankind and now serving after the order of Melchizedek (Hebrews 5:6).

The priestly ministry of the saints rises with the incense upon the heavenly altar. The twenty-four elders carry bowls full of incense which are the prayers of the saints (Rev. 5:8). As the seventh seal is opened, an angel bears to the golden altar that is before the throne, a golden censer full of the prayers of the saints. The prayers of all the saints ascend as sweet incense from the hand of the angel. These prayers would include the cries of the multitudes of martyrs that are slain and persecuted during the fifth seal. Worship and praise fills the clouds and the air with the glory of God. The sea of glass resembles the molten sea of Solomon's temple, and the bronze laver of the tabernacle, for purification is a necessary ritual in the temple of God.

The priestly images are also seen in Revelation chapter three. Jesus stands among the seven candlesticks and the overcomer has been promised to be a pillar in the temple of God (Rev.3:12). Truly the hour of incense has come (Luke 1:10).

The altar is also a priestly image. There are three altars in the Apocalypse -- the heathen altar upon which the martyrs were sacrificed (Rev. 6:9), the golden altar of incense that was before the throne of God (Rev. 8:3), and the altar of the temple that shall be in Jerusalem during trumpet six (Rev.11:1). The martyrs are found beneath the heathen altar. They have been sacrificed by the hands of wicked men and now they are cast beneath this altar as dung, as dung before men, but precious in the sight of God. An altar speaks of a religious power not a political power. The heathen altars of demonic men shall become slaughter sites of Christians. Whether these altars are literal or symbolic, they exist for the benefit of evil men, false religions, and unrighteous beliefs. Religion becomes more defiled in preparation for the worship of Satan.

Incense rises with the prayers of the saints. Holy incense[3] was a special formula. According to the book of Exodus, incense was a combination of sweet spices: stacte, a scent from the inner bark of the styrax; onycha, a marine mollusk; galbanum, a Syrian gum that holds the scent of the mixture; and salt.[4] According to the findings of Lightfoot, incense was made from spices and the amber of the Jordan - an herb known to few. It was also made from bitumen, or that which was from the Salt Sea often called Sodom's bitumen.[5] It is hard to believe that holy incense included an ingredient from the Salt Sea because the Talmudists assigned to the Sea of Sodom anything that was predetermined to rejection and cursing according to Talmudic law, and was forbidden to be used. A doctor of Talmudic law once said, "that he devoted the moneys of idolatry into the Salt Sea. Hence is that allusion 'and death and hell were cast into the lake of fire'"[6] However, God can take that which is designed for death and impart eternal life. Christ has done this for every believer and every overcomer. Christ shall do this for every believer and every overcomer (Exodus 30:34, 35).

The priestly image of incense referred to both the aroma and the sweet smoke substance that arose from the altar or censer. Incense was originally burned in portable censers but later upon the altar of incense that stood before the veil. Incense was burned every morning and evening by only the high priest of the Old Testament. During New Testament days, even the ordinary unqualified priest burned incense; and then at the end of time, false sacrifices and unholy incense shall be burned to the God of heaven by many. In Revelation, the four living creatures have bowls full of incense and the twenty-four elders had bowls full of incense (Rev 5:8).

B. True And False Worshippers

The high priest, once a year, took incense into the holy of holies to make atonement for sin. The congregation tarried for God's acceptance of the sacrifice. New Testament atonement has been made in the cross; therefore, if atonement for sin is reflected in the offering of this incense, then there is also reference to the daily cleansing of the heart before God.

The offering of the saint's prayers in the Apocalypse is accepted before the altar of God and the throne of God. These saints serve God day and night in His dwelling place, in the presence of God who will come to tabernacle among them (future tense). The incense of these martyrs is indeed a costly perfume that demands the sacrifice of their lives.

FALSE WORSHIP IN JEREMIAH'S DAY: JEREMIAH 44 : 17-23

False worship in Jeremiah's day was horrendous. They burned incense to the queen of heaven and worshipped her. Men and women of Jeremiah's day thanked the queen of heaven for plenteous food. What was God's judgment? Because of their false worship, their land was left desolate.

False incense shall burn again. God sees what men are doing today and will no longer bear it. And we see that the same thing happens in the Revelation. The first four trumpets bring disaster to the land, the sea, crops, and animals.

FALSE WORSHIP IN EZEKIEL'S VISION

And I looked, and there in the firmament that was above the head of the cherubim, there appeared something like a sapphire stone, having the appearance of the likeness of a throne. Then He spoke to the man clothed with linen, and said, "Go in among the wheels, under the cherub, fill your hands with coals of fire from among the cherubim, and scatter them over the city (Ezekiel 10:1, 2).

In Ezekiel's vision, a man clothed with linen went among the cherubim, (Ezekiel 10:1-22). The man in linen took coals of fire from among the cherubs and scattered them over the city in judgment. Similarly, in the Apocalypse, the censer that is filled with fire from the altar is cast to the earth. The plague begins.

THE REBELLION OF KORAH

The apostate forces of the end-time re-echo the rebellion of Korah. Korah who was a grandson of Levi, and Dathan, and Abiram from the tribe of Reuben, rebelled against Moses and Aaron. The Korathites were collaborators against the religious and political leadership of Moses. Insurrection mounted against the supremacy of Aaron as high priest and Moses as the law keeper. They asserted a self-authoritative voice that usurped the commandments of God. Moses claimed too much authority in view of their greed and desires. They complained with insults, "You have not brought us into a land flowing with milk and honey" (Numbers 16:11). They also desired to be priests of God, when only the chosen ones of the sons of Aaron were priests. The Korathites were temple singers (Numbers 16:4), and temple gatekeepers (2 Chronicles 20:19. They were set over things made in pans. They were bakers in the house of the Lord, but they desired the chosen position of priesthood. They considered themselves as holy as Moses and Aaron. But God said differently.

Moses called them to a show down at the door of the tabernacle. On the morrow, God was to show them who were truly called a priest and holy before Him. Each rebellious Korathite assembled with his brazen censer to offer incense before the Lord. Instead of accepting the incense, God did a new thing (Numbers 16:39); they fell alive into the pit (meaning hades or hell).

> *So Moses said to Aaron, "Take a censer and put fire in it from the altar, put incense on it, and take it quickly to the congregation and make atonement for them; for wrath has gone out from the Lord. The plague has begun" (Numbers 16:46).*

Even after the 250 were swallowed up by the fire of the Lord, the rebellion continued until 14,700 were killed.

Resembling the Korathite rebellion, false incense will burn to the gods of the heathen and false incense will also burn to the God of heaven. False incense shall not be accepted before the throne, but shall boomerang into the vengeance of God.

In the latter days, modern Kohathites will conspire against the true church of Jesus Christ. Rebellious mouths will mock the holiness of the church and recapitulate the sarcasm of the Kohathites: "We are just as holy as you." Incense shall be a valuable trading commodity with fallen Babylon (Rev.18:13) and Babylonian incense will burn worldwide unto the gods and goddesses within the imaginations of evil hearts. Incense in that day will be an abomination before God just as incense in the days of Isaiah became an abomination because their hearts were far from God; their hands were full of blood; and their souls were filthy unclean. A fire will be rekindled beneath the sacred pillars of the house of the sun and beneath the gods of the Baals. Cakes to the queen of heaven will again be baked as an offering (Jeremiah 44:19).

There is hardly a store, today, where you can't find incense — incense from "wild fire" to "herbal magic" for protection, good health, love, and much more. Our Babylonish world is full of incense.

The historical struggle between the Levites and the sons of Aaron shall be reiterated. The apostate church of Babylonian character will rage war against the true church of Jesus and in doing so they revolt against the laws of God. Even Satan himself will war against the saints. Believers shall fall away from the truth mocking and scoffing. "You have not brought us into the Promised Land. This is a land of tribulation and strife. There is no peace." But like Israel who fought her way into and through the Promise Land, the saints will encounter spiritual battles and persecution of a magnitude that has never been attested.

What a difference between the incense offered by the martyrs and the incense offered by the Korathites? The martyrs gave their lives for righteousness, but Korah and company lost their souls, being misaligned with self-righteousness. These who are martyred will serve in His temple day and night forever, but those in the rebellion of Korah lost their temple positions for eternity. The censer in the hand of the angel was able to bring victory for the believers, but the censers of Korah's men were hammered into flat plates for a covering of the altar. When will we learn that our chosen calling in Christ must be within the bounds of Christ's laws?

Man today arrogates his own priesthood, becomes a god, and burns incense before the gods of the New Age. Every man becomes perfect in his own eyes, but the judgment of God will declare who is holy. Defying Christ's laws, each man institutes his own laws of priesthood. All men can offer incense before the Lord, but not all is accepted. Only the incense offerings that comply with His will and His laws are acceptable.

The faithful are found worthy of persecution not punishment. Persecution is the consequence of obedience not judgment. Patience and faith in tribulation have the highest reward (2 Thessalonians 1:4-6, Hebrews 6:12, James 1: 3, 4).

God said to Isaiah and he speaks to us today. "Bring no more futile sacrifices; Incense is an abomination to Me" (Isaiah 1:13).

C. Vengeance for the Persecuted Church

Read Rev. 8:7-12

Hail and fire are cast upon the earth for the first trumpet. For the second trumpet a mountain of fire is cast into the sea. For the third trumpet, star wormwood falls from heaven, ablaze like fire. These three judgments are sequentially cast to the earth with the censer of fire from the altar of God (Rev. 8:5). The fourth trumpet struck the sun, moon and stars.

Christ's trumpet vengeance proceeds from the golden altar to avenge the persecution of the saints and a command comes from the four horns of the golden altar to the angels with trumpets. Christ's judgments proceed from His throne, from the golden altar. It is God who commands these angels, whether they are good or evil, to execute the trumpet vengeance.

In the Old Testament, incense was brought within the veil to make atonement, but incense in the Apocalypse proceeds from within the veil and is cast to the earth to bring vengeance. "And the Angel took the censer, filled it with fire from the altar, and threw it to the earth. And there were noises, thunderings, lightnings, and an earthquake" (Rev.8:5-6). The fire of Christ's vengeance is scattered throughout the world just as the fire from the Korah rebellion was scattered some distance away. There is a connection between the incense and judgment. The prayers of the martyrs are also linked with the vengeance upon evil men.

In Revelation, the angel with the censer and incense stands before the heavenly veil or the throne of God. Remember, judgment proceeds from the throne of God. A censer contained hot coals and incense is sprinkled upon it. The angel then fills the censer with fire from the altar of incense and casts it to the earth. The fire of God generates lightning, voices, thundering, and an earthquake.

The trumpet vengeances begin, but it is because of the prayers of the saints that God pours forth this vengeance. Because of the faithfulness of the saints, God can punish the unjust man that stands without excuse. Because of the holiness of the saints, the angel proceeds to cast fire upon the earth. The prayers of the saints are answered as the incense is accepted before God and the trumpets sound forth judgment. The martyr's divine calling to bring forth judgment is the role of the faithful church not the role of lucky believers who are saved during the tribulation.

During the seals, apostate forces eliminate what they call the pollution of the earth and a holocaust of fundamental Christians will be purged from the earth. But then during the trumpet period, God purges with his fire what He calls pollution. The prayers of the martyrs are answered. Those who persecuted the church at the command of their gods or spirit guides witness the destruction of their own gods. A great victory is won and the God of gods prevails over the gods of men.

God displays this vengeance for the duration of the first four trumpets upon the environment and mother earth. The physical heavenlies are literally shaken while the gods of this world are attacked. God attacks the environmental gods. Vengeance is sought for the saints who refused to worship the environmental gods. The earth which men worship is cursed and none of man's mystical rituals and enchantments will succeed in preventing its destruction.

Apostate forces will have reached their peak by the beginning of the trumpets, but by the end of the fourth trumpet, men will be in despair. Any prosperity that will exist is vanished by Christ's vengeance. The apostate forces that have honored nature will be devastated. Mother Nature becomes totally unpredictable and unreliable. Christ's vengeance will set fire to the earth to which man is so devoted.

Hail, fire, and blood burn the trees and all the green grass. A mountain of fire transforms the sea into blood. One third of the sea creatures die and one third of all ships are destroyed. These plagues mock the attempts of environmentalists to save the earth and the seas from pollution.

The lifeless objects that the martyrs refuse to worship are destroyed by fire from the altar of incense. Trees, which are central to pagan religions and mysticism, die because wood is the substance of carved images. The sun, moon, and star gods are darkened for a third of the day and night. Darkness presides which symbolically represents the sinfulness and debauchery of men's souls. These plagues mock witchcraft and the sun worshippers who will increase in the last days. As men's hearts become disillusioned with the strength of their many gods, the Antichrist will set himself up as God.

The normal direction of fire is upward, but the fire of God falls downward (Rev. 8:6). It burns and purges everything that opposes the character and purpose of God.

The miraculous and supernatural are witnessed in the hail. Only God could mix the extreme heat of fire with the extreme cold of hail (Rev. 8:7). In Josephus's day, hail caused houses to collapse and killed people.[7] What will be the destruction of hail in the last days?

Those who worship the earth will be punished by the earth. Man will starve for the delicacies of taste. Water will no longer quench man's thirst. Economic disaster will escalate astronomically. Earth magic, sky magic, and sea magic will be cursed with disasters because of man's sin. Later, during the vials of Christ's wrath, God destroys those who destroy the earth (Rev.11:18). Lack of environmental concern does not destroy the earth; sinfulness destroys the earth.

Christ's trumpets declare His vengeance, yet warn humanity to fear God because of further terrifying judgments yet to come. Christ has the right to enact His vengeance. "Vengeance is Mine, says the Lord" (Psalm 94:1-2). All throughout scripture, man called upon God for vengeance. "O

Lord God, to whom vengeance belongs - O God, to whom vengeance belongs, shine forth! Rise up, O Judge of the earth; Render punishment to the proud" (Romans 12:19). Finally, vengeance is displayed here in the Apocalypse during the first four trumpets.

FURTHER STUDY

1. Why do you think God accepted the incense offerings of the martyrs?
2. What kind of offerings does God expect of us today?
3. Could you be a preeminent martyr like Polycarp?
4. God has made us kings and priests unto Him. How is that true?

The Golden Censer of Revelation	The Censer of the Korah Group
Revelation 8:1-13	Numbers 16: 1-9, 17-40
During the seals, men become very evil and rebel against God.	Korah and company rebel against Moses and Aaron and not satisfied with their temple service wanting the priest-hood.
An angel from heaven with a golden censer and the prayers of the saints burned incense upon the golden altar.	Korah and company bring censers with fire and act as priests.
God is pleased with good fire and holy incense.	God was displeased.
Angel filled censer with fire from the golden altar and cast it to the earth.	Eleazar, son of Aaron, a rightful priest took the censers and scattered the fire.
The first Four Trumpets followed from the throne of God. The vengeance of God came upon the earth with thunder, lightning and an earthquake. 1. Hail, fire, and blood are cast to the earth and 1.3 of trees is burned. 2. Fire, like a great mountain, was cast into the sea and 1/3 of all life in the sea died. 1/3 of ships destroyed. 3. A great burning star falls and 1/3 of water becomes wormwood. 4. 1/3 of sun and moon and stars smitten	The earth swallowed them up. Fire consumed 250 men More followed the example of Korah and 14,700 die.
	Broad plates were made out of the censers that Korah and company used.

8. CHRIST'S TRUMPET WARNINGS

A. Warning Signs in the Heavens

Read Rev. Chapters 9-12

Justice and vengeance undoubtedly proceed from the throne of God and righteousness triumphs in the heavens. Star wormwood falls from heaven; the star of the fifth trumpet falls from heaven; and the dragon and his angels are cast out of heaven to the earth. The command to harvest the earth proceeds from the temple in heaven (Rev. 14:15). The heavenlies are scourged of all evil for we see that the dragon and his angels are cast out of heaven (Rev. 12:7-12) and Satan's final fall begins. Stars fall; the heavens are shaken. God purges the heavens and the earth while disasters occur on earth during the trumpet period.

Christ's trumpet signs will signal the brevity of time. Signs in the heavens will enable the righteous to discern the times (Matthew 16:3), but the unrighteous will blaspheme the signs of heaven. The whole heavens will be shaken and there will be signs in the sun, in the moon, and in the stars (Luke 21:11). The signs of the trumpets shall precede the Second Coming of Christ and these signs shall precede the earthly kingdom of God (Luke 21:31). These signs in the heavens will precede the redemption of Israel. He who can discern the signs will know and rejoice that their redemption is imminent and that the destruction of the unrighteous is sure.

The signs in the heavens shall be a witness to the sovereignty of God. The prophecies of Matthew, Mark, Luke, and John will come to pass. These signs will terrify the heathen because they have refused to be recipients of the mercies and promises of God. But, to the believer, these signs shall bring assurance of the eternal promises of God. The fulfillment of prophecy cultivates a healthy hope. Prophetic signs signal Christ's control. Hope thus encourages patience that we might endure a little longer the tribulation and persecutions of life. Jeremiah encouraged Israel with similar words. "Thus says the LORD, Learn not the way of the heathen, and be not dismayed at the signs of heaven; for the heathen are dismayed at them" (Jeremiah 10:3).

Then the fourth angel sounded: And a third of the sun was struck, a third of the moon, and a third of the stars, so that a third of them were darkened. A third of the day did not shine, and likewise the night. And I looked, and I heard an angel flying through the midst of heaven, saying with a loud voice, "Woe, woe, woe to the inhabitants of the earth, because of the remaining blasts of the trumpet of the three angels who are about to sound" (Rev. 8:12-13).

Signs and miracles are not always from God, but God has been very specific as to what His signs will be so that he who looks to Christ's word for guidance will understand and discern the end-times and rejoice. God is exact, for example, when He says that these heavenly bodies will not shine for one third of the day and the night, that's what it will be.

Signs were given at Christ's first coming to those who would believe. A star was a sign to the Wisemen who were eager to worship Him. The sign of angels in the heavens appeared to shepherds who were awaiting His coming. The dove was a sign to John the Baptist that this was the Christ. Signs then and now for His Second Coming are for the saints, not the world. It is not unscriptural to observe the times and the seasons. Much confusion occurred in the early church and even now because the church is not observing the times and the seasons carefully enough.

WORMWOOD

Amos warned the children of Israel of the judgment of God because they had turned justice to wormwood, and had laid righteousness to rest [as the KJV states] or they cast down righteousness to the earth [as the NKJV says] (Amos 5:7, 6:12). Now the nations will taste the wormwood from heaven; yet, star wormwood is the result of man's perverted justice.

Wormwood is the name of the star that falls from heaven and causes a 1/3 of the waters to become bitter. This is not the first time God had given man bitter water. God had just delivered Israel from the Egyptians and the Red Sea; they had traveled three days and found no water. When they came to Marah the waters were too bitter to drink. It was the tree of life that was cut and cast into the bitterness of life's swelling sea at God's command that made the water sweet (Exodus 15:23).

At the end of time, bitter waters are sent as a curse from God. Man has refused the fountain of living water for muddy cisterns of man's making. These muddy cisterns are bitterness to God; their backslidings were bitter in the sight of God. It was a bitter thing to forsake the Lord (Jeremiah 2:19), the end of a harlot is as bitter as wormwood (Proverbs 5:4), and the vine of Sodom is bitterness to the taste of God (Deuteronomy 32:32). God purges the earth of the bitter taste of wickedness.

To test whether a woman was unfaithful to her husband, the priest of Old Testament days would give her bitter water to drink. The curse would cause her thigh to rot and her belly to swell if she was guilty (Numbers 5:18-27). Bitterness was always a sign of unrighteousness in the Old Testament. The vengeance of God is determined upon the man who forsakes the righteous and living waters of God for man's polluted cisterns. Is it possible that the curse of star wormwood will only kill the unrighteous and guilty man, just as the guilty wife was cursed by the bitter waters administered by the priest?

Now according to the New Testament the "wages of sin is death" (Romans 3:23) or we can say the bitterness of sin is death. Man's unrighteousness is the victim of the star wormwood. Many men die when they taste the bitter waters of the earth.

We see from the above illustrations that bitterness also had an association with water. Contrariwise, Isaiah used water to describe peace and righteousness. "Oh, that you had heeded My commandments! Then your peace would have been like a river, and your righteousness like the waves of the sea" (Isaiah 48:18).

When star wormwood falls from heaven, don't drink the waters.

B. Destruction in Thirds

During the trumpets 1/3 of the trees are destroyed, 1/3 of the seas become blood, 1/3 of the waters become wormwood, 1/3 part of the sun, moon, and stars are smitten, and 1/3 of men are slain in the Euphrates battle. This pattern of thirds shows that God Almighty is in control.

This is not the first time God has destroyed by thirds. Destruction appears as a pattern of thirds in the Old Testament and in Jewish history. Ezekiel, at the Lord's command, demonstrated His coming judgments. He took a barber's razor and before the people of Jerusalem shaved his head. He divided a third and cast it into the fires. He slashed a third of the hair with a knife and a third was scattered or cast into the wind.

> One-third of you shall die of the pestilence, and be consumed with famine in your midst; and one-third shall fall by the sword all around you; and I will scatter another third to all the winds, and I will draw out a sword after them (Ezekiel 5:12).

Zechariah prophesied that in the day of the Lord, two thirds would be cut off and die, but that a remnant would remain. That remnant was often expressed as one third.

> "And it shall come to pass in all the land," Says the LORD, "That two-thirds in it shall be cut off and die, But one-third shall be left in it: I will bring the one-third through the fire, Will refine them as silver is refined, And test them as gold is tested. They will call on My name, And I will answer them. I will say, 'This is My people'; And each one will say, 'The LORD is my God' " (Zechariah 13:8–9).

When we see God passing judgment in thirds, it becomes a sign to the believer that God is in control.

C. Trumpets Warn and Announce

Christ's trumpets are very significant in the Apocalypse just as the blowing of the shofar was vital and helpful to the welfare of Jewish society. The Law of Moses was sounded forth with the blast of the shofar (Exodus 19:19); and during the apocalyptic trumpets, God judges those who have broken the laws of Moses. The walls of Jericho crumbled at the sound of the trumpet (Joshua 6:20), but the apocalyptic trumpets crumble the empire of Satan. The O.T. shofar announced the accession of a new king (1 Kings 34:39); but at the sound of the seventh trumpet, heavenly voices prophetically announce the King of kings. "The kingdoms of this world are become the kingdoms of our Lord; and of his Christ: and he shall reign forever and ever (Rev. 11:15).

The Old Testament shofar also announced the ingathering of the exiles from Babylonian captivity (Isaiah 27:13), but the apocalyptic trumpets will proclaim the ingathering of the final harvest. Judaism taught that the shofar would announce the resurrection of the dead,[1] and at the conclusion of the seventh trumpet, the Rapture and resurrection will explode with immortality and eternal life.

God's sovereignty will be recognized and honored in Israel during the trumpet period. The message and miracles of the Two Witnesses will demonstrate the sovereignty of God. The judgment of God will proclaim His sovereignty in those days as the Messiah King prepares to reign.

Rosh Hashanah was the Jewish Feast of Trumpets. The shofar was blown to announce the Feast of Trumpets in the seventh month Tishri, and at the beginning of a new year. Rosh Hashanah was a time to remember God's sovereignty; God was affirmed King over Israel and the world. The end-time trumpets will also remind the Jewish people of God's sovereignty and His promise to be King over all the earth.

The feast of Rosh Hashanah was a call to repentance. Israel was allotted ten days between Rosh Hashanah and Yom Kippur to repent. Three books were opened on Rosh Hashanah, one for the righteous, one for the wicked, and one for the average person. The names of the righteous were written in the Book of Life on Rosh Hashanah. Men greeted each other on that day with the words, "L'shanah tovah tikatevu,"[2] "May your name be inscribed in the book of life." Is it not time for Israel to repent?

The festival of Rosh Hashanah was instituted by God and given to the nation of Israel (Num. 29:1–6). Judgment was to begin on Rosh Hashanah and end ten days later on the Day of Atonement. Judgment on Rosh Hashanah according to Judaism was not limited to Israel, but embraced the whole world. It was believed that God took note of the sins of all mankind. The judgment of God was inevitable, and only averted by repentance. Repentance was necessary because the books of judgment were sealed for another year.

Similarly, the days of the apocalyptic trumpets will be days of repentance for the Jews. Israel will turn to her God. The book of life will be open and those not found in the book of life will be cast into the lake of fire. The Mishna prescribed that each man concentrated upon the blast of the shofar. In doing so, he was responding to the call of repentance. If a man failed to listen to the blast, he was in danger of the judgment of God.[3]

D. The Warning of the Two Witnesses:

Read Rev. 11:1-19

By considering the duration and events of the trumpets, we can determine when the first 3½ years of the Antichrist treaty would occur. The duration of the fifth trumpet is only five months (Rev. 9:5) and the duration of the sixth trumpet is for one year, one month, one day and one hour (Rev. 9:15). This totals to approximately a year and a half. Then the abomination of desolation is for 3½ years following the death of the two witnesses. Therefore the first half of Daniel's seventieth week, needs two years more to complete the seven years of the treaty. We must allow time for the temple to be built; yet, there is no indication from the Apocalypse that the temple is built during the seal period, but during the ministry of the Two Witnesses only. The Antichrist kills the two prophets and sets up the abomination of desolation at the close of the second woe or the sixth trumpet. Therefore, we can conclude that the first 3½ years of Daniel's seventieth week would coincide with the first six trumpets.

During the vengeance of Christ, trumpets 1 to 4, the temple is rebuilt, the Two Witnesses proclaim and demonstrate the truth, and God brings vengeance upon the earth for the persecution of the saints. God gives the church and the Jews true justice at this time. There is actually peace and prosperity for Israel during this time.

At the same time as the heavens are purged and the vengeance of God is enacted, our faithful God empowers two great prophets to minister to the Jews during the first four trumpets. The Two Witnesses sound out warnings to Israel and a future John prophesies.

Who are these Two Witnesses? Firstly, we must remember that they are but men, regardless of the miracles and wonders they achieve for the people of God and against the heathen. As men they die at the hand of the Antichrist and the Antichrist repudiates his negotiations and initiates the abomination of desolation, but as servants of God they are raised by the power of God.

We know that the second woe is passed at the time the Two Witnesses are killed (Rev. 11:14). "Then the seventh angel sounded." The seventh trumpet coincides with the third woe which comes quickly. This tells us that the Two Witnesses were ministering to the world before the seventh trumpet.

Elijah

The Two Witnesses are prophets ordained of God to minister for 3½ years. Dressed in sackcloth they resuscitate the dramatic role of Old Testament prophets. They emulate the miracles of Elijah. The heavens ceased to rain for 3½ years at the command of Elijah (2 Kings 1:12, James 5:17) and the witnesses will be able to command the heavens that it not rain for the duration of their ministry which is for 3½ years. Notice the repetition of 3½. Elijah caused fire to consume groups of fifty because they had inquired of Beelzebub the god of Ekron (2 Kings 1:12). The Witnesses for 3½ years shall be invincible devouring their enemies by fire at will. This fire that projects from their mouth does not resemble the demonic powers of sorcerers that I associate with the fire that proceeds from the mouth of the Beast, but they are endued with divine power to execute judgment in all the earth. The Two Witnesses may also destroy Baal worshippers in honor of the true God as Elijah did.

The wonders of the Two Witnesses happen at the same time as the first four trumpets because the source of power is the same. The four trumpets proceed from the throne because of the prayers of the saints and the Two Witnesses are anointed by God.

Malachi prophesied that Elijah would proceed the day of the Lord (Malachi 4:5). John the Baptist partially fulfilled this prophecy, but this prophecy will again be fulfilled immediately before the day of the Lord. In Elijah's day there were seven thousand who had not bowed a knee to

Baal and at the death of the Two Witnesses seven thousand will be killed in the city of Jerusalem (Rev.11:13). This act is perhaps the vengeance of God for the death of the Two Witnesses and in honor of those who did not bow to Baal in Elijah's day.

Elijah was carried away in a chariot to heaven, and the angels buried Moses such that no man knew where he was buried. Because both disappeared and did not die as other men, many interpreters of the scripture say that the witnesses will be Elijah and Moses. John the Baptist came in the spirit and power of Elijah, but he was not Elijah. It is equally possible that the witnesses shall come in the spirit and power of Elijah and Moses.

MOSES

Moses was Israel's deliverer from the bondage of Egypt. God empowered Moses to burden ten plagues upon the Egyptians. The Two Witnesses will recapitulate the miracles of Moses. Like Moses they shall turn rivers into blood, and cast plagues upon the earth, as they will. Moses was familiar with the thunder of God at the giving of the law on Mount Sinai. The Witnesses also will be familiar with the seven thunders of God which utter their voices of judgment at this time.

TWO OLIVE TREES

The two witnesses are also likened to the two olive trees of whom Zechariah speaks (Zechariah 11:4). In Zechariah's day these were Zerubbabel the governor of Judah and Joshua the high priest. The Two Witnesses like Zerubbabel are chosen signet rings (Haggai 2:23). They are Christ's voice of power and authority to the whole world.

After the Babylonian captivity, the Spirit of the Lord stirred these leaders and the remnant of Israel, who had re-gathered in the Holy Land to rebuild the temple. The witnesses of Revelation are equated with the two olive trees of Zechariah because shall not God also stir the hearts of the Two Witnesses to rebuild the temple?

THE TRIBULATION TEMPLE

In the fullness of time, Israel, under the leadership of Christ's two chosen olive trees, will rebuild the temple in Jerusalem. It is my belief that during the sixth seal, the Islamic mosque on the temple mount will be destroyed by an earthquake. The sixth seal witnesses a great earthquake such that every mountain and island was moved out of place (Rev 6:14). Then the temple is rebuilt during the first 3½ years of Daniel's Seventieth Week (trumpets 1-6) and before the Antichrist invokes the abomination of desolation within that temple. The enemy of Israel endures such torment and anguish during the first six trumpets at the hand of God, and at the command of the two witnesses, thus Israel is able to safely rebuild the temple.

The Antichrist makes a covenant with Israel; this covenant, I believe, promises religious freedom to Israel and the right to rebuild the temple. Such a covenant would be necessary and applicable after a global persecution and religious purging of fundamentalism.[2] The Jewish nation would be concerned for her religious identity; but after 3½ years, the Antichrist breaks that covenant.

There is a unique comparison between the events of Zechariah's day and the days of the first six trumpets. As it was in the days of Zerubbabel, the temple will be built in troublesome times. The seven lamp stands are in the midst of the two olive trees in Zechariah's vision, and in Revelation also. At the same time that the temple was being built in Zechariah's day, the eyes of the Lord are going to and fro through the whole earth (Zechariah 4:10). Then according to Amos the eyes of the Lord purge the Gentile nations. "Behold, the eyes of the Lord God are on the sinful kingdom and I will destroy it from the face of the earth" (Amos 9:8-31).

The Two Witnesses can also provide protection from the enemy so that the temple can be completed. "And if anyone wants to harm them, fire proceeds from their mouth and devours their enemies. And if anyone wants to harm them, he must be killed in this manner" (Rev. 11:5). It is not until the temple is built and their ministry is complete that this divine protection from God is lifted and the two witnesses are killed. The same happened to John the Baptist. This prophet was beheaded when his ministry was completed so that men would then look to the Christ. Unfortunately, many look to the Antichrist in that terrible day.

These two witnesses not only provide protection but have a unique ministry to the Jews. Recapitulating the ministry of Zerubbabel and Joshua, the witnesses will have a unique ministry in rebuilding the temple. Like John the Baptist, this prophet like Elijah will deliver a message of repentance to Israel and unite the hearts of the fathers and the sons.[3]

The miracles of these witnesses testify to the power of God. The rebuilding of the temple becomes a sign to the believer. The nations are warned not to come up against Israel or they shall receive the judgment of God. The Two Witnesses take on the role of an Old Testament Prophet, who always warned of coming judgment.

> *When you are in distress, and all these things come upon you in the latter days, when you turn to the Lord your God and obey His voice. '(For the Lord your God is a merciful God) He will not forsake you nor destroy you, nor forget the covenant of your fathers which He swore to them (Deuteronomy 4:30-31).*

The Two Witnesses plague the whole earth (Rev. 11:6). Their enemies are the nations of the world. Peoples from many nations rejoice and celebrate their death because the whole globe will have been a victim of their plagues and torments.

> *And those who dwell on the earth will rejoice over them, make merry, and send gifts to one another, because these two prophets tormented those who dwell on the earth (Rev. 11:10).*

The temple must be built in order for the Antichrist to establish himself in the temple as God. The Antichrist performs his evil acts for the duration of the last 3½ years of Daniel's week (the seventh trumpet). It makes sense to assume that the Antichrist kills the Two Witnesses when he sets up the abomination of desolation within the city. There is possibly a struggle in the city at this time when the Antichrist assumes control.

LAND AND SEA

The angel with the little book stood with one foot upon the sea and one foot upon the land (Rev. 10:2). John makes literal references to the land and the sea in the Apocalypse. There is an interesting interpretation that is worth considering. The Jewish people of Bible days used the word *land* to refer to Israel and used the word *sea* to refer to the heathen countries of the world. Babylon was not referred to as *land* or *sea* but just *Babylon*. This defining of Babylon may show us that Babylon refers to a religious grouping not a political grouping.

The Jewish writer, Rabbi Solomon divided the whole world into, *"the land of Israel"* and *"without the land,"* the countries of the heathen. Every foreign region he called the region of the sea, except Babylon. [4]

To interpret *"land and sea"* in the Apocalypse as *"Israel and the Gentile nations"* gives further proof that the Two Witnesses minister to the whole world, for the angel of the seven thunders stood upon the sea and upon the earth (Rev. 10:2,5,8). The magnitude of their witness shall be great and powerful. What they prophesy will come true. Israel will witness the rebuilding of the temple. They will administer plagues of warning. Miracles and disasters shall culminate by the power of their word. Finally the whole world will witness not only their death but their literal resurrection. As a result of their ministry, Israel shall return to her God; the heathen shall refuse to repent; and Satan's wrath shall then be enraged through the Antichrist.

E. Warnings of the Future Prophet John

Read Rev. 10:1-10

The seven thunders have not been uttered. Only John knows what the thunders uttered. John the Apostle who figuratively ate the contents of the little book will prophesy the fate of the seven thunders (Rev. 10:11). This causes us to wonder if this John-like prophet is one of the Two Witnesses or if he is a third prophet of end-times.

The ministry of these later-day prophets is not confined to Israel and the Jewish people. John was told that he would prophesy again not just to Israel but to many peoples, nations, tongues, and kings (Rev. 11:10). Irenaeus wrote about this great prophet, "When the close of the times draws nigh a great prophet shall be sent from God to turn men to the knowledge of God."[5]

FURTHER STUDY

1. What do you think is the significance of the fig tree dropping its late figs in Rev. 6:12?

PART D:

CONFLICT OF THE KINGDOMS
HEAVENS ARE PURGED

Trumpets 5,6,7

9. THE TWO WOES OF IRONIC JUSTICE

TRUMPETS 5, 6

Read Revelation 9

The final three trumpets are three woes of demonic origin. The first woe is a plague of locust from the bottomless pit, a dwelling place of the dead and demonic spirits. For the second woe, evil angels are loosed from the Euphrates River. For the third woe, Satan who then dwells on the earth, will demonstrate his wrath for 3½ years. Ironically, while man is being plagued by demonic locusts and by a demonic horse-like army, man continues to worship Satan. Ironically the gods of the underworld become the enemies of wicked men and we witness the kingdom of darkness fighting against its own kingdom. Jesus knew the irrevocable law of destruction: "Every kingdom divided against itself is brought to desolation, and every city or house divided against itself will not stand" (Matthew 12:25). Satan destroys his own kingdom.

Seven Trumpets			
Trumpets 1-4	5th Trumpet	6th Trumpet	7th Trumpet
Vengeance of Christ	1st Woe Demonic Locust	2nd Woe Demonic Horsemen	3rd Woe Abomination of Desolation
2 years	5 months	1 year, 1 month, 1 day, 1 hour	3 1/2 years

We have discussed the vengeance of Christ which happens during the first four trumpets. In this chapter we are looking at the events of the fifth and sixth trumpets.

A. Demonic Locusts: Trumpet 5,

Read Rev. 9:1-12

> *The shape of the locusts was like horses prepared for battle. On their heads were crowns of something like gold, and their faces were like the faces of men. They had hair like women's hair, and their teeth were like lions' teeth. And they had breastplates of iron, and the sound of their wings was like the sound of chariots with many horses running into battle. They had tails like scorpions, and there were stings in their tails. Their power was to hurt men five months (Revelation 9:7–10).*

These locusts are different from any locusts that have ever existed. These locusts attack people, but not crops. In fact, the locusts are told not to hurt the grass, other green herbs, or trees. The common locusts of our earth have no king over them, but these demonic locusts have the destroyer, himself, as their king. Neither do ordinary locust ascend out of the abyss. Real locusts do not wear crowns, have the faces of men, hair like women, nor teeth as lions. However, when I was shopping one day, I read an article saying that in America a bat was found having the face of a man. You wonder if these locusts are not as literal as described.

If they are real insects, then they are a creation of evil as a result of the corruptness of mankind. Harmful insects and weeds were creations that came into being after man had sinned and were a part of sin's curse; so these may come into existence because of the magnitude of evil.

Their sting is as a scorpion's sting. Their slender tails end in a sting. There are scorpion stings that are very painful and poisonous and can be fatal to humans. In Mexico there are a thousand deaths a year from scorpion bites. Whip scorpions squirt or spray acetic acid on antagonists. Their chemical war tails are fatal.[1] What is most interesting to me about the scorpion is that it is nocturnal. Just like evil and Satan, scorpions love darkness.

These locusts of the fifth seal, however, do not kill their victims, but only torment them. These locusts, of the Apocalypse, ascend out of the abyss (αβυσσος). The abyss is the underworld of the spirits and the abode of the dead and of demons. The abyss is the lowest part of the underworld in the ancient cosmology of Greece and the ancient mystics called it the divine abyss. The sorcerer, witch, channeler, and shaman of the New Age enter this different world through the subconscious mind.

Mystical methods such as meditation, visualization, yoga, and biofeedback bend the mind from reality into a new alpha mind reality where the individual becomes vulnerable to evil spirits. Human-like creatures appear regularly in the mystical darkness of the mind.[2] Is it possible that the mystical man will be tormented in the mind by these locust-like creatures? Could the wrath of Satan be a real struggle in the following manner? Imagine the following.

Mental torture causes men to want to die; yet, they are unable to die. What other disease is like that? Previously the demons have remained as friendly spirit guides, but now they become demonic criminals of the mind and emotions; yet, ironically, man repents not of his sorcery.

We know that Babylon becomes a dwelling place of demons as the depths of the abyss are opened. John says, "Babylon the great is fallen, is fallen, and is become the habitation of devils, and the hold of every foul spirit, and a cage of every unclean and hateful bird" (Rev. 18:12). Babylonish men and women will then taste the tortures of the hellish abyss as these hungry demonic locusts prey on them. These demonic locusts will attack those who associate with mystery Babylon and the occult. It is impossible for the believer who has separated himself from idolatry, meditation, witchcraft, sorcery, and shamanism to be attacked by these demons.

From the heavens above to the deepest abyss, God proves that He is in control. The abyss is so deep it is unfathomable, discernible only by God. Now God unleashes the abode of death and demonic powers because of spiritual darkness and deception.

The apostate church stumbles in confusion. Demons attack the throne of the Babylonish whore. The abyss is the dwelling place of spirit guides who are unleashed to display their true character. What was once seemingly good spirit guides, now torment man's mind and body. The sting of their tails brings mental and physical torture. The righteous are protected from the effects of demonic guides because they have refused to seek their aid.

Psychological torment is possible here because they longed for death and could not find it. The mind is so tormented that they cannot even commit suicide. The very demons and spirit guides, from whom men sought wisdom, turn against men to hurt them for five months. The spirit guides that men worshipped cannot give them the eternal rest that they seek in death.

Christ takes control of the kingdoms of the earth, the heavens, and the abyss. Even demonic forces are used by God to bring forth revenge, an ironic revenge as demonic powers turn on their victims. Even the demons could not kill because of the command of Christ (Rev. 9:5).

The nature of these locusts characterizes the apostate church that falls to the demons it worships. They wear deceptive crowns that appear to be gold. The apostasy that appears to be a godly spirituality is rather an evil authority. They are effeminate with their long hair like women which reminds me of the worship of female gods. They destroy with lion-like teeth. Lions characterize Babylon. Their breastplates are human-like instead of Christian-like. They are clad in breastplates of iron, not breastplates of righteousness.

B. Demonic Horses: Trumpet 6

> *And thus I saw the horses in the vision: those who sat on them had breastplates of fiery red, hyacinth blue, and sulfur yellow; and the heads of the horses were like the heads of lions; and out of their mouths came fire, smoke, and brimstone. By these three plagues a third of mankind was killed—by the fire and the smoke and the brimstone which came out of their mouth for their power is in their mouth and in their tails; for their tails are like serpents, having heads; and with them they do harm (Revelation 9:17-19).*

The angels that are loosed from the Euphrates River must be evil angels. David recalled many plagues upon the Egyptians in Moses's day and said: "He cast upon them the fierceness of his anger, wrath, and indignation, and trouble, by sending evil angels among them" (Psalm 78:49).

God sent evil angels to administer the plagues upon Egypt and I believe for the fifth trumpet also.

A third of man is destroyed by the plagues of demonic horses. There are three plagues symbolized by the fire, smoke, and brimstone that proceed from the mouth of this army of horsemen.

Is this a real army of men from Babylon? If so then the smoke, fire, and brimstone are possibly the effects of large chemical war that destroys 1/3 of the earth. But why is this destruction translated as a *plague*? Most translations have said: "By these three plagues was the third part of men killed" (Rev. 9:18). When you examine the Greek originals, the word *plagues* is in parentheses.

Biblical wars were never called plagues. This plague is not Armageddon, but a plague approximately three years before Armageddon. Plagues are sent because of sin just as a plague was sent when the children of Israel made the golden calf (Exodus 32:35, Numbers 31:16, and Psalm 101:29). Plagues were often stayed by repentance and incense burning (Exodus 9:34), but no plague is stayed during the abomination because there is no repentance.

> But the rest of mankind, who were not killed by these plagues, did not repent of the works of their hands, that they should not worship demons, and idols of gold, silver, brass, stone, and wood, which can neither see, nor hear, nor walk. And they did not repent of their murders, their sorceries, or their sexual immorality or their thefts (Rev. 9:21, 22).

The people of the last days shall be as Pharaoh. Regardless of the plagues, man sins more and his heart becomes more hardened (Genesis 19:24).

How we interpret these strange apocalyptic creatures depends upon how we view and emphasize end-time judgments. Many writers place a strong emphasis upon political issues when they interpret these woes; therefore, the apocalyptic creatures are depicted as creating a literal battle. But if we emphasize the spiritual battle that is raging between good and evil, then these creatures could even exist in the unseen world or the spirit world. Evil spirits could take on the form of demonic horses. The plagues they create can be both physical and psychological.

The Unseen World of Evil Spirits

There are seven reasons why the army of horses could be evil spirits or demonic creatures of the unseen world.

1. The powers of sorcery, magic, alchemy, divination, astrology, and geomancy originate from the Euphrates area. The origin of this plague is also in the Euphrates River.

2. This unseen world according to the occult is called the astral world, the Invisible Sea. It is a different reality and dimension of life for those following a new age philosophy. Those who follow meditative ways and tune into the spirit world find beyond rational reality a different world, a world of spirits that resemble creatures such as are described in the Apocalypse. Occult comic books today depict spiritual battles, and strange creatures of the unseen world. The demi-gods of the Greeks were half human and half animal-like.

3. The army of two hundred million horsemen is described as demonic. Their tails are like snakes. The fire and brimstone are the very substances of the abyss from where

they came and of the lake of fire. Babylon in the Bible is described as a lion and these creatures had lion-like heads.

4. The fire and brimstone that shoots forth from their mouth implies the power they use. The nature of fire and brimstone describes the nature of their spoken word. They have demonic power to speak words and see destruction.

Brimstone is inflammable sulphur, a non-metallic element with a yellow color. It melts at 113 degrees centigrade and burns with a blue flame, producing a suffocating sulphur-dioxide gas. The brimstone here is different from that which destroyed Sodom and Gomorrah. The fire and brimstone that destroyed Sodom and Gomorrah fell from heaven, but the fire and brimstone from the mouth of these demonic horses are not from heaven but from the abyss from where these beasts originate. Brimstone from God purifies but brimstone from the pit destroys.

Judgment is however described in similar terms as proceeding from the mouth of God.

> For Tophet was established of old, yes, for the king it is prepared. He has made it deep and large; its pyre is fire with much wood; the breath of the LORD, like a stream of brimstone, kindles it (Isaiah 30:33).

The brimstone that is likened to the breath of the Lord does not literally proceed from his mouth, but is figurative of the judgment of God and purifying work of God by fire. The fire from the mouth of the Two Witnesses would not be literal either, but symbolic of the fiery judgments that occur by the spoken word of these prophets of God. Similarly, the brimstone of these horses could be symbolic of the destructive judgments that arise from the abyss.

The horses wore a spiritual armor of darkness. Their breastplates were not made of iron as the breastplates of the locust. They were not of righteousness as the breastplates of the saints. They were neither like the breastplates of the priests who wore breastplates of judgment. These were breastplates of fire, jacinth, and brimstone. They were breastplates of apostasy. The wrath and corruptness of Satan's armor stands in opposition to the armor of the saints that will enable them to overcome the plagues of Satan.

5. Brimstone and fire have a strong connection with the occult world as well as with the judgment of God. The alchemists symbolize the lower world in terms of fire or sulphur.[3] Three fundamental symbols of Rosicrucianism represent sulphur, salt and mercury[4]. These three according to Rosicrucianism are the three beginnings of nature[5].

The occult sees in man four basic elements, fire, earth, air and water. Over each of these four elements of creation, God demonstrates His authority. Although we must be cautious not to interpret scripture from satanic symbols, they do prove interesting in light of the apocalyptic imagery.

6. Mystery Babylon does fall to demonic power. John describes the great harlot in chapters 17 and 18. Mystery Babylon is described as a cage and a prison for everything foul and demonic spirit (Rev. 18:2). The downfall of Mystery Babylon begins with the fifth and sixth trumpet, but the grand finality of Mystery Babylon will not be until the day of

the Lord and the Battle of Armageddon. The vengeance of God ironically opens the fire gates of the abyss and the occult world experiences torment from the pit of the abyss. The occult world of Mystery Babylon that once sought the souls of men and murdered prophets and saints will taste, during the trumpet period, the vengeance of God (Rev. 18:13, 24).

The vengeance of God is witnessed upon Babylon after the Babylonian captivity. The vengeance of God is sought because Babylon had destroyed the nation of Israel. The following verses describe Christ's vengeance.

> *Flee from the midst of Babylon, And every one save his life! Do not be cut off in her iniquity, for this is the time of the Lord's vengeance; He shall recompense her. Babylon was a golden cup in the Lord's hand that made all the earth drunk. The nations drank her wine; therefore the nations are deranged. Make the arrows bright! Gather the shields! The Lord has raised up the spirit of the kings of the Medes. For His plan is against Babylon to destroy it, Because it is the vengeance of the Lord, The vengeance for His temple (Jeremiah 51:6-11).*

The voice of those who flee and escape from the land of Babylon declares in Zion the vengeance of the Lord our God as the vengeance of His temple.

In the days of the Apocalypse, Babylon will be destroyed again by the vengeance of God. This is that same vengeance that descends from the throne and the temple of God or His dwelling place when the censer that was filled with fire from the altar of God was cast into the earth (Rev. 8:5).

7. The heavens have just been purged. Satan has been cast out of the heavenlies to the earth and all evil angels have been cast upon the earth. The torments of the three woes ascend from the bottomless pit. Demons are released from the pit and the earth is filled with smoke of the pit (Rev. 9:2). The earth is filled with demonic powers.

At the same time as these two demonic plagues occur, the Two Witnesses rule in Jerusalem and have powers to stop the rains and cause famine and plagues upon their enemies. No army will succeed in entering Israel at this time. The Two Witnesses have power to stop them. The demonic locust and demonic horses could not be armies of men from any nation. The Two Witnesses maintain peace and safety so that the temple can be rebuilt. God has also sealed the 144,000 so that they cannot be hurt.

The Two Witnesses perform miracles and evil spirits from the pit create horrors; yet, every incident in the Apocalypse is orchestrated by God. When the sixth angel sounded his trumpet, a voice came forth from the golden altar that was before God. God commanded the angel to loose the four angels that were bound in the great river.

The spiritual weapons of our warfare have the power to witness a great victory during the trumpet period. Just as God protected Israel from every plague that fell upon Egypt, God can also protect His people from harm during these plagues of Satan.

Further Questions:

1. How would the armor of God help believers during this time?

2. Do you think the church is ready to bind such demons from the bottomless pit? Why?

3. Are the demonic horses a literal army or are they an army of demonic spirits?

Three Woes: The Wrath of Satan

	Who?	When	Happening	Result
	Demonic Locust	1st woe 5th trumpet	Locust from the bottomless pit	Men Tormented 5 months
Satanic Plagues	Demonic Horses	2nd Woe 6th Trumpet	Four Demonic Angels From Euphrates	A Third Of Man Destroyed
Abomination of Desolations 3 1/2 years	Antichrist And False Prophet	3rd Woe 7th Trumpet	1. Image of beast. 2. Desecration of the temple 3. Persecution	Wrath upon those who take the mark

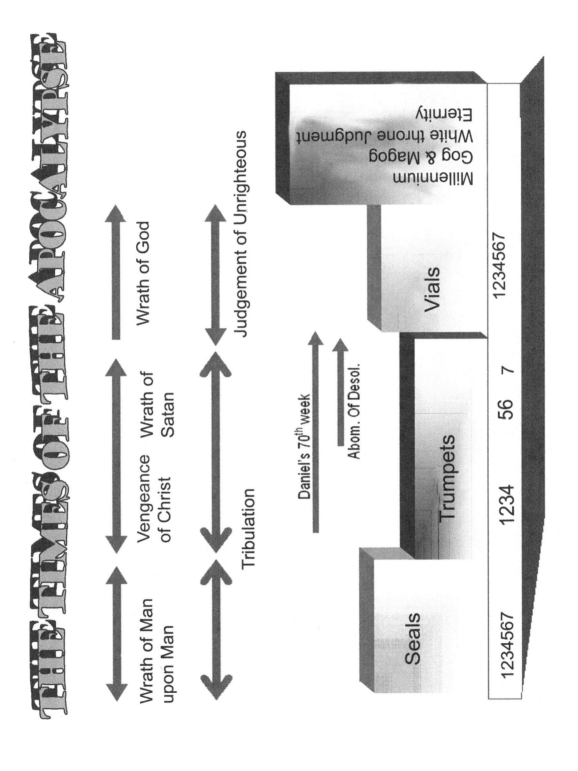

89

10. The Wrath of Satan

Read Revelation 12 and 13

*And war broke out in heaven: Michael and his angels fought with the dragon; and the dragon and his angels fought, but they did not prevail, nor was a place found for them in heaven any longer. So the great dragon was cast out, that serpent of old, called the Devil and Satan, who deceives the whole world; he was cast to the earth, and his angels were cast out with him. Then I heard a loud voice saying in heaven, "Now salvation, and strength, and the kingdom of our God, and the power of His Christ have come, for the accuser of our brethren, who accused them before our God day and night, has been cast down. And they overcame him by the blood of the Lamb and by the word of their testimony, and they did not love their lives to the death. Therefore rejoice, O heavens, and you who dwell in them! Woe to the inhabitants of the earth and the sea! For the devil has come down to you, having **great wrath,** because he knows that he has a short time" (Revelation 12:7-12).*

The Antichrist appears as the evil one just after the apocalypse speaks of Satan falling from heaven and attacking the earth with great wrath. Satan possesses the Antichrist, who then executes the wrath of Satan.

In order to establish his kingdom and require the worship of all, Satan must dispose of all other worship. Therefore, he has five main peoples to possibly exert his wrath upon, the apostate church, Islam, the true church, mystic religions, and the Jewish faith. These five religions must be destroyed or merge that he might establish his own kingdom.

A. Antichrist and Mystery Babylon:

Read Revelation 18

After the Harlot woman, Babylon, has served the purpose of the Antichrist, he destroys her. All must worship the Antichrist. Babylon represents the apostate church whether she is Rome and the Catholic Church, Islam, or another religious apostate organization. In order for the Antichrist to receive all worship, Babylon the great must be destroyed. Demonic powers arrest the kingdom of Babylon and she becomes a nest for every foul evil spirit (Rev. 18:2).

God remembers Babylon's iniquities and she is rewarded double for leading the nations into idolatry, witchcraft, and fornication. In one hour, a brief time, the powers of the harlot woman face judgment and ruin. Because she deceives the world by her sorceries and witchcraft, she falls prey to the most foul of demonic spirits. Satan collaborates with the Antichrist to devastate Babylon's authority and power. Satan's wrath is only the beginning of Babylon's destruction. When Christ returns, the roots of evil, witchcraft, pride, sorcery, and greed shall dissolve in the fires of hell where the Antichrist and the False Prophet are cast.

Babylon, the great whore, receives double sorrow. The securities and assurances that were a part of her position as queen of the universe leave her sunk in a mire of endless doubt and despair. With great sorrow, she slumps into extinction. Mirthful shouts to her multitudinous gods and goddesses are choked and transformed into wild weeping that resembles the ecstatic chants to that demonic Dionysus. The apostate worship of the earth and the queen of heaven are warped into an iron web of satanic worship. Perhaps this is what was meant when Hippolytus wrote:

> Then the lawless one, being lifted up in heart, will gather together his demons in man's form, will abominate those who called him to the kingdom, and will pollute many souls; for, he will appoint princes over them from among the demons."[1]

The rich men, traders, and merchants of the earth are mad at her destruction because by her rituals, evil practices, and fornications they had become rich. The soothsayer's wealth sees corruption. The wealth of slave traders is bound with satanic shackles. Articles of worship like cinnamon, ointments, frankincense and oil will rot with the decay of Babylon. The wealth of the world shall fold into the wallet of the Antichrist. Babylon shall plummet like a millstone into a bottomless sea.

B. Antichrist and Israel

THE DECEPTION

The Antichrist deceives the nation of Israel. A deceptive alliance is made with Israel, but the details of that deception are not outlined in scripture, so we speculate and read between the lines. After many false christs have appeared the Antichrist rises as the ultimate deceiver. Israel expects the Messiah to bring peace, so he will most likely promise peace. Israel expects the Messiah to rebuild the temple, so he permits the Jews to rebuild under the leadership of the Two Witnesses during the time of Trumpets 1-6. He allows the temple to be rebuilt that he may sit as god in the temple of God. The Antichrist does not hinder the ministry of the two witnesses for 3-1/2 years; therefore, we conclude that he presents himself as one who is pro-Israeli and pro-Jewish when he is really the summation of all anti-Semitism. The church of Jesus Christ has just been severely persecuted by apostate forces; therefore, as a deceiver, the Antichrist probably promises freedom of religion for the Jewish people.

The early church fathers speculate deeper into the deceptiveness of the Antichrist. Hippolytus sees the Antichrist as one "'who restores them that he may be worshipped by them as God."[2] He sees the restoration of Israel from all parts of the globe as Satan's trickery that he might force upon them the worship of himself.

> *Above all, moreover, he will love the nation of the Jews, and with all these he will work signs and terrible wonders, false wonders, and not true, in order to deceive his impious equals ... loving, says he, the Scriptures, reverencing priests, honoring his elders, repudiating fornication, detesting adultery, giving no heed to slanders, not admitting oaths, kind to strangers, kind to the poor, compassionate. And then he will work wonders, cleansing lepers raising paralytics, expelling demons, proclaiming things remote just as things present, raising the dead, helping widows, defending orphans, loving all, reconciling in love men who contend, and saying to such: "let not the sun go down upon your wrath" and he will not acquire gold, nor love silver, nor seek riches.[3]*

> *Then when he is elevated to his kingdom, he will marshal war; and in his wrath he will smite three mighty kings, those of Egypt, Libya, and Ethiopia. And after that he will build the temple in Jerusalem, and will restore it again speedily, and give it over to the Jews. And then he will be lifted up on high against every man; yea, he will speak blasphemy also against God, thinking in his deceit that he shall be king upon the earth.[4]*

Victorianus claimed that the Antichrist would change his name to deceive and be accepted by the Jewish nation. He visions the Antichrist calling the nation to circumcision.[5]

During the first six trumpets, the Antichrist is seen in the Apocalypse as a wonder-worker. When he survives his deadly wound, the whole world wonders at him (Rev. 13:3). Man admires the Antichrist as the great warrior (Rev. 13:5). With fear, men fall down and worship him. With great wonder the globe sees the image of the Beast come to life. There has been much speculation about the image that talks. Some see it as a computerized genius, or as a scientific clone. Personally, I see the life of the beast as the power of sorcery and enchantment. Demons shall inhabit the image.

FLOOD OF WRATH

Read Rev. 12:13-17

The Apocalypse focuses upon the leopard beast that rises from the sea. Blasphemy against God betrays him as being any messiah. The eyes of Israel are opened when he kills the Two Witnesses. His abomination of the temple consummates any doubt as to his identity; he is not the Christ.

Israel is persecuted because Christ was born of her seed (Rev. 12:13). The church is persecuted because she is the seed of Christ. Both persecutions are a part of Satan's wrath and war against the Lamb.

As the seventh trumpet sounds, the abomination of desolation begins and the Antichrist desolates the temple. At this time, Israel flees to the mountains for protection. The wrath of Satan is described as a flood. Whether this flood is a literal flood, or an army, or any other means, is not important. However, it is important to realize that whatever means he exercises, the miraculous hand of God delivers the Jews. Only God can stop real floods. Only God can stop an army as powerful as the Antichrist's army. By this time, he has already conquered Egypt, Libya, and Ethiopia (Ezekiel 30: 1-5). In the light of today's news, Egypt, Libya and Ethiopia are in trouble. A small nation like Israel without God is no contest for the Antichrist and Satan, but with God, she shall triumph.

PROTECTION

Read Rev. 12:1-2, 6, 13:14

God protects Israel. God prepares a safe place in the wilderness for His people. Jesus warns those who live in Judea to flee when they see the abomination (Mark 13:1; 4).

Israel is described as a "woman clothed with the sun, with the moon beneath her feet and wearing a crown of twelve stars" (Rev. 12:1). She is clothed with the beauty and power of God. She is clothed with the victory of the heavens. The exaltation of Israel is a contrast to the fall of Satan from the heavens. This portrait of Israel is beautifully framed with love; while at the same time, disasters are splitting the heavens with judgment. An angry God is shaking the heavens; yet, God protects Israel. The sun and moon are darkened, and the stars are falling from heaven; yet, this woman clothed with the sun, is being lifted up into the Almighty arms of God like an eagle that bears its young upon its wings. God repeats the exodus deliverance. 'You have seen what I did to the Egyptians and how I bore you on eagles' wings and brought you to Myself (Exodus 19:4).

The world is being ravaged by famine but Jehovah nourishes Israel for 3 ½ years just as Elijah was fed by the brook Cherith during 3½ years of drought. God kept Israel in Moses's day through the wilderness of Sin and Sinai and nourished her with manna and quail supernaturally. Again in the wilderness, God will provide and feed His people. They shall be protected from the face or presence of the serpent. Instead, they witness the face of a just God.

He is the God of the valleys as much as He is the God of the hills. Ben Hadad king of Syria, in the days of Ahab, attacked Israel with the aid of thirty-two other kings. Because he thought that the God of Israel was the God of the hills and not the valleys, God gave Israel a great victory in that day upon the plains (1 Kings 20:28). God is the God of the secret places too, for in the hills of the earth, God shall protect Israel.

C. Antichrist and the Church

Hippolytus believed that the woman clothed with the sun is the church that endures persecution by the hand of the Antichrist and that the twelve stars are the twelve apostles. Hippolytus also sees the church being miraculously preserved during the reign of Antichrist and gives reference to Luke

21: 18. "And there shall not a hair of your head perish". He referred to Isaiah and believed that the church should hide until the indignation is completed.[6]

> Come, my people, enter your chambers, and shut your doors behind you; Hide yourself, as it were, for a little moment, until the indignation is past. For behold, the LORD comes out of His place to punish the inhabitants of the earth for their iniquity; The earth will also disclose her blood, And will no more cover her slain (Isaiah 26:20-21).

Lactantius believed the same. He believed that when the abomination comes, the righteous would separate from the evil and hide in solitude.[7] It makes human sense to hide from such furry. No man shall be spared in that hour.

When the early church fathers interpreted the woman clothed with the sun to be the church; this confirms that the early church fathers believed that the church would go through the tribulation, even the tribulation of the Antichrist.

This would be the second persecution of the righteous during the events of the Apocalypse. Apostate forces have already martyred many from the fifth seal. Now the saints are persecuted because they refuse to take the mark of the Beast.

Cyprian believed that the end of the world and the time of the Antichrist were imminent; yet, he admonished the church to be prepared as soldiers of Christ, and be able to shed their blood for Christ.[8] It is possible that Cyprian recognized the two periods of persecution when he said:

> Blessed shall they be who overcome the tyrant then. For they shall be set forth as more illustrious and loftier than the first witnesses; for the former witnesses overcame his minion only, but these overthrow and conquer the accuser himself, the son of perdition. With what eulogies and crowns, therefore, will they not be adorned by our King, Jesus Christ?[9]

Hippolytus describes the satanic demands of the Antichrist in this way: He will order incense-pans to be set up by all everywhere, that no man among the saints may be able to buy or sell without first sacrificing...[10]

God permits the Antichrist to persecute the church and overcome the flesh but not the spirit. The word overcome in Revelation refers to both the Antichrist and the church.

> And they overcame him by the blood of the Lamb and by the word of their testimony, and they did not love their lives to the death. (Rev.12:11)

> It was granted to him (the Antichrist) to make war with the saints and to overcome them. And authority was given him over every tribe, tongue, and nation. (Rev.13:7)

> When they finish their testimony, the beast (the Antichrist) that ascends out of the bottomless pit will make war against them, overcome them, and kill them (Rev.1:7).

> These will make war with the Lamb, and the Lamb will overcome them, for He is Lord of Lords and King of kings; and those who are with Him are called, chosen, and faithful (Rev. 17:14).

Here, the church is a contestant in the great final tug-of-war between evil and good, between God and Satan. As far as winning the terrestrial and temporary crown, Satan is the overcomer; but as far as winning the heavenly and eternal crown, the saints are the overcomers. Patience and faith are the badges of the overcomer (Rev. 13:10). Here, under the rule of the Antichrist these badges are more notably won than in any time in history, for greater shall be this persecution. A new song is sung in glory (Rev. 15:3) for suffering cannot destroy the song of victory. Fear cannot destroy the song of hope. Persecution cannot destroy the song of eternal life, for death is "swallowed up in victory" when Christ was resurrected. He that has an ear to hear must listen because both sides cannot win.

The church is not an overcomer only because her life was a witness to righteousness but because of the righteousness of the Lamb. It is Christ that gives the final tug to victory; that tug is empowered from the cross, the resurrection of Christ, and the enabling power of the Holy Spirit. It is Christ in us with all hope and power to overcome.

The resurrection and Rapture does bring deliverance for the remnant. The 144,000 are raptured from Mount Zion after the mark has been prescribed for mankind. They are redeemed from the earth and from among men. The sickle from heaven first reaps the good harvest and men are gathered into the portals of heaven (Rev 14). Then the song of Moses and the song of the Lamb are sung in glory. Both Jews and Gentile believers rejoice in the God of their salvation (Rev. 15:3).

The martyrs and all those who refuse the mark live and reign with Christ a thousand years. Yes, many shall die because they refuse the mark, but what is there to fear in death when the resurrection is the next event in history? Here, is where the saints must have patience in order to be overcomers. Imagine! – being slain for not accepting the mark of the Beast. Your head rolls down the hill side. Then forty-five days later, approximately, you return to earth with a new glorified body and head to help Christ defeat the Antichrist. What a story!

The image of Nebuchadnezzar is a type of the image of the Beast. The three Hebrew children Shadrach, Meshach and Abednego refused to bow down to the image. These Babylonian names had only earthly significance. Respectfully their Babylonian names meant *royal and great scribe, guest of a King,* and *servant of Nebo.* Their Hebrew names have divine and eternal significance. Hananiah means *Jehovah is gracious.* Shadrach means *Who is what God is?* Mishael means *Jehovah is keeper.* What names in the face of fire! These are names of faith that the church must know and trust when faced with tribulation.

FURTHER STUDY

1. The Antichrist is that beast that arises from the sea. Describe him. Read Revelation 13: 1-9.

2. What are the rewards of the overcomer according to Revelation?

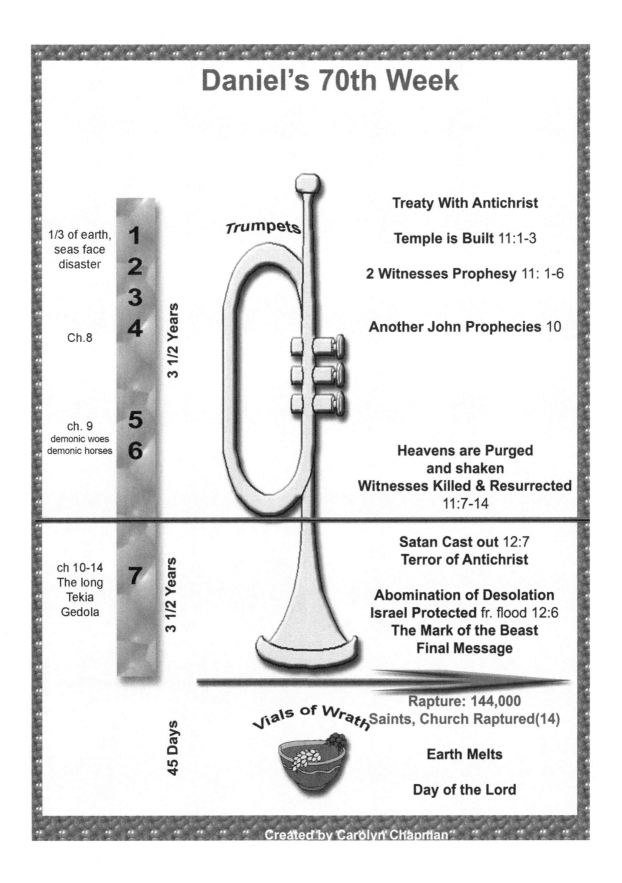

Daniel's 70th Week

Trumpets

1/3 of earth, seas face disaster

1
2
3
4

Ch.8

ch. 9
demonic woes
demonic horses

5
6

3 1/2 Years

Treaty With Antichrist

Temple is Built 11:1-3

2 Witnesses Prophesy 11: 1-6

Another John Prophecies 10

**Heavens are Purged
and shaken
Witnesses Killed & Resurrected**
11:7-14

ch 10-14
The long
Tekia
Gedola

7

3 1/2 Years

Satan Cast out 12:7
Terror of Antichrist

**Abomination of Desolation
Israel Protected** fr. flood 12:6
**The Mark of the Beast
Final Message**

Vials of Wrath

45 Days

Rapture: 144,000
Saints, Church Raptured(14)

Earth Melts

Day of the Lord

Created by Carolyn Chapman

11. REIGN OF ANTICHRIST

THE SEVENTH TRUMPET: WRATH OF SATAN

A. Who is The Antichrist?

THE SATANIC THREE

Read Rev. 12:3-12; 13:1-17

The apocalyptic triad of evil and destruction incorporates Satan, the Antichrist and the False Prophet. Satan is portrayed as a dragon, the Antichrist as a leopard, and the False Prophet as a lamb-like beast with horns.

Dragons are imaginary mythological creatures usually associated with the gods. They were a symbol of evil that needed to be destroyed. Fire is known to spew from their mouths. The figure of a dragon has been worshipped by many heathen religions. Vrtra, the dragon, is a Hindu god. Ancient Babylon worshipped the monstrous dragon. According to ancient Mesopotamia and Ugaritic thought, the dragon is associated with the Deep, and the Sea.[1] Isaiah tells us that God will destroy the dragon that is in the sea (Isaiah 27:1.2).

Together, Satan (the dragon), Antichrist (the leopard), and the false prophet (the lamb), reign upon the earth for 3½ years. These 3½ years constitute the abomination of desolation and the duration of the seventh trumpet commencing with the breaking of a treaty between Israel and the Antichrist and concluding with the Battle of Armageddon.

For this final 3½ years, the holy city of Jerusalem shall be trodden by the Gentiles (Rev. 11:2). Satan, with his angels, has just been cast out of heaven to the earth and the two witnesses have been murdered by the Antichrist and raised by the power of God. Satan, knowing that he has been cast out of heaven and knowing that his time is very brief (Rev. 12:12), energizes all his power with great wrath. But having been cast out of heaven, Satan has lost his spiritual powers in the heavenly places and administers his wrath with his own personal power and with all earthly power and authority.

In heaven there is great rejoicing because of his fall. "Now is come salvation, and strength and the kingdom of our God (Rev. 12:10)." But John also says, "Woe to the inhabitants of the earth and of the sea" (Rev. 12:12). Woe to men of Israel, the earth, and the Gentiles of the sea.

Satan's wrath is directed towards the nation of Israel, the church, and anyone or any nation he pleases. This period of the tribulation is called, *the Wrath of Satan* (Rev. 12:12). God permits the Antichrist during these 3½ years to perform his evil acts by the power of Satan (Rev. 11:2). In the chart on the wrath of Satan, I have included the fifth and sixth trumpets because of the demonic nature of the two plagues, namely the plague of the locust and the horsemen. Also, the three woes parallel the last three trumpets. The word "woe" separates these trumpets from the trumpets of Christ's vengeance.

The leopard beast, representing the Antichrist, does not arise up out of the sea until after Satan is cast out of heaven. The power and authority of the Antichrist before this time is more peaceful. It is possible that when Satan falls to the earth, the deadly wound of the Antichrist is healed by Satan so that he is restored to greater, yet more demonic authority and power. At the commanding voice of the triad are the numerous angels or stars of heaven that Satan drags to earth with him.

Several common factors exist among the triad of demonic power. Firstly, the leopard and the lamb-like beast are empowered by Satan (Rev. 13:2,12). The False Prophet exercises the same power as the Antichrist. The False Prophet is of an ecclesiastical order because of the lamb-like horns counterfeiting the Lamb of God; yet, he spoke as Satan himself. He spoke with dragon power and not by the power of the Holy Spirit (Rev.13:11). Both the Antichrist and the False Prophet execute the will and wrath of Satan.

Both speak blasphemous words. Antichrist blasphemes the God of all gods, His name, His tabernacle, and those in heaven. Revenge probably lies at the root of his hatred for those in heaven. Michael and his angels have just conquered Satan and have cast him to the earth. Satan and his angels no longer have a voice before the throne of God. His kingdom in the spiritual realm is destroyed. His power to accuse the saints before the throne of God is removed forever (Rev.12:10)

Both Satan and the Antichrist are worshipped by those whose names are not written in the Lamb's book of life. Not only does the False Prophet direct men's worship to the Antichrist (Rev.13:12), but he also causes or enforces men to worship the dragon (Satan). The word *"cause"* is "ποιει" from the Greek root word "ποιεο" meaning to create, to make, to do, to work, to perform, to produce, and to accomplish.[2] He is given the authority to execute or enforce the mark as a sign of allegiance to the Antichrist. He executes the killings of all those who do not receive the mark of the Beast.

When the Antichrist spoils the powers of the apostate church, the False Prophet will assume leadership of the new satanic apostasy. If the False Prophet becomes the head of the ecclesiastical order of the day, then the worldwide leaders of the previous apostate church may become the enforcers of demonic worship and the mark of the Beast. Hence, if Rome is Babylon, the religious order of the Antichrist has immediate authority over the economical issues and policies of the globe such that no man can buy or sell unless they wear the mark. If Rome is Babylon the Great, the Antichrist usurps the ecclesiastical powers of fallen Rome so that the false prophet expropriates the role of a pope in authority and power over ecclesiastical issues to ordain and legislate the will and desire of Satan.

The Antichrist will use the powers of the Church of Rome and other apostate forces until they serve him no longer and then he destroys ecclesiastical Babylon the whore. When a demonic form of worship is legislated through the channels of the fallen church, then the mark of the Beast is executed. His powers of authority have already been established throughout the world and can be quickly enforced.

Satan has always been the great deceiver. Acting according to the character of Satan, the Antichrist and the False Prophet are great deceivers. "For many deceivers have gone out into the world who do not confess Jesus Christ as coming in the flesh. This is a deceiver and an antichrist" (2 John 7).

Evil and deceit play together in the game of death. "Deceit is in the heart of those who devise evil" (Proverbs 12:20), and the Antichrist is the summation of all evil. He causes deceit to prosper.[3] His deceit is witnessed with false peace accords, flattery, lies, and with magic.

The False Prophet deceives by his mighty miracles and wonders. The miracles are deceptive in that they re-enact the miracles of Christ's servants, the Two Witnesses. He makes fire fall from heaven for all to see. His miracles will falsely acclaim divine power to reinforce the position of divinity that the Antichrist assumes upon the throne of David. He deceives the world by giving life and power to the image of the Beast. He falsely acclaims and demonstrates the divine ability to give life. Irenaeus identifies the wonders performed by the False Prophet as wonders performed by magic, demons, and apostate spirits that are at his service.[4] Hippolytus wrote:

> Under the eye of the spectators he will remove mountains from their places, he will walk on the sea with dry feet, he will bring down fire from heaven, he will turn the day into darkness and the night into day, he will turn the sun about where so ever he pleases; and in short, in presence of those who behold him, he will show all the elements of earth and sea to be subject to him in the power of his specious manifestation.[5]

Both the dragon (Satan) and the leopard (Antichrist) have seven heads and ten horns. This shows that they share the same authority and cooperate with the same mind and purpose. These seven heads give reference to the ecclesiastical power he has through the apostate church, that possibly being the Catholic Church out of Rome, or Islam, or the Mystical new age, or apostate Christianity, or a combination of apostasy.

The ten horns signify the ten nations that rule with the Antichrist and go out to battle with him for one hour.

The dragon, however, has seven crowns upon his head while the leopard has ten crowns upon his ten horns. The seven crowns upon the heads of Satan mocks the divine authority of God. Seven represents the seven mountains upon which sat Mystery Babylon mother of harlots (Rev. 17:9). Seven also represents seven kings. However the ten crowns upon the Antichrist represent the ten kings that rule with him for one hour for the Battle of Armageddon. Antichrist is the eighth and is of the seven (Rev.17:9-11). It is puzzling to know what that is. I know that the eighth son of Ishmael was Hadad. A descendent of Hadad could be the seventh leader of the next great kingdom of which five have fallen, one is, and one is yet to be (Rev. 17:10).

There are ten kings of the earth that do not receive power until they rule with the Beast at the conclusion of the 3½ years of the Abomination of Desolation. They rule for only one hour with the Antichrist. Their one purpose is to destroy the Jewish nation and make war with the Lamb (Rev.17:12-14). Therefore, ten crowns upon the heads of the Antichrist may not refer to the kings of the European Community but to ten kings of the earth that commit themselves to fight with the Antichrist for that great battle of Armageddon. It is during the rule of this ten-toed-kingdom that Christ, the God of heaven, will set up His kingdom.[6] I believe that is more possible for the Eastern nations of the Old Roman Empire, which are the Islamic nations, to be the ten nations that fight with the Antichrist for the great battle of Armageddon.

There is a difference between the leopard beast (the Antichrist), and the lamb (False Prophet). The leopard arises out of the sea (Rev.13:1) and the two-horned beast arises from the earth. The Antichrist is the political figure that arises from dwelling in the Gentile nations of the world. The False Prophet is the spiritual figure during the tribulation which arises possibly from within Israel herself represented by the "Land."

The word "sea" in scripture often implies a place of turmoil (Psalm 65:5, 12), and a place of despair and separation (Psalm 68:22). The sea is a place for things that are thrown out. Mountains are cast into the sea (Psalm 46:2). Sin is cast into the sea (Micah 7:17). Jesus cast the demonic swine into the sea (Matthew 8:32). The "sea" could refer to the dwelling place of demonic spirits and angels. Is it ironic or meaningful when Jesus casts the demons out of the man of the Gadarenes, they flee to the sea? Also, according to Isaiah, the Antichrist is a reptile that lives in the sea that shall be destroyed in the day of the Lord. The Apocalypse of John confirms this destruction of the Antichrist in the day of the Lord.

> *Then the beast was captured, and with him the false prophet who worked signs in his presence, by which he deceived those who received the mark of the beast and those who worshipped his image. These two were cast alive into the lake of fire burning with brimstone. (Rev.19:20)*

In that day, the Lord with His severe sword, great and strong, will punish Leviathan the fleeing serpent, Leviathan that twisted serpent; and He will slay the reptile (monster) that is in the sea (Isaiah 27:1).

The Person and Nature of the Antichrist

The early church fathers describe clearly the insidiousness of the Antichrist. The word *insidiousness* implies his deceitfulness, his falseness, and his perniciousness. Lactantius saw him as a murderer, as an intolerable ruler, self-centered, and deceitful. With deceit he will fuse the divine with the human. According to Hippolytus his passion and wrath are determined to destroy mankind. Hippolytus identifies him as the unrighteous judge of Luke 18. Irenaeus called Satan "the apostate angel" and the Antichrist one who will *"bruise"* mankind like eggs that are crushed in the hand. Irenaeus saw him as the illegitimate king and leader of apostasy.[7] His counterfeit endeavors only defy a Holy God.

According to the Apocalypse, the Antichrist is a combination of beastly creatures. He is firstly depicted as a leopard. The leopard lurks and prowls until it is ready to pounce upon its victim. The ancient Grecian Empire from which Antiochus sprung was also pictured as a leopard (Daniel 7:6). The Antichrist will re-enact the character of Antiochus and very possibly arise from Syria as Antiochus Ephiphanes did.

Secondly, the Antichrist is sketched having the feet of a bear. The bear in Daniel's dreams depicted the Medo-Persian Empire (Daniel 7:5, 20). The Antichrist will be aided by the strides of modern Persia, Iraq and Iran. Lastly, the Antichrist is sketched having the mouth of a lion. The first beast of Daniel's dream was a lion that represented Ancient Babylon (Daniel 7:4). The Antichrist will act with the strength of all these nations that are depicted in Daniel's dream. The empire of the Antichrist is greater than the sum of all these other nations. All these nations at the end of time are Islamic.

Note the order of the beasts in Daniel's dream, lion, bear, and leopard. John's reference to these beasts follows in the opposite order.

> Now the beast, which I saw was like a leopard, his feet were like the feet of a bear, and his mouth like the mouth of a lion. The dragon gave him his power, his throne, and great authority. (Rev. 13:2)

In Daniel, the Antichrist is referred to as the little horn, the king of the north with a fierce countenance, and that vile person. In the Apocalypse he is the leopard beast from the sea, and in Paul's writings he is the man of sin (2 Thessalonians 2:3, 22). In Isaiah he is the king of Assyria (Isaiah 10:12-17, 24). In Jeremiah he is the prince of Tyre (Ezekiel 28:2). It is only in the epistles of John that the word *Antichrist* is used and John makes only one reference to a man that shall arise in the later days.

> "Little children, it is the last hour; and as you have heard that the Antichrist is coming, even now many antichrists have come, by which we know that it is the last hour (1 John 2:18).

In all other verses, John refers to the *spirit of antichrist*. This spirit characterizes the Antichrist as one who denies the Father and Jesus the Son of God, who was God incarnate in human flesh. When the Antichrist sits in the temple as god and when he makes war against the Jews and Christians, he ultimately denies the Father and the Son with all blasphemy. Again, Islam denies the deity of Christ but the Catholic Church does not.

Who is a liar but he who denies that Jesus is the Christ? He is antichrist who denies the Father and the Son.

> And every spirit that does not confess that Jesus Christ has come in the flesh is not of God. And this is the spirit of the Antichrist, which you have heard was coming, and is now already in the world (1 John 2:22, 4:3).

The Antichrist spirit develops and grows because of the demonic root of pride. Pride is demonstrated in humanism, Epicureanism, mysticism, human potentiality, and monetarism. Pride was the downfall of the king of Tyre and the king of Babylon. Pride is the nature of Lucifer.

The Antichrist exalts himself above all the gods of the earth. He regards not the god of his fathers, the goddesses of nature, or any god (Daniel 11:37). He exalts himself above everything that is called god (2 Thessalonians 2:4). He exalts himself above the God of gods (Daniel 11:36). He will sit in the temple of Yahweh and declare that He is Yahweh. With pride, he acts according to his own will (Daniel 11:16). With pride He blasphemes God, robs all worship, and makes war against the King of kings. Today, what is not called god?

For when Antichrist is come, and of his own accord concentrates in his own person the apostasy, and accomplishes whatever he shall do according to his own will and choice, sitting also in the temple of God, so that his dupes may adore him as the Christ.[8]

He honors the god of fortresses -- a foreign god (Daniel 11:38.39). Fortress implies securities which makes me wonder if money is not his god. A false security and refuge does Satan offer while destroying the temporal and eternal securities of the people. Some say the god of fortresses is the god of war.

His Power and Authority

The mouth identifies the power, authority, action and character of the individual force. The word *"mouth"* has an interesting chronology in the Apocalypse. Representing the evil forces there is the mouth of the demonic horse, the Antichrist and Satan. The power of the two hundred million demonic horses and horsemen is in their mouth and in their tails. Fire, smoke and brimstone rush from their mouths. Satan spews water out of his mouth like a flood after the woman. The mouth of the Antichrist speaks great things and blasphemies. From the mouth of the dragon, beast, and false prophet leap three unclean spirits like frogs. Antichrist like a lion, roars terrible things and blasphemies against God, his name, his tabernacle and those that dwell in heaven (Rev. 9:18, 19, 3:16, 12:1, 13:5, 16:13, 13:2, 5, 33).

Representing the righteous forces we have the mouth of one like unto the Son of Man, the two witnesses, the earth, and the Lamb with a sword in His mouth. A sharp two-edged sword proceeds from the mouth of the Son of Man. Fire proceeds from the mouth of the two witnesses to slaughter their enemies. The earth opens her mouth and saves Israel. The lukewarm of the Laodicean Church were spewed out of Christ's mouth. Out of the mouth of the Lamb goes a sharp sword to strike the nations. The sword from His mouth slays the forces of the Antichrist in that great Battle of Armageddon. The sword of righteousness shall prevail and conquer. The Word of our God shall stand forever. (Rev. 1:16, 11:5, 12:16, 19:15, 21)

The mouth of the Antichrist is a summation of satanic mystical powers that have been silenced in the heavens and now exert upon the earth their final voice of witchcraft, sorcery, mystical enchantments, and magic. By the deceptions of magic he will show great signs and wonders.

As king, the Antichrist makes war against the Jews, the Christians, and the Prince. John questions the ability of anyone to make war with him (Rev. 13:4). As lawmaker he changes laws, yet he destroys righteous and just laws.

The humility and condescension of love resurrected the sons of God, but the fall of Satan shall resurrect an antichrist. Christ willingly left heaven to bring salvation for mankind, but Satan fell from heaven to bring wrath upon mankind. Christ was the incarnation of all righteousness and love but the Antichrist will be the embodiment of all evil. As the embodiment of Satan, the Antichrist is a destroyer, a murderer, a liar and full of deceit. As a destroyer, the Antichrist casts down the sanctuary of God and casts truth to the ground. He makes desolate the land that he treads. With the force of a flood he attempts to annihilate the people of God (Daniel 8:23, 25). As a murderer, he conquers with an army, slaughters the mighty and holy people, and appoints women into battle (Daniel 8:12, 24, 11:17). As a deceiver he is cunning. He understands dark and secret sayings. He seizes kingdoms with intrigue. He conjures treaties only to break them. He wields Jewish dissenters of the law to perpetrate his abominations. He speaks lies at political conferences (Daniel 8:23, 25, 11:30, 27).

Daniel dreamed of four great kingdoms. These four kingdoms were depicted by the great image of Nebuchadnezzar (Daniel 2:31-45). The head of gold represents the Babylonian kingdom, the breasts and arms of silver the Medes and Persians, the thighs of brass the Grecian Empire, and legs of iron represent the Eastern and Western Roman Empire. The kingdom of the Antichrist develops from this fourth kingdom (Daniel 7:17-29). This forth kingdom, according to Daniel, is the kingdom of the Roman Empire. The European Community is the renewing of that old Roman Empire. The ten toes of iron and clay have not yet been fulfilled. The ten toes represent ten kings that shall arise in the last days and rule under the Antichrist. It is during the rule of these ten kings that God shall establish His kingdom that will endure forever.

The Antichrist not only arises from within the boundaries of the Old Roman Empire but he shall most possibly arise from Syria, as did Antiochus Ephiphanes. "In the latter days of the four kingdoms of Greece, this king of fierce countenance shall arise" (Daniel 8:22-15). This verse informs us that the Antichrist will also arise from the old kingdom of Greece. The land of Syria lies within the boundaries of both the Roman Empire and the Grecian Empire. Lightfoot interprets Gog of Ezekiel to have been the Grecian Empire that profaned the temple, the holy ones, and the law by the hand of Antiochus Epiphanes.[9] The book of the Maccabees recognizes Antiochus not only as the king of Syria but as king of Asia.[10]

According to scripture, there is no mention of any other nation or king of the north that complies with the fulfillment of the Antichrist. The little horn of Daniel is the only king in scripture that is called the *king of the North*. The little horn has full association with Syria under the rule of Antiochus and therefore, this little horn that refers to the Antichrist, may be from Syria.

Many modern-day prophets consider other nations such as Spain, Germany, or Russia, as the country of the great Antichrist. Their speculation is based upon past and present historical occurrences, but my speculation is narrowed to what the scriptures suggest. Do we base our prophetical truths upon history or scriptural evidence?

The scriptures focus upon Syria more than any other nation. Daniel places emphasis not upon other nations of the world, but upon the four nations of Daniel's dream and the four kingdoms that arise out of the Grecian kingdom of which one is Syria. "And in the latter time of the kingdom."

This refers to the divided Grecian Empire.[11] If what I understand is true, Syria will join with other eastern nations of the Mediterranean -- Islamic nations. Is it also possible that Greece shall rise with greater power in these last days? Is it possible that the eastern nations of the Old Roman Empire will rise to greater power than the western part of the Old Roman Empire? Lactantius seemed to think so. He believed that all prophecy pointed to the destruction of Rome that would allow the Eastern Roman Empire to rule again. This already happened once during the Byzantine period of history.

> *...because the Roman name, by which the world is now ruled, will be taken away from the earth, and the government return to Asia; and the East will again bear rule, and the West be reduced to servitude.*[12]

Since World War II these eastern nations of the Old Roman Empire have become independent and stronger than at any time in history since the days of the Old Roman Empire. Damascus became the capital of an independent Syria during World War II. Syria gained independence April 17, 1946 by the League of Nations and a French mandate. Israel became a nation on May 14, 1948 by the League of Nations and an English Mandate. Lebanon became independent on November 22, 1943; Jordan on May 25, 1946; Cyprus on May 14, 1960; and Iran on April 1, 1979. The strength of these eastern nations is rising. These nations are arising with new youth and vitality. The population of these nations, under the age of fifteen, ranges from 35 to 50 percent.

Rabbi Riskin, who was dean of the Ohr Tora institutions and who was chief rabbi of Efrat, wrote concerning the light of the Hanukkah minora. Hanukkah celebrates the victory that the Maccabees had over Greek-Syrians and Antiochus. Rabbi Riskin's article very interestingly shows how the minora should be a light on the inside and outside of their homes.[13] The victory that God gave Israel in that day should be remembered by not only the Jewish people but by all nations. God is on their side and nations should remember that. He said that Israel's greatest threat was not intermarriage or assimilation, but he said, "Our main threat comes from the nations that have conspired for so long to destroy us."

There is no nation like Syria that has been such a conspiring enemy. There was constant battle between Israel, Judah, and Syria during the generations of the divided kingdom of Israel. It was only during the reign of King David that Israel reigned in Damascus the capital of Syria. The Messiah shall sit upon the throne of his father David. Again, Syria will be ruled from Jerusalem. Is this a constant fear of Syria?

B. Antiochus IV Ephiphanes

SIMILARITIES

Antiochus IV Epiphanes, a descendent of Grecian Alexander the Great, ruled as a Seleucid king in Syria. He is the little horn that arose from the divided Grecian Empire. Antiochus was the first fulfillment of Daniel's prophecy concerning the vial king that would bring abominations to Israel. The second fulfillment will be the abomination of the Antichrist during the tribulation period. Because Antiochus was of Syria, the Antichrist will most likely also arise out of Syria. Syria from the dawn of history has been the enemy of Israel.

Many early church fathers believed that the Antichrist would arise out of Syria. Lactantius wrote,

> And when his works shall be accomplished, another king shall arise out of Syria, born from an evil spirit, the over thrower and destroyer of the human race, who shall destroy that which is left by the former evil. He shall fight against the prophet of God. He will command fire to come down from heaven, and sun to stand and leave his course, and an image to speak...he will attempt to destroy the temple of God, and persecute the righteous people.[14]

Antiochus lived fourteen years in Rome and learned the foundational strategies that finally made the greatest empire of history. He was a Stoic converted to the Epicureans who put pleasure first. The Antichrist also shall be a man that knows the ways of the world and the ways of Rome.

Durant, the famous historian has said, "Antiochus IV was both the most interesting and the most erratic of his line, a rare mixture of intellect, insanity, and charm."[15] He was a man of deceit. The Maccabees write, "and spake peaceable words unto them, but all were deceit."[16] The Antichrist is also a man of such diversity. He performs great wonders, yet he makes desolate the nations.[17] He deceives in the name of peace. He is worshipped, yet cunningly conquers to exalt himself.

Antiochus enforced one law and culture. As an ardent Hellenist, he coerced his subjects to embrace Greek ideals and customs. He constrained Jews to participate in games that they regarded as indecent. He taxed Jews for one third of their grain crops and one half of their fruit.[18] He seized Jerusalem without fighting, and plundered its wealth. Bacchides enforced these outrageous instructions with an innate ruthlessness, subjecting the Jews to many forms of injustice.

Day after day Bacchides tortured distinguished citizens and publicly flaunted the spectacle of a captured city, until his criminal excesses provoked the victims to reprisals.[19]

The history of the Maccabees details other atrocious acts of Antiochus.

> They put to death certain women who had caused their children to be circumcised. And they hanged the infants about their necks, and rifled their houses, and slew them that had circumcised them...wherefore they chose rather to die, that they might not be defiled with meals, and that they might not profane the holy covenant: so then they died.[20]

The Antichrist in accordance with the prophecy of Daniel will also enter Jerusalem peaceably and set up the abomination of desolations (Daniel 11:24). The Antichrist being empowered by Satan will enact the wrath of Satan with unimaginable cruelty.

ENFORCES ONE FAITH

Antiochus forced the worship of foreign deities and the partaking of food that the Jews deemed unclean. He pillaged the temple treasury and banned the religious practice of daily sacrifices for three years and six months. He forced the Jews to forsake their ancestral law of circumcision.

Upon their altars he sacrificed swine, which was the gift to the vile god Dionysus. The temple was rededicated to Zeus and used for the worship of Baal-Shamaen. A Greek altar was built over the Jewish altar. Jews who refused to eat pork or who possessed the book of the law were jailed or murdered. The book of the law was burned. Jews were compelled to work on the Sabbath and to sing wild and sensuous songs in homage to Dionysus. Antiochus forced Jews to erect shrines to the Greek deities. The Samaritans, who complied with Antiochus, called their temple *"The Temple of Jupiter Hellenios."*[21] Hippolytus informs us that:

> *Antiochus Epiphanes the king of Syria... issued a decree in those times, that all should set up shrines before their doors, and sacrifice, and that they should march in procession to the honor of Dionysus, waving chaplets of ivy; and that those who refused obedience should be put to death by strangulation and torture.*[22]

Eerdmans Bible Dictionary says:

> *The "god of fortresses" (KJV "forces"; cf. NIV) whom Antiochus IV Epiphanes wished to honor above all other gods (Dan. 11:37–38) was probably Zeus Olympios. Antiochus promoted the worship of this deity with great zeal, seeking to make it the principle of religious unity within his kingdom (and to gain for himself divine acclaim by identifying himself with this deity). He built a magnificent temple to him in Antioch, desiring to dedicate the Jewish temple in Jerusalem to Zeus Olympios and the Samaritan temple on Mt. Gerizim to Zeus the Protector of Strangers (2 Macc. 6:2; Dan. 11:31; 1 Macc. 1:44–47).*[23]

Similarily, the Antichrist worships the god of fortresses (Daniel 11:38).

Antiochus was invited to invade Judea by the sons of Tobias. Let us hope that renegade Jews will not betray Israel to the hand of the Antichrist. If Antichrist is of an Islamic nature, let's hope that Israel is not deceived and turn against Christianity. If Antichrist is of a mystical practice, let's pray that the miracles of mysticism will not deceive the Jews.

Jews were to worship as Greeks or die. Similarly the Antichrist will enforce not the worship of many gods but the worship of one, Satan. An image will be erected to himself, the embodiment of Satan. The Antichrist will exalt himself to the position of the only God. Daily sacrifices will be removed. The temple will be desolated with abominations.

Early church fathers write the following concerning the abomination by the Antichrist.

> *He will enwrap righteous men with the books of the prophets, and thus burn them..."*[24]

> *Because they give not glory to him he will order incense pans to be set up by all everywhere, that no man among the saints may be able to buy or sell without first sacrificing; for this is what is meant by the mark.*[25]

There is another unique similarity between Antiochus and the Antichrist. Antiochus allured his whole kingdom to be *"one people."*[26] The Antichrist, in order to establish worldwide power will follow the present-day directives toward a one-world government and a one-world religion. Only, his mandates will exceed a union of paganism and Christianity. His one faith will be the worship of himself, the satanic Antichrist.

A treaty was made between Antiochus and certain rebels of Israel. But, more important is the treaty between Israel and the Antichrist. The prophecy of Daniel 11:23 has fulfillment in the Antichrist as well. The word *treaty* in the Hebrew is translated, "they join themselves to him". What a tragedy when Israel joins themselves to the Antichrist.

DIFFERENCES

Although Antiochus and the Antichrist are very similar in character and in their historical roles, there are four important differences. According to Durant, Antiochus loved women,[27] but the Antichrist will hate women. Daniel prophesied that he would give "no regard" to women; hence many feel that he may be homosexual. This disregard for women most fittingly refers to his disregard for the female goddesses. This interpretation better parallels his disregard for the god of his fathers and his disregard for all gods. "He shall regard neither the God of his fathers nor the desire of women, nor regard any god; for he shall exalt himself above them all (Daniel 11:37). The Antichrist also forces women to aid him in his battles; therefore, they turn against him (Daniel 11:17).

Antiochus labelled his coins, *Antiochus Theos Epiphanes* meaning God *Made Manifest*."[28] But, he did not dictate the worship of himself as god. Durant says that, "Antiochus thought of establishing and requiring the worship of himself as a god." [29]

Walter K. Price thinks differently.

> The evidence is strong that Antiochus IV not only encouraged the worship of Zeus, but he encouraged the worship of himself also. On many of the coins that survive from that day can be seen the figure of Zeus whose features closely resemble those of Antiochus IV Epiphanes. One which has been seen in the British Museum, a silver tetra drachma, has the head of Antiochus IV as if he were Zeus, crowned with laurel. Its inscription reads: "Of King Antiochus, God Manifest, Victory-bearer."[30]

The Antichrist, however, will evoke all men's worship.

Thirdly, Antiochus does not perform great wonders or miracles but the Antichrist performs great deceptive wonders. Irenaeus calls these wonders, magic.

> Let no one imagine that he performs these wonders by divine power, but by the working of magic ... since the demons and apostate spirits are at his service, he through their means, performs wonders.[31]

Antiochus came to a tragic end. According to Durant, Antiochus died in Persia as a result of epilepsy, madness, or disease.[32] However, according to Hippolytus, Antiochus was eaten up of worms and died.[33] In the histories of the Maccabees we read concerning the death of Antiochus that he proudly proclaimed that he would make Jerusalem the common burial place of the Jews, but the Almighty Lord smote him with pain of the bowels so that the worms rose up out of his body. He pleaded with God and said,

> It is meet to be subject unto God, and that a man that is mortal should not proudly think of himself, as if he were God.[34]

God did not heed his cries and promises. He died.

Any Antichrist who arises like Antiochus will be judged by God. The Antichrist also, in his attempts to destroy the Jewish people, will be cut off by the appearing of our Lord and Saviour Jesus Christ. He shall be cast into hell where 'the worm dieth not and the fire is not quenched (Mark 9:44).

C. The Dan Connection

The idea that the Antichrist would arise from the tribe of Dan is rooted in Jewish tradition.[35] Many early church fathers thought that the Antichrist would arise from the tribe of Dan.

Jeremiah 8:16 says, "The snorting of Babylon's horses were heard from Dan." The king of the north according to Daniel was Antiochus and the vial one (the Antichrist) who was to come. This above verse might allude to the enemies of Israel who approached from the north very close to Dan that was in the North.

This city of Dan was in the north and bordered on Syrian land. Dan was the northern most city in all Israel. Dan was included in the prophetical view of the Promise Land that Moses had from the top of Mount Pisgah. Today, Dan is called Tell Dan or Tell El-Qaida.

Hippolytus was certain that the Antichrist would spring from the tribe of Dan.[36] Dan was considered the counterfeit lion to the Lion of Judah. Both were called 'a lion's whelp (Jeremiah 8:16).

> Judah is a lions' whelp; from the prey, my son, you have gone up. He bows down, he lies down as a lion; and as a lion, who shall rouse him? (Genesis 49:9).

> Dan is a lion's whelp, and in naming the tribe of Dan he declared clearly the tribe from which Antichrist is destined to spring. For as Christ springs from the tribe of Judah, so Antichrist is to spring from the tribe of Dan.[37]

Dan was the son of Jacob. Dan means *judge*. Daniel means *divine judgment*. Samson's mother was of Judah and his father was of Dan. Samson, a descendant of Dan judged Israel and brought judgment upon the Philistines. Will God allow divine judgment to fall by an Antichrist who is of the tribe of Dan? Will the Antichrist spring from the tribe that was birthed by a handmaid and not by a true wife (Genesis 30:6)?

Dan is not reckoned with the twelve tribes in the Apocalypse. Irenaeus believed this was because the Antichrist would arise from the tribe of Dan.[38] John in the Apocalypse omits Dan and includes instead the priestly tribe of Levi.

When Jacob was blessing his children upon his death-bed, he prophesied that Dan would "leap from Bashan" (Deuteronomy 33:22). Why would Dan leap from Bashan? Moses conquered Og the king of Bashan and all the sixty cities of Bashan. This was the land of giants that became the inheritance of Manasseh, the firstborn of Joseph (Joshua 13:12). This land was not the inheritance of Dan. Is it possible that Jacob in his blessing was prophesying of an Antichrist that would in the latter days arise from Bashan? Bashan today would include the Golan Heights and the southern part of Syria. A Jewish man from Dan could live in Bashan today.

Dan was the only tribe that had not claimed their God-given inheritance in the Promised Land. Being on the edge of Philistine territory, they were driven north when the Philistines became too warlike. The Danites settled in the extreme north. They destroyed Laish and called it Dan.

The tribe of Dan intermingled and intermarried with other tribes and other nations. Marital ties were made with the Philistines. Those of the Danite tribe in the south were assimilated into other tribes. The Danites in the north intermingled with the tribe of Naphtali and the peoples of Tyre (1 Kings 7:13). They were rebuked for not participating in war against the Canaanites. They lost their distinct identity as one of the tribes of Israel.

The Danites also lost their zeal for the laws of God. The Danites turned to idolatry. When fleeing northward they persuaded a grandson of Moses to go with them as their idol priest. Micah's idol was set up in Dan. When Jereboam assumed kingship of the Northern Kingdom of Israel, two idols were established for worship, one in Dan and the other in Bethel. Jewish tradition says that all his descendants were idol worshipers.[39]

The Danites also lost their identity because they were too vulnerable to the wars and struggles between, Syria, Assyria, and Israel. Ben-Hadad king of Syria conquered the city of Dan. The territory of Dan was also conquered by Tiglath-Pileser of Assyria.

There is an interesting story about a son of a Danite woman and of an Egyptian father who blasphemed the name of God. The son was taken outside the city and stoned to death (1 Kings 15:16-20) Christ's judgments took place outside the city. Could this blasphemous son prophetically reflect the deeds of the Antichrist who may also be the son of a Danite woman but the son of a heathen father? Such is the judgment of Armageddon (Leviticus 24:11). God will in that day judge all who blaspheme against His name outside the city and will destroy the Antichrist who will blaspheme God, his temple, and his people.

Jewish tradition says that Dan wanted Joseph killed more than all the other brothers because his father loved him more. From Dan's Confession, we read.

> *When Dan assembled his family at the last of his life, he spake: "I confess before you this day, my children, that I had resolved to kill Joseph, that good and upright man, and I rejoiced over his sale, for his father loved him more than he loved the rest of us. The spirit of envy and boastfulness goaded me on, saying, 'Thou, too, art the son of Jacob,' and one of the spirits of Beliar stirred me up, saying, 'Take this sword, and slay Joseph, for once he is dead thy father will love thee.' It was the spirit of anger that was seeking to persuade me to crush Joseph, as a leopard crunches a kid between its teeth. But the God of our father Jacob did not deliver him into my hand, to let me find him alone, and He did not permit me to execute this impious deed, that two tribes in Israel might not be destroyed."*

I speak thus, for I know that in the latter days you will fall off from God, and you will kindle the wrath of Levi, and rise in rebellion against Judah, but you will not accomplish aught against them, for the angel of the Lord is their guide, and Israel will perish through them [40]

However, Dan receives an inheritance of land during the millennium that includes the land of Syria, for the scripture describes his territories as, 'the border of Damascus northward" (Ezekiel 48:1). Contrary to what Irenaeus says, a remnant of the tribe of Dan will be saved.

Today, it is believed that the black Jewish believers of Ethiopia are from the tribe of Dan. The Falasha or Beta Israel, as they are called, consider themselves to be part of the Jewish people. It is interesting to note that the Ethiopian Orthodox Church sought to annihilate and demonize the Ethiopian Jewish population as the Antichrist. [42]

Antichrist, I believe will arise from with a Gentile nation (the beast from the sea), yet I believe that he will arise from the tribe of Dan, possibly a Jew living in Syria. I can't see the Jews falling for someone who isn't a Jew.

There is no proof in scripture that the Antichrist will arise from the tribe of Dan but there are plenty of questionable details that make you wonder at the possibility. There is enough proof for me.

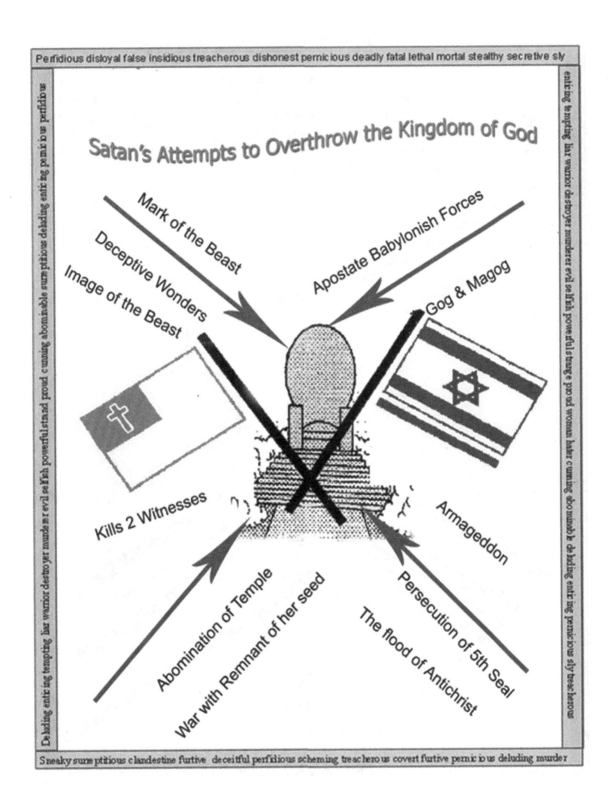

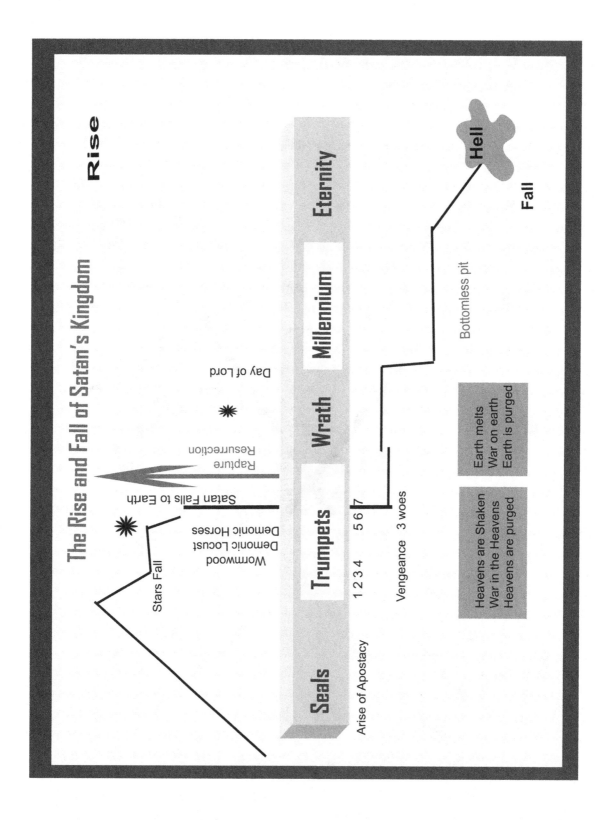

12. Christ's Trumpet Protections

A. Purging of the Heavens

During the plagues of the demonic locust and the demonic horses, I believe that the spiritual heavenlies are purged of demons, evil spirits, and wicked angels. The apostle Paul told us of the demonic powers in heavenly or high places.

> *For we do not wrestle against flesh and blood, but against principalities, against powers, against the rulers of the darkness of this age, against spiritual hosts of wickedness in the heavenly places (Ephesians 6:12).*

These spiritual forces will no longer be a threat to the believer but their power will be upon earth to destroy; therefore, the warning is *"woe, woe, woe"* to those who dwell on the earth. The star-hosts of Satan fall to deform and twist the minds of evil men. Evil spirits in the heavens fall downward to earth as the stars fall from heaven and the spirits in the underworld are unleashed upward to the earth. Evil spirits converge upon the earth and upon man.

Don't you think the heavenlies must be purged before the Harvest Rapture of the church into the heavens? Then the heavenlies must be purged before the earth is purged during the vials of Christ's wrath. The angels rejoice, but 'woe' is the message for men.

> *Therefore rejoice O heavens, and you who dwell in them! Woe to the inhabitants of the earth and the sea! For the devil has come down to you, having great wrath, because he knows that he has a short time (Rev.12:12).*

John envisioned Michael fighting against the dragon and his angels (Rev. 12:7). This war in heaven takes place during the trumpets and Satan is cast to the earth. Satan's power in the spiritual realm comes to an end. His entrance into the world enables him to fulfill his anger with the abomination of desolation that takes place during the long last trumpet, the seventh trumpet.

As a result of this war in the heavenlies, Satan is cast down to the earth and the heavens above the earth are purged. This is a tremendous victory for the cause of righteousness. Satan can no longer accuse a believer before the throne of God. His spiritual powers are limited to earth. Satan is silenced, but a shout from heaven proclaimed the great victory.

And war broke out in heaven, Michael and his angels fought with the dragon and the dragon and his angels fought; but they did not prevail, nor was a place found for them in heaven any longer. So the great dragon was cast out, that serpent of old, called the Devil and Satan, who deceives the whole world; he was cast to the earth, and his angels were cast out with him. Then a loud voice in heaven said, "Now salvation, and strength, and the kingdom of our God, and the power of His Christ have come, for the accuser of our brethren, who accused them before our God day and night, has been cast down (Rev.12:7-10).

A. The Purging of Fire

The church in Thyatira was encouraged to buy gold refined in the fire (Rev. 3:18). Why? Because purification was important for the church. Fire purges whatever it burns. Gold is not burned but refined. The fire of the Apocalypse refines the church and does not burn her if she is made of gold.

The word *fire* is used twenty five times in the book of Revelation but never once does fire destroy the church. Fire is that which God uses to judge the world justly. Fire won't burn the gold.

THE FIRE OF GOD

The fire of God is used to symbolize the acts of God's judgment. First, Christ is portrayed with eyes like a flame of fire in the first chapter of Revelation (Rev. 1:14, 2:18) and again in the 19th chapter when He comes again riding on a white horse. It is the eyes of Christ that knows the heart of man and can pass judgment fairly. Man has a choice to change his ways when he looks into the eyes of his Savior or fire will destroy him. Christ tells the Laodiceans church to anoint their eyes with eye salve that they may see (Rev. 3:18).

Second, fire is seen about the heavenly throne scenes three times. Seven lamps of fire before the throne represented the seven Spirits of God (Rev. 4:5). The Angel (Christ) standing before God had a golden censer. Smoke of the incense with the prayers of the saints was ascending before God, when the angel filled the censer with fire from the altar in heaven. This is a beautiful picture of Christ as High Priest.

Third, an angel is described as having feet like pillars of fire (Rev. 10:1). Is this Christ also?

Fourth, the overcoming saints stood on a sea of glass that was mixed with fire (Rev. 15:1-2). These praised God.

The fire of God only destroys because of evil. During the seventh seal and announcing the first trumpet is the angel with fire in the censer which is cast to the earth. Fire followed and 1/3 of the trees are burned and all green grass is burned up (Rev. 8:7).

For the second trumpet another angel sounded and a great mountain burns with fire and 1/3 of ships are burned.

Then, for the vials of God's wrath, those who took the mark of the Beast are tormented with fire and brimstone (Rev. 14:10). Not everyone is burned with this fire because an angel came from heaven that had power over fire and casts the remainder of the grapes into the winepress of the wrath of God (Rev. 14:18-19). During the fourth bowl, men are scorched with fire (Rev 16:8).

Then we find Babylon the great burning with fire (Rev. 17:16).

Hell then finally burns with fire and brimstone. Satan, the Antichrist, and the False Prophet are all thrown into that fire that is eternal (Rev. 20:10). Finally, the second death comes when anyone whose name is not in the book of life is cast into the lake of fire. God destroys evil – the unbelieving, abominable, murderers, immoral, sorcerers, idolaters, and liars.

C. Protection for the Saints

Read Rev. 9:12-21

The believer does not need to fear the tribulation plagues of Satan during the trumpets. God will not punish the righteous. The unrighteous man is plagued by Satan, not the righteous man.

> *But the rest of mankind (sinners), who were not killed by these plagues, did not repent of the works of their hands, that they should not worship demons, and idols of gold, silver, brass, stone, and wood, which can neither see nor hear nor walk (Rev.9:20).*

Those who survive the plague of the 5th trumpet do not repent; therefore, the survivors of the plague are unrighteous. We also know that there is no more repentance; therefore, no more forgiveness. But are there not some righteous people on the earth during the tribulation? If those who survive the plagues are *"the rest"* or *"the remainder"* who do not repent, then the plagues do not attack the saints. The righteous are protected from the demonic plagues. Why not? Israel was protected from the plagues of Egypt. While God judged Egypt, the Sons of Jacob in the land of Goshen escaped the plagues. They did not escape the terror of the enemy but God brought deliverance and brought them out of Egypt. So in the last days, the enemy will terrorize Christ's people but God will deliver them by a glorious resurrection and a Harvest Rapture.

We cannot argue that there were no righteous men or Christians upon the earth at this time. Many people later refuse the mark of the Beast. Many refuse to worship the image of the Beast. If men do not repent of their sins during the tribulation then these who refuse the mark are surviving righteous believers. The unrighteous remain unrighteous (Rev. 22:11), but the righteous remain righteous. Many die because they don't take the mark of the Beast but these live and reign with Christ for a thousand years.

> *And I saw thrones, and they sat on them, and judgment was committed to them. Then I saw the souls of those who had been beheaded for their witness to Jesus and for the word of God, who had not worshipped the beast or his image, and had not received his mark on their foreheads or on their hands. And they lived and reigned with Christ for a thousand years. But the rest of the dead did not live again until the thousand years were finished. This is the first resurrection. (Rev.20:4-5)*

Paul writes in Ephesians that the believer is sealed for the day of redemption (Ephesians

4:30). He is protected from the judgments of God and delivered from the wiles of the enemy but persecution from men continues. The Spirit of God keeps the believer until the Rapture. The believer is destined for the day of redemption. The martyrs die but are kept in the hand of Christ for the same day of resurrection.

D. Protection for 144,000

We must not forget that during the trumpet plagues God seals the 144,000. These are sealed before the hail falls, before the seas are turned to blood, before the grass and trees are burned, and before the sun is darkened. There is safety from the trumpet plagues upon the environment. God will provide water, food and protection for the 144,000. It is only those men that have not the seal of God in their foreheads that are plagued with the demonic locusts of the fifth trumpet (Rev. 9:4). The king of the bottomless pit has no power over Christ's chosen people whether they are Jews or Christians. Has not God promised that when you go through the waters, *"I will be with Thee."*? The plagues will not destroy the righteous. The righteous man needs only guard against unbelief and the falling away. The 144,000 do not see death but are raptured from Mount Zion. The church is raptured before the end of the mark of the Beast, before the Battle of Armageddon, and before the vials of Christ's wrath.

E. Miracles and signs of Protection

Not only are miracles and signs used as warnings, but God gives miracles as protections for the righteous from the vengeance of God and from the wrath of Satan. There are hidden miracles during the trumpets. Read the following verse carefully.

> In the same hour there was a great earthquake, and a tenth of the city fell. In the earthquake seven thousand people were killed, and the rest were afraid and gave glory to the God of heaven (Rev. 11:13).

The Two Witnesses are resurrected, and before the same hour has passed, an earthquake takes the lives of seven thousand people. The survivors of the earthquake are awed and glorify God. Who are these who praise God? Remember that the unrighteous repented not, so why would the unrighteous glorify God after an earthquake and after thousands have been killed? It must be Christ's people who praise Him. Why? The finger of God appoints the earthquake to destroy the enemy, but the hand of God clasps the righteous with love and protection. When they see this, they glorify God. God performs many miracles for His people in that day.

F. The Wilderness Woman Protected

> But the woman was given two wings of a great eagle, that she might fly into the wilderness to her place, where she is nourished for a time and times and half a time, from

the presence of the serpent. So the serpent spewed water out of his mouth like a flood after the woman that he might cause her to be carried away by the flood. But the earth helped the woman, and the earth opened its mouth and swallowed up the flood which the dragon had spewed out of his mouth. And the dragon was enraged with the woman, and he went to make war with the rest of her offspring, who keep the commandments of God and have the testimony of Jesus Christ (Rev.12:14-17).

WINGS OF AN EAGLE

After Satan is cast out of the heavenlies Israel is enraged by the face or presence of the serpent (Rev. 12:13). The battle that raged in the heavenlies is resumed on an earthly plain. This immediate presence of Satan begins the abominable reign of the Antichrist. When Satan perceived that he had lost his heavenly battle and was flung to the earth, he launched an assault against Israel because Jesus was that man-child born of Israel. So, Israel is that woman that flees into the wilderness. The Antichrist establishes his throne in Jerusalem. Ironically, Daniel recounts the abomination of desolation of the Antichrist as being borne upon wings.

> *Then he shall confirm a covenant with many for one week; but in the middle of the week He shall bring an end to sacrifice and offering. And on the wing of abominations shall be one who makes desolate, even until the consummation, which is determined, is poured out on the desolate (Daniel 9:27).*

What a contrast to the protective wings of the eagle that comes to the protection of Israel. The wings of Jehovah are mightier. "But to you who fear My name the Sun of Righteousness shall arise with healing in His wings" (Malachi 4:2). Although Israel is so vulnerable, she endures because of the great strength of Jehovah. On two great wings of an eagle she is carried into the wilderness for the duration of 3½ years during which the Antichrist shall manifest his abominations against the holy God.

Once before, Israel was born upon eagles wings. When they had faced the terror of Pharaoh, God delivered them into the Promise Land. "You have seen what I did to the Egyptians, and how I bore you on eagles' wings and brought you to Myself" (Exodus 40:4). The wilderness became the school ground for Israel to learn about her God. God nourished Israel in the wilderness for forty years with manna before they experienced abundance in the land of milk and honey (Exodus 40:4).

Then the wilderness becomes their place again during the trumpets. The wilderness was designated *"her place."* The same all-sufficient God will provide for Israel during the 3½ years of the reign of the Antichrist. God will protect and provide for Israel during the abomination of desolation. The wilderness is the abode of the eagle; but the wilderness was also a crude playpen where the nation of Israel developed and matured under the hand of Moses. The struggles of her wilderness experience taught her the ways of God. Again, engaged in a wilderness she will call upon Jehovah and see the mighty hand of God. Those who live in Israel are warned by God to flee to the mountains and caves (Matthew 24:16).

The two wings may be just figurative for possibly two nations who protect Israel. Some think that the two wings are two airplanes that rescue Israel but Israel my not have time to wait for two airplanes. Israel flees probably on foot.

MICHAEL THE ARCHANGEL

Michael the Archangel has been appointed by God to be the protector of Israel, not only on past occasions but also for the duration of the abomination of desolation. Daniel identifies Michael's role as chief prince of his people for end-time troubles.

> *Suddenly, a hand touched me, which made me tremble on my knees and on the palms of my hands. "But I will tell you what is noted in the Scripture of Truth. No one upholds me against these, except Michael your prince. "At that time Michael shall stand up, The great prince who stands watch over the sons of your people; and there shall be a time of trouble, such as never was since there was a nation, Even to that time. And at that time your people shall be delivered, everyone who is found written in the book (Daniel 10:21, 12:1).*

FLOOD SWALLOWED

When Satan tried to destroy Israel with a flood from his mouth, the earth swallowed up the flood (Rev. 12:15, 16). Without this divine protection, Israel would die as a nation and people.

Daniel also describes the acts of the Antichrist as a great flood (Daniel 9:26). This flood breaks the people but does not drown them. According to Daniel, the Antichrist assumes control peaceably while Israel is at ease, and seizes the nation by intrigues (Daniel 11:21-24).

This flood is not necessarily a literal flood. A literal flood is possible, considering the geography of the land for rainstorms can produce dangerous floods. However, Jehovah is Creator God not Satan. Satan has no control over the rain.

The word *flood* in scripture suggests a figurative interpretation. Terrors overtook Job like a flood (Job 27:20). David experienced a miraculous deliverance at the hand of God and prophesied of a similar deliverance for His people. The Lord sat enthroned at the flood, and the Lord sits as King forever.

> *For this cause everyone who is godly shall pray to You in a time when You may be found; surely in a flood of great waters they shall not come near him (Psalm 29:20, 32).*

Isaiah prophesied also of divine intervention from the floods of life.

> *So shall they fear the name of the Lord from the west, and His glory from the rising of the sun; when the enemy comes in like a flood, the Spirit of the Lord will lift up a standard against him (Isaiah 59:19).*

G. The Temple of God: Place of Safety

Then the temple of God was opened in heaven, and the ark of His covenant was seen in His temple. And there were lightnings, noises, thunderings, an earthquake, and great hail.

The temple was filled with smoke from the glory of God and from His power, and no one was able to enter the temple until the seven plagues of the seven angels were completed (Rev. 11:19, 15:8).

We have seen how God will protect His people from His vengeance, the plagues of Satan, the wrath of Satan, and the Antichrist; but the temple in the heavens is Christ's final secure home for His people. The temple of God is the dwelling place of God. It is that place where men shall dwell in the presence of God. Such a temple is not a literal building but the assembling of all believers into the presence of God. God does not need a literal temple in the heavens any more than there is a need for a temple in the new heavens and the new earth. The temple scenes in the heavenlies are symbolic of the high priestly duty of Christ and His intercessory mediation for mankind. The angels also minister in this presence of God. The temple is symbolic of a literal dwelling place with God.

The angel with the seventh trumpet shouts many prophetical declarations that are fulfilled by the conclusion of the seventh trumpet (Rev. 11:15-19). One prophetical statement is: "the temple of God was opened in heaven." Could this refer to the Harvest Rapture that occurs near the end of the seventh trumpet, when the dwelling place of God is made available to man? This open temple is referred to again immediately after many martyrs obtained victory over the Beast and appeared about the throne (Rev. 15:5).

The vials go forth from the temple of God. But, the Apocalypse declares that man cannot enter the temple until the vials of Christ's wrath are poured forth (Rev. 15:8). Some interpret this to mean that no man can be saved and enter heaven during the period of the vials of Christ's wrath. Since the Rapture had just occurred then this verse would verify that time of grace is finished. There is no second chance to repent. Revelation tells us that no man repented. Or perhaps, the anger of God and the holiness of God are so unbelievably demonstrated by His wrath that no one could possibly enter into His presence. This temple, however, symbolically represents that final ark of safety from the tribulations of this world.

H. The Final Warning

Read Revelation 14:6-12.

This message is important because it is delivered by angels. When Jesus came the first time, angels announced His coming to the shepherds. Angels delivered messages to Mary and Joseph several times. Why should his Second Coming be announced any less supernaturally? Angels will supernaturally give mankind of every nation a final warning to repent and worship God rather than worship the Beast. Missionary endeavors during the final tribulation under the Antichrist will be one-to-one witnessing and will face deathly consequences. The organized church of the remnant will be crushed and unable to pursue missionary tasks without extreme difficulty. The message of the angel will be imperative.

This message is important because it is the final warning. This final message shall go forth just as the mark of the Beast is demanded upon mankind. Man is warned not to associate with Babylon for she shall fall. God is faithful to warn people not to take the mark. There is no gain in receiving the mark because this mark will initiate the wrath of God.

The angel with the everlasting gospel says that the hour of His judgment has come. Why does it say that the hour of His judgment has come? Has not the world witnessed His judgment already by this time? But it is Christ Himself who administers the final judgment for the seven vials and on the day of the Lord. Man and Satan have an important role in the tribulations of the seals the trumpets. There is also a difference between the vengeance of God and the judgment of God. Vengeance reflects the anger of God because of the death of the saints. The judgment of God reflects Christ's hatred for sinfulness. Wrath reflects the intensity and conclusion of the judgment of which the angel is speaking.

The everlasting gospel is important because the grace of God will not be extended to man any longer. The temple door in heaven will be closed during the wrath of God (Rev. 15:8). No man shall be saved after the Harvest Rapture. For two thousand years the door has been open. The angel of the Lord said to the church of Philadelphia these words.

> I know your works. See, I have set before you an open door, and no one can shut it; for you have a little strength, have kept My word, and have not denied My name (Rev. 3:8).

Again the angel of the Lord said to the church of Laodicea these words.

> Behold, I stand at the door and knock. If anyone hears My voice and opens the door, I will come in to him and dine with him, and he with Me (Rev. 3:20).

> To him who overcomes I will grant to sit with Me on My throne, as I also overcame and sat down with My Father on His throne. He who has an ear, let him hear what the Spirit says to the churches (Rev. 3:20-22).

> The angel of the Lord that spoke to the seven churches is Christ. This is distinctly proclaimed by these words. "I will come in and dine with him." "I will grant to sit with Me on My throne with My Father" (Rev. 3:20, 21).

There is only one eternal message. The apostles preached about the grace of God and the same grace of God is offered here. Matthew said, "And this gospel of the kingdom will be preached in all the world as a witness to all the nations, and then the end will come" (Matthew 24:14). This gospel is the gospel of our Lord Jesus Christ.

The eternal message of the angels warns of the wrath of God and eternal judgment. The eternal judgment is different than the vials of Christ's wrath. Every man who receives the mark of the Beast shall endure the vials of Christ's wrath. These judgments are intense but brief. For forty-five days, God will judge all men on earth with the seven vials.

The believer gains victory over the mark and the Beast. This victory is not escapism but martyrdom. There are three necessary ingredients for victory: patience, obedience to Christ's commandments, and the faith in Jesus.

"Here is the patience of the saints" (Rev. 14:12). Patience is an essential trait of victory. The saints must at this time possess patience and hope in order to witness the glories that God had prepared for them. When the Bible describes tribulation, patience is often mentioned (Romans 12:12). Patience is an imperative companion to tribulation. Tribulation develops patience (Romans 5:3). Paul admonished the saints to rejoice in hope, to be patient in tribulation, and to continue to prayer (Romans 12:12). The final hour of history is no time to give up. Victory is around the next cloud of judgment.

John, who wrote this Apocalypse, bequeaths great encouragement. He calls himself not only a brother and fellow partaker in the tribulation but a brother and companion of the kingdom and of the endurance of Jesus Christ (Rev. 1:9). Tribulation is no time to mourn and bewail our imminent fate, but as John, we too can experience the Spirit on the Lord's Day and hear the voice of God. "Therefore be patient, brethren, until the coming of the Lord (James 5 7-9). Be patient that you might possess your souls (Luke 21:19). Endure, because the promises follow (Hebrews 10:36).

The angels give a message of comfort to the saints too.

> Then I heard a voice from heaven saying to me, "Write: 'Blessed are the dead who die in the Lord from now on.' " "Yes," says the Spirit, "that they may rest from their labors, and their works follow them" (Rev. 14:13).

The righteous man shall have rest but the unrighteous man shall have no rest day or night for eternity (Rev. 14:11). The angels pronounce blessings to him who keeps His commandments (Rev. 14:12). Some in the church have considered the commandments as Old Testament laws and legalistic chains not fit for the day of grace but here the commandments are necessity to the eternal blessings of God. The believer must keep His commandments or face the judgment too.

Victory also demands the faith of Jesus. Jesus faced persecution and death knowing that the final result was victory. When persecution torments the church, the faith of Jesus within the believer will see victory not defeat.

There is a comparison here between those who take the mark and those who do not take the mark. Those who do not take the mark are patient, they refuse to disobey God, and they have the faith of Jesus Christ. Obviously, those who take the mark are not waiting patiently for His coming; they disobey God and love not Jesus. The mark of the Beast is a sign of allegiance. There is no deception or confusion as to what the mark is and why it is given. It is a mark with eternal significance not merely political or monetary significance. Man will encounter the same ultimatum that Elijah gave to the nation upon Mount Carmel.

> And Elijah came to all the people, and said, "How long will you falter between two opinions? If the Lord is God, follow Him; but if Baal, follow him." But the people answered him not a word (1 Kings 18:21).

Christ's final trumpet warning is loud and clear. Man finally decides to worship God or the Beast, to obey the commandments of God or receive the mark, to keep the faith of Jesus or experience the wrath of God, to die in the Lord or never find rest.

Further Study

1. What else could God do to protect Israel?

2. List all the times God has protected you.

3. What is the secret to overcoming?

13. The Harvest Rapture

Read Rev. 14

This narration harmonizes with all scripture pertaining to the Rapture and resurrection that will be synonymous.

> And I looked, and behold a white cloud, and upon the cloud one sat like unto the Son of man, having on his head a golden crown, and in his hand a sharp sickle. And another angel came out of the temple, crying with a loud voice to him that sat on the cloud, Thrust in thy sickle, and reap: for the time is come for thee to reap; for the harvest of the earth is ripe. And he that sat on the cloud thrust in his sickle on the earth; and the earth was reaped. And another angel came out of the temple which is in heaven, he also having a sharp sickle. And another angel came out from the altar, which had power over fire; and cried with a loud cry to him that had the sharp sickle, saying, Thrust in thy sharp sickle, and gather the clusters of the vine of the earth; for her grapes are fully ripe (Revelation 14:14-18).

We find here someone who resembles the Son of Man standing in a cloud. He is wearing a golden crown and carrying a sharp sickle. The command comes forth from an angel who proceeds from the temple in heaven to thrust in the sickle for the time has come to reap the harvest. So the angel thrusts in his sickle and reaps the harvest. This passage of scripture narrates for me the Harvest Rapture and resurrection of the church.

A. The Time is Ripe

The Harvest Rapture occurs when the time is fully ripe according to the scriptures. The farmer does not reap his harvest until it is entirely ripe. Mark informs us that no time is ever wasted once the grain ripens. "But when the grain ripens, immediately he puts in the sickle (Mark 4:29). The sickle thrashes the wheat with great speed. Similarly the Greek word *harpadzo* (rapture) denotes a quick action, a snatching away. The angel of Revelation 14 is told that the harvest of the earth is

125

ripe. The wheat is gathered at the end of time and the wheat harvest of Israel always preceded the harvest of the grapes. The second angel has power over fire and commands another angel to thrust in the sharp sickle and gather the vine of the earth for the vine is ripe. With power over fire, this angel has the authority to execute judgment. The vine of the earth is ripe with sin and wickedness. Joel prophesies of the vintage harvest.

> *For there I will sit to judge all the surrounding nations. Put in the sickle, for the harvest is ripe. Come, go down; for the winepress is full, the vats overflow for their wickedness is great (Joel 3:12, 13).*

The destiny of the harvest of the first sickle remains untold, but we are clearly informed of the destiny of the harvest of the grapes. But if the harvest of the grapes gathers the wicked men of the earth, then the harvest of wheat gathers the righteous. If the grapes are hurled into Christ's wrath, we can safely assume that the righteous are rescued in a Harvest Rapture. The wheat harvest is the Rapture of believers in Christ who refuse the mark of the Beast. This is the Rapture. God separates the wheat from the tares. The wheat is stored in His heavenly garner and the grapes are trodden in the wrath of God. The redemption of the righteous has come and the judgment of the wicked is being fulfilled. In the fullness of time, Christ came as a babe in the manger and in the fullness of time, Christ shall return as a kingly Groom.

B. It's The Last Trump

> *For the Lord himself shall descend from heaven with a shout, with the voice of the archangel, and with the trump of God: and the dead in Christ shall rise first: Then we which are alive and remain shall be caught up together with them in the clouds, to meet the Lord in the air: and so shall we ever be with the Lord (1 Thessalonians 4:16,17).*

The Harvest Rapture eventuates at the last trump. The seventh trumpet, as far as scripture reveals, is the last trumpet which is 3½ years long. According to this verse in Thessalonians, the Rapture will occur at the last trumpet. The Rapture of the one hundred forty-four thousand and the Harvest Rapture occur during the time of the seventh trumpet or the last trumpet, very closely together.

An angel during the sixth trumpet prophesies that in the days of the sounding of the seventh trumpet, the mystery of God should be finished (1Thessalonians 4:16, 17). What is this mystery that is completed except the mystery of the church? She is raptured into glory at a time when the mystery of iniquity has filled the earth. The mystery of the church is the mystery of redemption and salvation that culminates at the Harvest Rapture. It's the mystery that was hid from the prophets, yet made known throughout the church. According to Paul it is the mystery of Christ and the church. "This is a great mystery, but I speak concerning Christ and the church" (Ephesians 5:32).

At the very beginning of the seventh trumpet, voices in heaven shout prophetically, "The kingdoms of this world are become the kingdoms of our Lord (Rev. 11:15). By the end of the seventh trumpet the kingdom of God is harvested. The last blast of the trumpet is 3½ years long.

The true sons of His kingdom are separated from the false sons of the kingdom. The message of the gospels proclaimed that the kingdom of heaven was at hand. Now, in Revelation, the kingdom of God sees its ultimate fulfillment in the resurrection of believers and His earthly kingdom arrives not long after.

In ancient Israel for twenty-nine days before the feast of trumpets, the ram's horn was blown. The last blast was longer. It was called the *Tekia Gedolah*[1] meaning *The Great Blowing*. When we examine John's account of the trumpets, we clearly see that the duration of the seventh trumpet is over a longer period of time compared to the other trumpets. During the seventh trumpet, the third woe of the red dragon takes place. The Antichrist and False Prophet execute their wrath. We also wonder if the series of trumpet blows for the feast of trumpets may resemble the seven trumpet blasts of the Revelation.

When Abraham was requested to offer up his son upon the altar, God provided a ram in the thicket. Judaism taught that the ram represented Messiah. They also instructed that the left horn of this ram became the shofar that was blown on Mount Sinai at the giving of the Law. This blowing of the ram's horn became known as the *first trump*. The shofar blown on Rosh Hashanah is considered to be the right horn of this same ram. The blowing of this second horn is called the last trump.[2] (See chapter 10, 11.)

C. There are Clouds

Revelation 14:14

The Harvest Rapture of Revelation 14 satisfies the scriptural requirement of 1 Thessalonians 4:17 because a cloud is present also. We shall be caught up in clouds to meet the Lord in the air. Daniel speaks of one like the Son of Man coming with the clouds of heaven (Daniel 7:13). The word 'cloud' is used five times in the book of Revelation. The two witnesses ascend to heaven in a cloud. Four of these occur during the seventh trumpet. Both the angels who thrust in the sickle are in the clouds. The angel who appears like the Son of Man and wearing a golden crown is in the white cloud with a sickle in his hand.

D. It's Harvest Time

The barley harvest of Israel was about mid April. Two weeks later the Jordan River overflowed its banks. Then another two weeks later began the time of the wheat harvest. The wheat harvest lasted seven weeks (Deuteronomy 16:9). Summer fruit, a harvest of figs, were picked and the grapes were cast into the winepress about August or September. Finally in November the olives were gathered.

At the end of time the harvest shall be a reaping of righteous men not wheat, a reaping of wicked men not grapes. Both the righteous and the wicked are left to grow together unto the end and the seventh trumpet is the time of the end (Matthew 13:39).

The angel that stood upon the sea and the land prophesies before the seventh trumpet that time would come to an end during the sounding of the seventh trumpet (Rev. 10:6). The timing of the Harvest Rapture is at the end. Only the seven vials and the day of the Lord is yet to come. A pre-tribulation rapture, on the other hand, is not at the end of time as we find the Harvest Rapture to be.

> *"The enemy who sowed them is the devil, the harvest is the end of the age, and the reapers are the angels. Therefore as the tares are gathered and burned in the fire, so it will be at the <u>end of this age</u>. The Son of Man will send out His angels, and they will gather out of His kingdom all things that offend, and those who practice lawlessness, and will cast them into the furnace of fire. There will be wailing and gnashing of teeth. Then the righteous will shine forth as the sun in the kingdom of their Father. He who has ears to hear, let him hear! (Matthew 13:39–43).*

Matthew speaks of the Son of man dispatching forth His angels to gather all the offensive persons in His kingdom (Matthew 13:47-49). The Son of Man comes in a cloud with the angels to reward the subjects of His kingdom. "For the Son of Man will come in the glory of His Father with His angels, and then He will reward each according to his works" (Matthew 16:27). Similarly, in the Revelation, the one with the sickle is likened to the Son of Man and coming with the angels to reap the harvest (Rev. 14:14-17).

The Harvest Rapture of Revelation distinctly portrays the angels as the reapers. An angel departs from the temple in heaven and cries to the man on the cloud. "Thrust in your sickle." Another angel comes from the altar with fire and cries out to the man with the sharp sickle, "Thrust in the sickle and gather the cluster of the vine of the earth and cast them into the wine press of the wrath of God." The angel thrusts in the sickle. The vials of Christ's wrath follow.

The grapes represent the wicked men, who take the mark, and whose name was not found in the book of life. God has determined that these must endure the vials of His wrath and His eternal judgment. But the wheat that is gathered into His barn represent those who are raptured into the heavenly kingdom. These shall escape the vials of Christ's wrath and His eternal judgments. One shall be taken and the other left behind (Matthew 24:40).

Even the daughters of Babylon will see their day of judgment upon the threshing floor at this harvest time. "The daughter of Babylon is like a threshing floor when it is time to thresh her; yet a little while and the time of her harvest will come" (Jeremiah 51:33).

The feast of harvest is also called the feast of weeks. The time of the Hebrew harvest began with the giving of the firstfruits. Harvest concluded with the *Feast of Ingathering* that occurred at the end of the year (Exodus 23:16, 17). The feast and celebration of the Harvest was after the corn and the vintage had been gathered. The Feast of Ingathering is also called the Feast of Tabernacles. The Feast of Tabernacles or the Feast of Ingathering was a time of great rejoicing. For seven days the people presented an offering by fire to the Lord. The eighth day of the feast was a holy convocation when an offering by fire was given to the Lord (Numbers 15:3). No man worked on that day called Atzeret .

When we compare the events of the Jewish harvest with the events of the end time, there is a great similarity. The rapture of the one hundred forty-four thousand is called the firstfruits of the harvest. The Rapture and resurrection at the end of the world could be equated to the Feast of

Ingathering. The offerings by fire for seven days could allude to the outpouring of Christ's wrath upon those who take the mark of the Beast.

E. Angels Are the Reapers

According to Matthew, the angels are the reapers of the harvest. "And He will send His angels with a great sound of a trumpet, and they will gather together His elect from the four winds, from one end of heaven to the other" (Matthew 24:31). The Harvest Rapture agrees with Matthew's record. Angels are in the clouds of heaven ready to reap the harvest.

F. Jesus Appears

Who is that in the white clouds? He is described as an angel like the son of man. Jesus is the son of man and Jesus was the Angel of the Lord in the New Testament. We shall meet the Lord in the clouds in the air (1 Thessalonians 4:10). On His head is a golden crown for He is already King. In His hand is a sharp sickle. The fast action of the sickle resembles the fast rapture that happens in a twinkling of an eye. We not only see Jesus as He is but we shall be like him (1 John 3:2). "We shall be conformed to His glorious body" (Philippians 3:20). Wow! We do return through the heavens dressed in white garments riding on white horses to accompany Christ in the Battle of Armageddon.

G. The Final Warning is Preached

Read Rev. 14

When we examine Revelation chapter fourteen, we discover that several events are congruent. At the same time that men are receiving the mark of the Antichrist, angels take the final message of the gospel to the ends of the earth. The angels warn mankind not to submit to the mark of the Beast (Rev. 14:9). The mark of the Beast occurs before the Rapture of the one hundred forty-four thousand. All these events occur at the last trump and we also know that the sickle is thrust in the earth for the final ingathering of the church shortly after the Rapture of the 144,000 who are the firstfruits. Will the Rapture not occur at the end of the same harvest in which the firstfruits are raptured? Yes.

Noah faithfully preached a message of repentance before the great flood. Man did not repent. Only Noah and his family believed God. God sent angels to warn Lot before He destroyed Sodom and Gomorrah. God sent angels before the first coming of Jesus. Angels brought a message of hope and peace to the shepherds who were caring for their sheep upon the Judean hills that first Christmas night. Mary and Joseph received warnings from angels who appeared to them in a dream. Angels shall again warn the peoples of every nation with a final everlasting gospel just before the Rapture and the judgment of God. Matthew speaks of a global message before the end of time.

"And this gospel of the kingdom shall be preached in all the word for a witness unto all nations, and then shall the end come" (Matthew 24:14). Man will not heed the angel's final warning.

The angels at His first coming conveyed a message of hope and peace, but the angel's message preceding His Second Coming liberates three powerful warnings. The first warning is to "Fear God." What a contrast to the message the shepherds heard the angels sing -- "fear not!" But men need to fear God in the face of imminent judgment. Angels warn the inhabitants of the earth to worship God who made heaven and the earth.

The second angel prophesies the fall of Babylon. The third angel warns man not to worship the Beast and his image. The angel cautions man not to accept the mark of the Beast. No Christian needs to fear what will be or not be the mark of the Beast. The angel's warning is so clear that no one in ignorance will accept this mark. The consequences were stated clearly by the angel of the Lord. The vials of Christ's wrath would be squeezed into a cup of Christ's indignation without measure, undiluted, and with full strength. Those who take not the mark are promised a rest, but for those who take the mark of the Beast, there is no rest day or night.

How faithful God is to warn the nations, before the day of judgment. Faithfulness is the testimony of the patient saints. Faithful are those who keep His commandments. Faithfulness is a treasure glittering forth from the martyrs for Christ Jesus (Rev. 14:12). The Lord is faithful to shorten these days so that all flesh is not destroyed.

A conflict is evident in regards to the harvest of the world. Matthew's account says that the tares are gathered first, then the wheat (Matthew 13:30-43). But, in the Revelation, the wheat is reaped first before the grapes are trodden by the wrath of God. There is one explanation that is visible as history and time leap forth into the millennium and eternity. The tares are burned and cast into the eternal hell that is prepared for the devil and his angels. Hell, which is the second death, is not until after the millennium and then after this, the New Heavens and the New Earth descend from God out of heaven. Here the wheat of the harvest fills the golden barns of Christ's eternal abode. We see the reversal ingathering of the wheat and tares.

With each of the seven throne scenes in the book of Revelation, more believers and martyrs are witnessed before the throne of God. Each possible rapture coincides with a new scene in heaven. However, if there is only one rapture and resurrection of the church, then that rapture must be the Harvest Rapture. Scripture verifies one rapture only.

The first resurrection is completed with those martyrs that are about the throne in the seventh throne scene. Some are beheaded, and others refuse the mark of the Beast (Rev. 20:4). Those who have been beheaded may refer to the saints who had patience and were killed by the sword in Revelation 13:10. (See chart 4A.)

We know, according to Revelation 20:4 that the final resurrection of the righteous is after the mark of the Beast and before the millennium; therefore, this final resurrection could be synonymous with the Harvest Rapture. Again, if there is only one resurrection and only one rapture, then these final martyrs under the persecution of the Antichrist must have been resurrected during the Harvest Rapture. Those who were resurrected for their faith under the reign of the Antichrist cannot precede those who are alive and remain until the coming of the Lord. The Rapture cannot transpire until the completion of the resurrection of the just for they occur together.

For the Lord Himself will descend from heaven with a shout, with the voice of an archangel and with the trumpet of God, and the dead in Christ will rise first. Then we who are alive and remain shall be caught up <u>together</u> with them in the clouds, to meet the Lord in the air (1 Thessalonians 4:14-17).

The dead in Christ are raised before the Rapture, for the Rapture cannot precede the resurrection. So, how can there be a pre-tribulation rapture when there are definite references to a resurrection of the just at the last trump.

Is there a possibility of several resurrections very close together at the end of time? This idea pivots upon the translation of 1 Thessalonians 4:17. "We shall be caught up together." Does *together* modify the verb *caught up* meaning that both the dead and those who remain go together or does it describe the final togetherness in the clouds of the air? Lexicons concur that *together* denotes coincidence of two actions in time, or at the same time, and that αϖνα means 'together, also, at once, at the same time.'

The Harvest Rapture is the only eschatological event that complies with all the evidence of scripture with reference to a Rapture and resurrection of the saints. In the fullness of time the groom shall appear and the trump shall sound. The mystery of God will be completed and no soul shall be saved here after. The glory of God and His heaven will dispel the darkness of those days. The prepared bride is escorted to her heavenly home.

FURTHER STUDY

1. Why do you think there are seven throne scenes in Revelation?

2. What is the role of angels in the last day?

PART E

KINGDOM'S FALL
AND
THE DAY OF THE LORD

14. The Prelude to the Day of the Lord

Vials of Christ's Wrath

Read Rev. 15, 16

A. The Qol

The Rapture has taken place. Seven vials or bowls are bursting with the wrath of God. These are the seven last plagues (Rev.15:1) and John names them the judgments of God that are true and righteous (Rev.16:6). God has been faithful to forewarn man of these judgments for an angel of the fourteenth chapter warns man that the wine of Christ's wrath is *"without mixture"* (Rev.14:10), it is with full strength, undiluted and strong. Judgment is the not the result of God's failure but man's. So the angel thrusts in the sickle and the grapes are harvested and cast into the winepress.

The first six vials of Christ's wrath are a prelude to the day of the Lord and the Battle of Armageddon. The day of the Lord more specifically refers to the seventh wrath, the final day of his wrath. This prelude to the day of the Lord is the *"noise,"* the *"voice,"* or the *"sound"* of the day of the Lord of which Zephaniah speaks. "The great day of Jehovah is near. It is near and rushing greatly, the (sound or noise) of the day of Jehovah" (Zephaniah 1:14).

The Hebrew word for noise is *qol*.[1] Qol interprets that which is heard not seen and that which precedes or qualifies an action. For example: the noise of war, the noise of the horses' hoofs, and the noise of chariots. The six vials precede and describe the nature of the climatic event, which is the Battle of Armageddon. *Qol* is also translated *proclamation*. The vials, as a prelude, proclaim the great day of the Lord. Before something arrives, you often hear it coming. Christ's *qol* is the sound of thunder; these judgments are the sound of Christ's voice, His doings, and His judgments. The six vials are the voices of Christ's judgment. The six vials are but the sound of His judgment compared to the dreadful shaking judgments in the day of the Lord. The six vials are the thunderings of the battle and the judgment. The six vials share but a sample of the cries and mourning that occurs in the day of the Lord. The cries in the day of battle are more thunderous and screeching.

A noise (qol) will come to the ends of the earth—For the Lord has a controversy with the nations; He will plead His case with all flesh. He will give those who are wicked to the sword,' says the Lord." Thus says the Lord of hosts: "Behold, disaster shall go forth from nation to nation, and a great whirlwind shall be raised up from the farthest parts of the earth. And at that day the slain of the Lord shall be from one end of the earth even to the other end of the earth. They shall not be lamented, or gathered, or buried; they shall become refuse on the ground (Jeremiah 25:31-33.)

However, we can rejoice because the Lord shall reign with majesty and strength. The Psalms comfort us with promise that the Lord on high is mightier than the *qol* of many waters (Psalm 93:4).

FORTY-FIVE DAYS

The words of Daniel lead me to believe that the vials of Christ's wrath and the Battle of Armageddon are for a period of 45 days. Daniel says, "Blessed is he who waits, and comes to the thousand three hundred and five and thirty days" (Daniel 12:12). This is 45 days longer than the 3½ years of the abomination of desolation. He who endures the vials of Christ's wrath and the day of the Lord is truly blessed because that person is alive to live during the millennial reign of Christ.

B. Judgment

The vials are Christ's *judgments*. At the eleventh hour, one of the angels with a final message says, "Fear God, and give glory to him for the hour of his judgment is come (Rev. 14:7)." These admonitions occur just before the Harvest Rapture and just before the vials are poured out, but not before the seals, nor before the trumpets. The word judgment is not used in the Apocalypse before this fourteenth chapter. It is then used six times to refer to the last seven plagues.

The plagues of Egypt were ten just as the law of the commandments was ten. Seven speaks of the divine law of grace; therefore, the vials of Christ's wrath are seven in number. The seventh vial is the Battle of Armageddon. With the consummation of that great battle, God proclaims: "It is done (Rev.16:17)." Jesus said, "It is finished" when he died but now the kingdoms of this world become the kingdoms of our Lord and Christ. "It is finished."

1st vial is upon the earth but is really upon man. Grievous sores fall upon those who take the mark of the Beast and those who worship his image.

2nd vial falls upon the sea. Every living soul dies in the sea.

3rd vial turns rivers and fountains into blood.

4th vial upon the sun causes men to scorch with fire, yet they continue to blaspheme the name of God and repented not.

5th vial is upon the seat of the Beast. His kingdom is full of darkness.

6th vial dried up the River Euphrates and prepared a path for the kings of the east.

7th vial upon the air brings to pass the greatest earthquake, thunders, lightenings, in all history. Hail, weighing hundreds of pounds, falls from the heavens. The Battle of Armageddon brings judgment upon the nations. Babylon causes all nations to drink of the wine of the wrath of her fornication (Rev. 14:8).

C. Wrath

Greek	Meaning	Scripture Reference	Translation of NJKV
ορүε orge	Wrath State of mind, Expression of the emotion	Rev. 6:16 Rev 6:17 Rev 11:18 Rev. 14:10	Wrath of the Lamb Day of wrath Your wrath Cup of his indignation NKJV
θυμος thumos	Anger, Outburst of a state of mind, Emotion	Rev. 12:12 Rev 14:8 Rev 14:19 Rev. 15:1 Rev. 15:7 Rev. 16:1 Rev 18:3	Wrath of Satan Wrath of Babylon's fornication, Wrath of God Wrath of God Wrath of God Wrath of God Wrath of Babylon's fornication
Both thumos and orge		Rev 14:10, Rev. 16:19 Rev. 19:15	Wrath of God which is poured out full strength into the cup of His indignation. Fierceness and wrath of God Fierceness and wrath of God

These seven vials are full of the wrath and the indignation of God. John employs two words to describe the wrath, anger, or indignation of God: *thumós* (θυμος) and *orgé* (ορүη). "The word "wrath" in Greek is *orgé*, a state of mind, in contrast to *thumós*, anger, which is an outburst of that state of mind with the purpose of revenge.[2]

In antiquity both words differed from each other. *Orgé* (wrath) gave orientation to revenge and punishment. Etymologically *thumós* originally denoted the emotion and *orgé* the expression of the emotion. The difference between these two words has been lost in the Septuagint translation and within the New Testament both *thumós* and *orgé* overlap in their meanings.[3]

John used both *thumós* and *orgé* to describe the wrath and anger of God. We must observe that *orgé* is used by John in the sixth and the eleventh chapters of Revelation and then he uses *thumós* from chapter fourteen onward to refer to the wrath of God.

The word *thumós* thus gives no reference to the wrath of God until after the trumpet period, just as the word judgment is not used until the fourteenth chapter in which chapter the Harvest Rapture occurs also. John is making a very important distinction here between the different periods of the tribulation. Previously, John spoke of the orgé of God, the *thumós* of Satan, and the *thumós* of Babylon, but it is not until the fourteenth chapter that John used the term 'the *thumós* of God" (θυμοσ~ Του θεου). Could John be making this distinction by his use and order of the words *orgé* and *thumós*? *Thumós* denotes violent movement and God definitely exhibits violent movements and acts during these last seven vials.[3]

The seven vials alone are a manifestation of the wrath (*thumós*) of God, not the plagues or the seals and the trumpets. The seal period is the wrath of man and the trumpet period is the wrath of Satan. We may also conclude that the seals and trumpets do not overlap with God's wrath.

Wrath is not the same as judgment. Wrath is a process or emotion within God.[4] This emotion affects man and brings forth judgment. Wrath reflects Jehovah's divine reaction and reckoning with evil. Both Israel and the church deals with a personal divine will, not merely an irrational or impersonal force. The character of God determines the nature of His wrath and vengeance. In the Apocalypse the divine wrath of God determines the final fate of mankind and the nations.

The Old Testament employs the words ebrah, סרי and aph, 'אפ to describe the dreadfulness of the day of the Lord. In the book of Daniel *ebrah* is translated both *thumós* and *orgé* are uniquely combined in the Septuagint, the New Testament and in the Apocalypse to emphasize the dreadfulness of the day of Christ's wrath.

John combines both words with his final two references to the wrath of God. Now the great city was divided into three parts, and the cities of the nations fell. And great Babylon was remembered before God, to give her the cup of the wine of the <u>fierceness of His wrath</u> (Rev. 16:19 *thumós* and *orgé*).

Again John uses both words together. Now out of His mouth goes a sharp sword, that with it He should strike the nations. And He Himself will rule them with a rod of iron. He Himself treads the winepress of the <u>fierceness and wrath</u> of Almighty God (Rev. 19:15).

The Old Testament combines *thumós* and *orgé* at least forty-three times. I bring your attention to only a few. The Lord spoke to the children of Israel and said: "each day for a year, shall ye bear your iniquities, even forty years, and ye shall know my fierce anger (Τον θυμοσ τη~ μου)." The Zondervan Septuagint text translates it more correctly as *My fierce anger*. Most translations do not follow suite and the KJV translates it, *my breach of promise*. This is a very unique translation. Christ's wrath in the Old Testament was promised to all who did not keep his laws, or breached their promise with God and disobey Him.

> *"After the number of the days in which ye searched the land, even forty days, each day for a year, shall ye bear your iniquities, even forty years, and ye shall know **my breach of promise.** " (Numbers 14:34, KJV 1900)*

> *"According to the number of the days during which ye spied the land, forty days, a day for a year, ye shall bear your sins forty years, and ye shall know **my fierce anger**" (Numbers 14:34). The Septuagint Version of the Old Testament Translated into English)*

> *Therefore I have poured out My indignation on them; I have consumed them with*

the fire of My wrath; *and I have recompensed their deeds on their own heads,"* says the Lord God (Ezekiel 22:3).

> *Who can stand before His indignation and who can endure the fierceness of His anger? His fury is poured out like fire, and the rocks are thrown down by Him (Nahum 1:6). Christ's fierce anger is like rain for it falls upon a man while he is eating (Job 20:23).*

His wrath does not wait for a man to finish his eating or to repent. There is coming a day 'as a thief in the night' when a man will not a have another chance.

> *Behold, the day of the Lord comes, Cruel, with both wrath and fierce anger, to lay the land desolate; and He will destroy its sinners from it (Isaiah 13:9, Septuagint)[5].*

The day of the Lord comes with cruelty and with no remedy; God will not change his mind in that day. Concerning the wrath of God, Daniel wrote: "what has been determined shall be done" (Daniel 1:36). In that day sinful man will have to face the judgment of God just as Moses had an encounter with God face to face (Exodus 33:11, Deuteronomy 5:4). Facing the judgment face to face is seen in the Apocalypse when Christ himself treads out the winepress and the unrighteous are punished in the face of Jesus and His angels.

Christ's fierce anger is something that is *poured out like* fire (Nahum 1:6). Fire denotes fury, destruction, and heat. Revelation also describes the wrath and anger of the Lord as "fire".

> *I beheld, and indeed the fruitful land was a wilderness, and all its cities were broken down at the presence of the Lord, by His fierce anger (Jeremiah 4-26).*

> *He himself shall also drink of the wine of the wrath of God, which is poured out full strength into the cup of His indignation. He shall be tormented with fire and brimstone in the presence of the holy angels and in the presence of the Lamb (Rev. 14:10).*

D. Indignation

The day of the Lord is translated as the day of Christ's indignation. Indignation means anger, wrath, outrage, fury.

Two times in the book of Daniel the word *orgé* is translated indignation. Daniel's day of indignation is at an appointed time and at the end of time. These days of indignation in the book of Daniel refer to the wrath of the Antichrist (Daniel 8:19, 11:30, 36) and the abomination of desolation, not the wrath of God. In Daniel the Antichrist shows indignation against the holy covenant, but in Zephaniah, Christ shows indignation against the nations of the world for not obeying his holy covenant.

The same words are used to describe the anger of man and the anger of God, but there is a difference (Ephesians 4:31). It is a sin and a folly for man to show anger against others, but with

God it is the proper and just out-flowing of the righteousness of God. Human wrath is wrapped tightly with self-interest, but God is concerned with the revelation of righteousness. Divine anger is never estranged from Christ's essential righteousness. Without this divine anger of God, man could not have the eternal hope of peace for true peace only comes with divine righteousness.

The wrath of God in the New Testament is both present and eschatological. Those who do not believe are already destined to the eternal wrath of God that shall happen in the future.

> He who believes in the Son has everlasting life; and he who does not believe the Son shall not see life, but the wrath of God abides on him" (John 3:36).

We are by nature born as the children of wrath. Only Christ's mercy can spare man from the present curse of His wrath and its future fulfillment. It is by wrath that the greatness of mercy is measured and by mercy the greatness of wrath.

> Only he who knows the greatness of wrath will be mastered by the greatness of mercy. The converse is also true: Only he who has experienced the greatness of mercy can measure how great wrath must be. For the wrath of God arises from His love and mercy. [5]

Those who accept mercy are freed from wrath and those who despise mercy remain under its curse.

Jesus alone can deliver man from the coming wrath (1 Thessalonians 1:10, Romans 5:9). He alone is able to open the seals of judgment and mercy. The work of Christ, in freeing man from the wrath to come is a two-fold effect - the cross, and the resurrection. Believing on the Christ of the cross frees a man from the present condemnation of sin and the future wrath of God. Those who are in Christ Jesus are raptured before the vials of the wrath of God; yet, these judgments are merely a taste of the eternal fires of hell from which the believer is delivered. The truth and power of the resurrection of Jesus Christ grants the church the assurance that God approved the work of the cross and grants the church the assurance of a resurrection for all the saints. The ascension of Jesus Christ provides the assurance of a future rapture and deliverance from the wrath to come.

As judge of the earth, Christ's responsibility is justice, which is the manifestation of the wrath and anger of God. God is slow to wrath, but the final wrath of God comes as a thief in the night. The aim of divine wrath is to bring to completion the divine rule of holiness. Morality and the commandments of God cannot be ignored. Man in the Old Testament was destined to wrath if he disobeyed the commandments of God, heeded not His word, or worshipped other gods. Paul uses both *thumós* and *orgé* when explaining the wrath of God that is promised unto them that do not obey the truth.

But to those who are self-seeking and do not obey the truth, but obey unrighteousness —indignation and wrath (Romans 2:8).

Only holiness can pass judgment upon sin. The perfect holiness of the Messiah exercises Christ's judgment. Even the angels that proceed from the temple in heaven to execute these judgments wore garments that were pure and white. No one can enter the temple of heaven during this horrible display of Christ's wrath. The holy smoke in the temple from the glory of God arises in contrast to the filthy smoke and pollution of Babylon. Even the sea of glass before the throne was mingled with the holy fire of Christ's judgment. Standing upon this sea of glass are holy Jewish and Gentile believers singing the song of victory and judgment. The sea is stained with the fire of Christ's revenge on behalf of those who gain the victory over the mark and number of the Antichrist. Now, those who receive the mark and the number of the Beast are subjected to the judgment vials of God.

FURTHER QUESTIONS

1. How are the vials of God worse than anything yet prophesied?
2. What does holiness have to do with the final judgment?

15. The Great Day of God Almighty

A. One Concluding Day of Darkness

The feast of harvest is also called the feast of weeks. The time of the Hebrew harvest began with the giving of the firstfruits. Harvest concluded with the Feast of Ingathering that occurred at the end of the year. The feast and celebration of the Harvest was after the corn and the vintage had been gathered. The Feast of Ingathering is also called the Feast of Tabernacles. The Feast of Tabernacles or the Feast of Ingathering was a time of great rejoicing. For seven days the people presented an offering by fire to the Lord. Does this fire depict the seven vials of God's wrath by fire?

The eighth day of the feast was a holy convocation, when an offering by fire was given to the Lord. No man worked on that day called Atzeret. Atzeret translated withdrawal, conclusion and convocation. Atzeret was the eighth day of a festival.[1] The day of the Lord is truly described by the word Atzeret meaning conclusion and withdrawal. The day of the Lord is the end and conclusion of all things. The day of the Lord is the conclusion of God's wrath, the conclusion of man's world, the conclusion of Satan's rule, and the conclusion of the reign of the Antichrist.

The seven days of this Old Testament feast could parallel the forty-five days of the vials of God's wrath which is approximately 7 weeks. Then the eighth day of the feast could parallel the day of the Lord.

The day of the Lord occurs after the sun is turned into darkness and after the moon is turned into blood (Joel 2:3). The day of the Lord is a day of complete darkness. This day of the Lord occurs after Elias has come to warn the people (Malachi 4:5). The day of the Lord occurs after the angels of heaven have warned the world of His wrath to come. In that day, judgment is executed upon the nations and there is no more chance to repent. The day of the Lord occurs after Satan falls to earth because he too is punished in that day. The day of the Lord is at the close of the reign of Antichrist who is, at this time, cast into the lake of fire (Rev. 19:20, Isaiah 27:1). What a conclusion!

The day of the Lord is a day of darkness and destruction when God shall avenge all nations (Obadiah 1:15) and destroy all wickedness and pride (Isaiah 2:12). This is a day of battle (Ezekiel 13:5) when Christ shall return to earth and destroy the kingdoms of evil. There is no light in that day (Amos 5:18, 20) and there is nothing good about that day. It is not a day in which to rejoice;

therefore, the day of the Lord is not the day of Jesus Christ, but it is a day of battle (Rev.16:14, Zechariah 14:1-2, Ezekiel 13:5, Jeremiah 46:10).

Darkness shall invade the whole earth for one whole day and then in the evening there shall be light. A new day is born. A new Sabbath of the millennium of Christ is born. Zechariah clarifies this in his prophecies.

> It shall come to pass in that day that there will be no light; the lights will diminish. It shall be one day which is known to the Lord—Neither day nor night. But at evening time it shall happen that it will be light (Zechariah 14:6-7).

> For behold, the stone that I have laid before Joshua: Upon the stone are seven eyes. Behold, I will engrave its inscription', Says the Lord of hosts, 'and I will remove the iniquity of that land in one day (Zechariah 3:9).

The Apocalypse also emphasises the brevity of the day of the Lord as being only one hour. The ten kings rule with the Antichrist in battle against the prince for one hour (Rev.17:12) and Babylon the Great falls in one hour (Rev.18:10).

The five events of the day of the Lord include the greatest earthquake of history, the Battle of Armageddon, the Second Coming, the final fall of Babylon, and the Great Supper of our God. All these events occur in one day. The day of the Lord has always been noted as 'that day' not *those days*.

B. The Battle of Armageddon

Read Rev. 16: 12-20

Three frogs that proceed from the mouth of the dragon, False Prophet, and the Beast initiate the battle of Armageddon. These evil spirits deceive the kings of the earth to battle against the Messiah. This is the sixth and seventh bowl of the wrath of God.

BATTLE INSIDE THE CITY

Even though demonic powers deceive and initiate this great battle, these demonic spirits act according to the will of God for it is the Lord who gathers the nations against Jerusalem.

> For I will gather all the nations to battle against Jerusalem. The city shall be taken, The houses rifled, And the women ravished. Half of the city shall go into captivity, but the remnant of the people shall not be cut off from the city (Zechariah 14:2).

Jerusalem means inheritance *of peace*, a name that seemingly contradicts history and the events of Zechariah's prophecy. Only the fulfillment of prophecy justly propositions the true meaning. Christ's ultimate design for Jerusalem will vindicate safety, and in the day of the Lord Jerusalem shall be called, "The Lord our Righteousness" (Jeremiah 33:16).

Zechariah chapter12 shares the victories of the city in that day so eloquently. Read it. The armies that besiege her will be led to confusion. The leaders of Israel will be as firebrands and devour the enemy on every side and the Lord defends the city. It is there in the city at the beginning of the great battle that the house of David shall see the Messiah, the one whom they pierced.

The city is attacked but a remnant is saved. The city and people of God shall be spared from total ruin only because Jesus returns upon the Mount of Olives to fight against the nations.

GREAT MOURNING

This leads to great mourning. The Apocalypse speaks of a weeping that happens when the entire world shall see Him return.

> *Behold, He is coming with clouds and every eye will see Him, even they who pierced Him. And all the tribes of the earth will mourn because of Him even so, Amen (Rev. 1:7).*

The mourning of Israel in that day is compared to the mourning for Hadad-rimmon. "On that day the mourning in Jerusalem will be as great as the mourning for Hadad-rimmon in the plain of Megiddo" (Zechariah 12:11)

Hadad-rimmon was a vegetation god of the Canaanites and Syrians.[2] Hadad, according to west Semitic meant "storm god" and rimmon meant "storm god" according to ancient Akkad. Baal is the "thunder god". According to Ras Shamra texts, Hadad is the proper name for Baal. According to the Syrian Ugaritic tablets, youthful Baal was named Hadad, meaning *rider of the clouds*.[3] One of the Baals was called Baal-Hadad. In honor of their gods, the mourning cries were extremely loud. When the vegetation died each year the worshipers thought that the god had died, so they mourned his death.[4] When Messiah returns again, the thunderings and cries of honor for Christ shall exceed the mournful cries for the death of Baal, for the qol of Jehovah is louder than the qol of Baal.

SYRIA

Naaman, the Syrian captain, called upon the prophet Elisha of Israel to heal him of his leprosy. Naaman was very grateful to the God of Israel and said that he would worship Him. In order to do so Naaman asked Elisha to send down two mules loaded with earth so that he could offer unto the Lord. They believed that a god could only be worshipped on his own land. Naaman also hoped that God would be merciful when he had to accompany king Ben-Hadad into the house of Rimmon. So we know that during the days of Naaman, there was a temple in Syria to the god Rimmon (2 Kings 5:15-18).

Hadad, as a name, has a strong reference to the Arab peoples of Syria and Edom. The eighth son of Ishmael was called Hadad (1 Chronicles 1:29). Hadad the Edomite was a satanic adversary of Solomon and he was a mischievous and bitter enemy of Israel who reigned in the land of Edom.

What does it means when it says that the Antichrist is called the eighth of the seven? (Rev. 17:11). Will the Antichrist's kingdom be the seventh kingdom? Five are fallen, one is, and one is yet to come. That makes seven. Or does it give reference to Hadad, being a servant of Baal, just as the Antichrist is a servant of the Devil.

Then there is the famous king of Syria during the reign of the prophets Elijah and Elisha called Ben-Hadad. He besieged Samaria and several cities of Israel. After taking Ahab's children, wives, silver and gold, he wanted the right to take from the people whatever he wanted. Israel had had enough of this mischief. Ben-Hadad prepared again to attack Israel with the aid of thirty-two kings. While they were in a drinking stupor, Israel defeated the Syrian armies and their allies even though they were more numerous.

In a year's time Syria attacked again. This time the king boasted that the God of Israel was only the God of the hills and not the plains. But on the seventh day, God proved Himself to be the God of the valleys. Is it possible that the victory on the seventh day is prophetic in the light of the Battle of Armageddon? Armageddon shall conclude the six thousandth year of history and usher in the seventh thousandth year, the millennial reign of Christ.

Ben-Hadad then sought the mercy of Israel. Girded as poor hopeless creatures, some Syrians sought to make a covenant with Ahab. They promised to return the cities that were taken from Israel. Israel disobeyed that day and made a league with the nation of Syria. How many foolish leagues has Israel made with Syria and how many more shall she make? The prophet illustrated with a parable how disobedient Ahab was (1 Kings 20:35-43). His final words of the parable were:

> Then he said to him, Thus says the Lord: Because you have let slip out of your hand
> a man whom I appointed to utter destruction, therefore your life shall go for his life, and
> your people for his people (1 Kings 20:42).

Breaking the treaty, as Syrian kings always did, Ben-Hadad returned again. This time Elisha saved Israel because God had revealed to him the strategy of the enemy. God also opened their eyes so that the men of Israel saw the armies of God that had come to their aid. The eyes of the enemy, however, were blinded and they were defeated. Similarly, the armies of God, which are the saints, aid Christ in the battle of Armageddon.

Later in history Joash defeated Ben-Hadad the grandson of Ben-Hadad three times. Syria is destined for defeat according to the scriptures. Both Jeremiah and Amos were definite in their prophecy concerning the kings of Syria.

> I will kindle a fire in the wall of Damascus, and it shall consume the palaces of Ben-Hadad (Jeremiah 49:27).

> But I will send a fire into the house of Hazael which shall devour the palaces of Ben-hadad (Amos 1:4).

Is Syria conscious of her destiny? Is this a reason why Syria is continually an enemy of the Jewish people? In the day of the Lord, Syria shall fall. If the Antichrist arises from Syria as did Antiochus, then these stories of the kings of Syria are meaningful to the final judgment of God upon the nations of the world. If the king's name 'Hadad' is significant then these battles have a greater significance. Not only is the enemy of Christ's people destroyed but the gods of the enemy, The Baal 'storm god' of Syria and every other god of this world is destroyed at the appearing of Jesus Christ.

BATTLE OUTSIDE THE CITY

Jesus himself treads the winepress outside the city because the Jewish people are excluded from His wrath and just as the city of God is holy, so that which is outside the city represented sin and uncleanness. All dung was cast outside the city of Jerusalem. The judgment of stoning was outside the city. The atonement bird for leprosy was set free outside the city (Leviticus 14:53). A house infected from leprosy was carried outside the city (Leviticus 14:45).

The nations of the world are gathered together in Megiddo and the battle of Armageddon may begin there, but the nations advance to Jerusalem and Armageddon is fought in the valley east of Jerusalem. The valley lies east of the temple mount and west of the Mount of Olives. This valley is known as the Valley of the Son of Hinnom (2 Chronicles 28:3, Jeremiah 19:2, 32-35), the Kidron Valley (Jeremiah 31:4), Armageddon (Rev.16:16), the Valley of Jehoshaphat (Joel 3:2, 14), the Valley of Decision, and the Valley of Slaughter (Jeremiah 7:32).

Eusebius called the Valley of Jehoshaphat,[4] the Valley of Hinnom. Jerome called it the Kidron Valley.[5] Lightfoot, from his Judaic studies and Talmudic studies recognized it as the Valley of Hinnom and part of the Kidron. By various aspects the valley has been known as the final place of judgment. This is a shared belief of Jews, Moslems, and Christians.[6] As a result of the great earthquake, all the land from Geba that is in the land of Megiddo to Rimmon south of Jerusalem shall be turned into a plain. The battlefield outside the city may possibly extend into the north and include the valley of Megiddo.

> *Thus says the Lord: Go and get a potter's earthen flask, and [take] some of the elders of the people and some of the elders of the priests. And go out to the Valley of the Son of Hinnom which [is] by the entry of the Potsherd Gate: and proclaim there the words that I will tell you, and say, Hear the word of the Lord, O kings of Judah and inhabitants of Jerusalem. Thus says the Lord of hosts, the God of Israel: Behold, I will bring such a catastrophe on this place, that whoever hears of it, his ears will tingle. Because they have forsaken Me and made this an alien place, because they have burned incense in it to other gods whom neither they, their fathers, nor the kings of Judah have known, and have filled this place with the blood of the innocents (they have also built the high places of Baal, to burn their sons with fire [for] burnt offerings to Baal, which I did not command or speak, nor did it come into My mind), therefore behold, the days are coming, says the Lord, that this place shall no more be called Tophet or the Valley of the Son of Hinnom, but the Valley of Slaughter. And I will make void the counsel of Judah and Jerusalem in this place, and I will cause them to fall by the sword before their enemies and by the hands of those who seek their lives; their corpses I will give as meat for the birds of the heaven and for the beasts of the earth (Jeremiah 19:1-7).*

> *Let the nations be wakened, and come up to the Valley of Jehoshaphat; For there I will sit to judge all the surrounding nations (Joel 3:12).*

> *Therefore wait for Me, says the Lord, Until the day I rise up for plunder; My determination [is] to gather the nations To My assembly of kingdoms, To pour on them*

My indignation, All my fierce anger; All the earth shall be devoured With the fire of My jealousy (Zephaniah 3:8).

I will also gather all nations, And bring them down to the Valley of Jehoshaphat; And I will enter into judgment with them there On account of My people, My heritage Israel, Whom they have scattered among the nations; They have also divided up My land (Joel 3:2).

Multitudes, multitudes in the valley of decision! For the day of the Lord is near (Joel 3:14.

There is only one battle of Armageddon and it is fought outside the city of Jerusalem. There is too much biblical evidence and importance upon this valley in Old Testament writings to think otherwise. The valley outside the city is very significant in Jewish history. The Garden of Gethsemane sat on the western floor of this valley (John 18:1). Jesus wept here great drops of blood as He prayed. Perhaps His thoughts and anguish that day reflected not only His own death but also the death of millions during the final Battle of Armageddon. The Potter's Field was also in the valley. Judas the Iscariot died and was buried here in his own place, a place of idolatry, witchcraft, blood, and filth.

The Kidron is noted as a place to throw temple debris (2 Chronicles 29:16). Altars of incense were crushed and cast into the Kidron. Articles of Baal were burned there (2 Kings 23:4). The idols of Asherah and others were burned in the Kidron (2 Kings 23:4).

During Old Testament days, the valley of Hinnom was a place of idolatry. Idols to the god Baal were erected there. In the valley was the sacred grove of the Canaanites called Topheth meaning very appropriately "fireplace" or "oven". Later the Topheth cult became the center of Baal worship for apostate Jews. Their first born infants were offered as live sacrifices to the god Molech.[9] Incense was burned to the gods of wood and stone.

The Valley of Kidron was also known as the *'common sink'* of the whole city of Jerusalem. The valley was a great burial place. The city sewers dumped their stinking debris into the valley. The valley is famous for its uncleanness. In the valley were two palm trees called the door of Gehenna, for it was believed that the fire burned continually to consume the dross.[7] To the Jew, the valley metaphorically represented Gehenna or hell. The mention of this valley in the New Testament is only mystical and metaphorical, and denotes the place of the damned. Hence, scripture speaks of a lake of fire and brimstone. What better place for the Battle of Armageddon? What better place could be chosen for the death of the Gentile nations? It is in this valley that the nations of the world shall view the carcasses of evil men when they come to Jerusalem to worship during the millennium (Isaiah 66:23, 24).

What an appropriate place for the final judgment of Christ's wrath to occur - in the valley of the "oven" or "fireplace." Just as the apostate sinners during the seal period left the saints beneath their altars, so God will bring every apostate force into the valley where their demonic idols once stood and demolish them forever.

C. Army Tactics

Out of the complete darkness of that day shines the brightness of His coming. The King of kings arrives ready for war and riding upon a white horse. His armies follow him from heaven also riding upon white horses.

God shall employ plagues to destroy the enemy in that day.

> *And this shall be the plague with which the Lord will strike all the people who fought against Jerusalem. Their flesh shall dissolve while they stand on their feet, their eyes shall dissolve in their sockets, and their tongues shall dissolve in their mouths (Zechariah 14:12).*

Confusion by the miraculous hand of God blinds men's eyes just as the army of Ben-Hadad was blinded. Confusion brings panic and distress. Men's flesh becomes refuse in the valley of Hinnom. Confusion causes one man to slay another while the armies of God are invisible.

> *It shall come to pass in that day that a great panic from the Lord will be among them. Everyone will seize the hand of his neighbor, and raise his hand against his neighbor's hand (Zechariah 14:13).*

> *I will bring distress upon men, and they shall walk like blind men because they have sinned against the Lord; their blood shall be poured out like dust, And their flesh like refuse (Zephaniah 1:17).*

Men are slain by the sword that shall proceed from the mouth of the Messiah. "And the rest were killed with the sword which proceeded from the mouth of Him who sat on the horse. And all the birds were filled with their flesh" (Rev. 19:21). The sword slays nations who become a sacrifice of Jehovah in that day. The sword slays wickedness as the hand of the Lord seeks justice for 'unrighteousness' and He judges and makes war (Rev.19:11). The sword is raised in all the earth. The sword is vital in the day of the Lord just as the Word of God is vital in executing the truth.

> *A noise will come to the ends of the earth—For the Lord has a controversy with the nations; He will plead His case with all flesh. He will give those who are wicked to the sword,' says the Lord (Jeremiah 25:31).*

> *For this is the day of the Lord God of hosts, A day of vengeance, That He may avenge Himself on His adversaries. The sword shall devour; it shall be satiated and made drunk with their blood; For the Lord God of hosts has a sacrifice in the north country by the River Euphrates (Jeremiah 46:10).*

> *A noise will come to the ends of the earth—For the Lord has a controversy with the nations; He will plead His case with all flesh. He will give those who are wicked to the sword,' says the Lord." Thus says the Lord of hosts: "Behold, disaster shall go forth from nation to nation, and a great whirlwind shall be raised up from the farthest parts of the earth. "And at that day the slain of the Lord shall be from one end of the earth even to*

the other end of the earth. They shall not be lamented, or gathered, or buried; they shall become refuse on the ground (Jeremiah 25:31-33).

D. The Army of God

Read Rev. 19:11-21

The Army of God makes warfare in that day. This army comes from heaven. They are dressed in fine linen that is the clothing of the saints. Notice that their dress is not described in terms of warfare. There are three verses that clearly explain that Christ shall return with His saints or holy ones.

> *Then you shall flee through my mountain valley, for the mountain valley shall reach to Azal. Yes, you shall flee as you fled from the earthquake in the days of Uzziah king of Judah. Thus the Lord my God will come, and all the saints with You (Zechariah 14:5).*

> *... So that He may establish your hearts blameless in holiness before our God and Father at the coming of our Lord Jesus Christ with all His saints (1 Thessalonians 3:13).*

> *Now Enoch, the seventh from Adam, prophesied about these men also, saying, "Behold, the Lord comes with ten thousands of His saints, "to execute judgment on all, to convict all who are ungodly among them of all their ungodly deeds which they have committed in an ungodly way, and of all the harsh things which ungodly sinners have spoken against Him (Jude 14, 15).*

The army of God is so amazing. They are invincible while the wicked fall by their own swords. The army rides upon horses that fly. They run and climb with supernatural strength. They march and fight without any confusion. No sword can slay them for they are armored with immortality. Just as the day of the Lord is described as a thief in the night, so the saints appear as thieves in the night. The strength of the army is as strong as their leader.

> *Their appearance is like the appearance of horses; And like swift steeds, so they run. They leap with a noise like chariots over mountaintops. They devour the stubble like the noise of a flaming fire and like a strong people they are arrayed in battle. Before them the people writhe in pain. All faces are drained of color. They run like mighty men. They climb the wall like men of war. Everyone marches in formation and they do not break ranks. They do not push one another, but everyone marches in his own column. Though they lunge between the weapons, they are not cut down. They run to and fro in the city; they run on the wall; and they climb into the houses. They enter at the windows like a thief. The earth quakes before them. The heavens tremble, the sun and moon grow dark, and the stars diminish their brightness. "The Lord gives voice before His army, For His*

camp is very great; for strong is the One who executes His word. For the day of the Lord is great and very terrible; Who can endure it?"(Joel 2:4-11).

E. The Fall of Mystery Babylon

Read Rev 14:8, 16:19, and chapters 17 & 18

The world mourns the destruction of Babylon but Heaven rejoices. To describe Babylon before her fall, John pictures her as an invincible queen and harlot that rides upon a beast. She rules over the kings of the earth. Her global power controls the wealth of the world.

Three images sketch the fall of Babylon: a demonic prison house, a city on fire, and a millstone.

1. Demonic Prison House

Babylon first becomes "the habitation of devils and the hold of every foul spirit and a cage of every unclean and hateful bird" (Rev. 18:2). The first fall of Babylon comes when billions of demons are let loose in the earth to torment man. Men within her grasp of belief are imprisoned by the power of demons in their lives. A prison house and a cage imply bondage, no release, and a capture beyond man's will. The demonic locust and demonic horsemen have such control and bondage over man. Just as the Antichrist unmasks his true evil nature, Satan will also destroy and torment men's minds and souls by this demonic energy force that men once sought after and worshipped as divine. Demonic possession leaves Babylon mad. Babylon shall become mad as hell itself. The second of the three angels sent by God to give the final warning, shouts to the people. "Babylon the great is fallen." This happens in part before the day of the Lord and the Battle of Armageddon because the Antichrist hates the whore and destroys her.

2. A City on Fire

Secondly, Babylon is pictured as a glorious city on seven hills, but now she is burning, ablaze with fire. Babylon's ecclesiastical, political, and economical power is lost. The Antichrist and the ten kings shall hate the whore. They deny all apostate worship and they burn Babylon and make her desolate (Rev.17:16).

Isaiah compares the destruction of end-time Babylon by the Antichrist to the destruction of the first Babylon by the Medes (Isaiah 13:17). Modern Babylon is destroyed by the armies of the Antichrist called 'the Medes" in Isaiah. The Antichrist acclaims complete control of the globe and total worship by all men. When men see the demonic madness of Babylon, they are glad to worship the Beast. In all this, Christ's will is performed (Rev.17:17).

Then, in the day of the Lord, Babylon faces the judgment of God for the last time. As the seventh trumpet is sounded, the greatest earthquake ever destroys many cities. God does not forget

Babylon. His rod of judgment strikes the city of apostasy in that day. She too experiences the cup of Christ's wrath (Rev. 17:19).

3. A Millstone

When I searched the Internet for some clue as to what the millstone might mean for our study, everything pointed to a new I-tune called "Millstone". It gave me the impression that life was a burden and full of confusion. The author no longer prays. He's a different man now who lives on a ship with fools. He is sinking with a milestone around his neck.[8] Well, life without Christ is just like that.

The third image of Babylon's destruction is that of the millstone.

> *Then a mighty angel took up a stone like a great millstone and threw it into the sea, saying, Thus with violence the great city Babylon shall be thrown down, and shall not be found anymore (Rev. 18:21).*

Why is she pictured as a millstone? There are hand millstones that range from fifteen to twenty-four inches in width and there is the ass-millstone that is about five feet in diameter and must be turned by animal power. The ass-millstone would sink to the deepest sea very quickly and never rise again. So shall be the fall of Babylon. She falls in one hour as the Apocalypse has emphasized. Nothing will be able to prevent the fall of the city, so the city falls into oblivion and never exists again. The weight of a millstone suggests the surety of her fall. The sins of Babylon reach into the heavens (Rev. 18:5), but the weight of her sin sinks her deep to sudden spoil.

It took a mighty angel to lift the millstone which suggests firstly that it was probably an ass-millstone and second, that there is a power in the heavenlies greater than the sins, sorcery, and power of Babylon. No matter how smug and secure the great whore feels; Christ's power shall break her vanity, her wealth, her sorceries, her crafts, her sins, and her existence.

There is a second snap shot of the millstone in the next verse.

> *"The sound of harpists, musicians, flutists, and trumpeters shall not be heard in you anymore. No craftsman of any craft shall be found in you anymore, and the sound of a millstone shall not be heard in you anymore." (Revelation 18:22)*

The death of Babylon is emphasized by the burial of the millstone. The millstone is silent for no beast or man is there to turn it.

In the dream of Nebuchadnezzar, Christ is portrayed as the stone that falls upon the ten toes of the final kingdom of men (Daniel 2:35). This stone falls at the Second Coming and crushes the kingdoms of evil. This has a similar action as the millstone. The crushing of Babylon in that day symbolically represents the crushing of all evil. The cup that Mystery Babylon has served to the world and to the saints is the same cup of judgment served back to her. This is a cup of suffering, a cup of wrath, a cup of torment, a cup of vengeance; that God returns in double portion.

With the fall of Babylon great mourning is heard worldwide. Notice the emphasis on that mourning (Rev. 18:8-20).

Now that Babylon the whore is stripped of her wealth, silk finery, precious jewels, and worldly pleasures, she stands naked before Christ's judgment. All that is left is the 'smoke of her burning', 'dust on their heads', uncontrolled weeping, ashes of the city, darkness, silence, and lifelessness. (Rev. 18:23).

What men considered dainty and good is taken away. What men had desired and lusted after vanishes before the throne of God. In the day of the Lord the beauty of Babylon disintegrates as the cities of Sodom and Gomorrah (Isaiah 13:19-22).

What a contrast to the mourning in the city of Jerusalem! While Babylon displays eternal ruin as her "smoke rises up forever and ever" (Rev. 19:3), the city of Jerusalem rebuilds with eternal triumph in the coming of her King. The Jewish nation will mourn in repentance when they see the nail prints in His hands, but the daughters of Babylon mourns selfishly for her great loss of material wealth. The soul of Babylon has no tears of repentance and her cup of plenty is tainted with a mixture of Christ's wrath and indignation. But the cup of persecution bubbles into a cup of blessing for the saints. God knows the heart of both cities. God defends Jerusalem in the day of the Lord, while God demolishes Babylon.

In contrast to the great mourning on earth is the command in heaven to Rejoice! The righteous are told to rejoice over the destruction of evil, not mourn, for justice finally gives her sentence upon all apostasy.

The righteous shall rejoice when he sees the vengeance: He shall wash his feet in the blood of the wicked, So that men will say, Surely [there is] a reward for the righteous: Surely He is God who judges in the earth (Psalm 59:10-11)

BABYLON TODAY?

Read Rev. 17

If Iraqi Babylon is the great whore, then the city will have to be restored for she stands in ruin and much of Babylon's character restored.

*"**Babylon** (Arabic: بابل, Babil; Akkadian: Bābili(m);[1] Sumerian logogram: KÁ.DINGIR.RA^{KI};[1] Hebrew: בבל, Bābel;[1] Greek: Βαβυλών, Babylōn) was an Akkadian city-state (founded in 1867 BC by an Amorite dynasty) of ancient Mesopotamia, the remains of which are found in present-day Al Hillah, Babil Province, Iraq, about 85 kilometers (55 mi) south of Baghdad. Babylon, along with Assyria to the north, was one of the two Akkadian nations that evolved after the collapse of the Akkadian Empire. All that remains of the original ancient famed city of Babylon today is a mound, or tell, of broken mud-brick buildings and debris in the fertile Mesopotamian plain between the Tigris and Euphrates rivers. The city itself was built upon the Euphrates, and divided in equal parts along its left and right banks, with steep embankments to contain the river's seasonal floods."[9]*

In the early church, Rome was called Babylon. It would not take much today to visualize Rome as the modern whore that sits upon seven hills. Let us summarize what the Bible says about mystery Babylon

1. She has murdered the prophets.

2. Babylon makes the nations drink of the wine of her fornication. (Rev. 14:8)

3. God gives Babylon the cup of His wrath. (Rev. 16:19)

4. She is called Mother of Harlots and Mother of the earth's abominations.

5. She becomes a dwelling place of demons and a prison for every foul spirit. (Rev. 18:2)

6. In one hour her judgement comes. (Rev. 18:10).

7. Babylon is thrown down by a great millstone. (Rev. 18:21)

8. She also sits on many waters which are peoples, multitudes, nations and tongues (Rev. 17:1, 17:15).

9. She is called Mystery, Babylon the Great, The Mother of Harlots and of the abominations of the earth (Rev. 17:5).

10. The Beast will hate her and destroy her by making her desolate, naked, by eating her flesh and burning her with fire (Rev. 17:16).

11. God will judge her who corrupted the earth and killed His servants (Rev. 19:2).

12. She is rich (Rev. 17:4, 18:12-14).

13. She is called a city many times that sits on a hill.

14. Babylon glorifies herself (Rev. 18:7). "I sit as queen," she says (Rev. 18:7).

How does the Roman Catholic Church fill these fourteen shoes? She has murdered many prophets of the Lord. Her many idols have led millions to worship Mary and other saints which can be considered as fornication. She is everywhere as one who sits upon the nations.

Has the Vatican become a dwelling place of demons? In one sense, she has. Father Gabriele Amorth, age eighty-five, who has been the Vatican's chief exorcist for twenty-five years, says he has dealt with 70,000 cases of demonic possession.[10] He also says that sex abuse scandals is proof that the Devil is at work inside the Vatican. "Cases of alleged demonic possession have soared in the past 20 years. Various officials within the Catholic Church blame growing interests in Satanism and demonology."[11] We also read on the Internet that a Vatican- recognized university is offering a course in exorcism and demonic possession for a second year."[12] I do know that demonic possession will increase in the last days.

Rome is one of the greatest cities in the world in every way. The Vatican has a coin with a picture of a woman sitting as queen. "The popes declare that they are antichrists when they use the title *Vicarius Filii Dei*. They believe they are Christ's and God's substitute ... the very meaning of the word antichrist."[13]

I never cease to be amazed at the religious and political glue between Islam and the Catholic Church. The Catholic Ustashe, as well as the Islamic Hanjar fought to exterminate the Serbs, Jews, and Romany in their region. Between 600,000 and one million people were murdered in the most brutal massacres of the Nazi period.[14] The largest mosque in Europe is on the Esquiline Hill in Rome beside a Catholic Cathedral.[15] Pope John Paul II gave permission for it to be built and the pope kissed the Koran — a book that denies the deity of Jesus Christ.[16]

The following is supposition, yet interesting. What if Rome became the capital city of the European Union? With the largest mosque and a Catholic cathedral on Esquiline Hill, a religious unity could be devastating and evil. Catholic/Islamic Rome could be a great Babylon.

On the other hand, what if the eastern countries of the old Roman Empire become stronger than the western nations of the Roman Empire, as the early church Father's believed would happen? If a leader rises to rule Egypt, Ethiopia, and Libya, he will make the eastern part of the old Roman Empire strong. This man, I believe, will be the Antichrist and make a treaty with Israel.

There is a third option for what Babylon represents. Maybe Babylon represents the apostate, mystical New Age belief that is becoming stronger and stronger. This Babylon can become possessed by demons easily and fulfill the image of Babylon as a demonic prison house. This Babylon is truly associated with idolatry, witchcraft, and sorcery which God hates and the Revelation speaks much of these sins of which the world refuses to repent (Rev. 18:23). But the New Age is not a city, but the philosophy of the New Age can rule the Vatican.

Maybe the religious powers of Rome, Islam and the New Age blend together somehow. I don't know. We need to keep an open mind and ask God to help us understand when these things are being fulfilled.

F. Israel in that Day

Except to say that Israel mourned when they saw their king, John does not explain how the Jewish nation fits into the day of the Lord. The Old Testament, however, enlightens us concerning this significant role. The apocalyptic day of the Lord is a time of judgment for the Gentile nations of the world not Israel. Israel faced her day of judgment when Babylon left her in ruins.

Israel in the later day shall be sifted from the nations. God is a master sifter. He knows where each grain of wheat falls. It is the world that is mad and confused in that day, not God. Every act of the day of the Lord is performed by the divine counsel of God and conforms perfectly to His divine plan and purpose. The Jewish nation is spared. God becomes their shelter and support. Jesus returns to establish the kingdom of David, not destroy it.

> *For surely I will command, and will sift the house of Israel among all nations, As grain is sifted in a sieve; yet not the smallest grain shall fall to the ground (Amos 9:9).*

> *The Lord also will roar from Zion, And utter His voice from Jerusalem; The heavens and earth will shake; but the Lord will be a shelter for His people, And the strength of the children of Israel (Joel 3:16).*

With the mourning that rises from the city of Jerusalem, a spirit of grace and supplication shall descend from God.

And I will pour on the house of David and on the inhabitants of Jerusalem the Spirit of grace and supplication; then they will look on Me whom they pierced. Yes, they will mourn for Him as one mourns for his only son, and grieve for Him as one grieves for a firstborn (Zechariah 12:10).

A promised relationship is birthed that day between the Messiah and Israel.

I will bring the one-third through the fire, Will refine them as silver is refined. And test them as gold is tested. They will call on My name. And I will answer them. I will say, This is My people; And each one will say, The Lord is my God (Zechariah 13:9).

Israel shall possess the lands around her. No wonder Israel is a stumbling block to the nations.

Therefore, as I live, Says the Lord of hosts, the God of Israel, "Surely Moab shall be like Sodom, And the people of Ammon like Gomorrah—Overrun with weeds and saltpits, And a perpetual desolation. The residue of My people shall plunder them, and the remnant of My people shall possess them (Zephaniah 2:9).

The King of kings shall display the children of Israel as jewels in His crown. The throne of David is established forever in Zion.

The Lord their God will save them in that day, As the flock of His people. For they shall be like the jewels of a crown, lifted like a banner over His land (Zechariah 9:16).

G. The Great Supper of Our God

Read Rev. 19:6-21

Then he said to me, "Write: 'Blessed are those who are called to the marriage supper of the Lamb!'" And he said to me, "These are the true sayings of God." Then I saw an angel standing in the sun; and he cried with a loud voice, saying to all the birds that fly in the midst of heaven, "Come and gather together for the supper of the great God". ... Then I saw an angel standing in the sun; and he cried with a loud voice, saying to all the birds that fly in the midst of heaven, "Come and gather together for the supper of the great God, that ye may eat the flesh of kings (Rev. 19:9, 17)

This great supper of God revolves around three important facts: guests are invited, there is food and drink for the guests, and there is a sacrifice. I don't believe that God literally spreads a table in heaven for those who have been resurrected and raptured. This supper is a celebration of the King of kings and Lord of lords not the bride's arrival in heaven. The supper is in honor of Christ's righteous judgments, not the righteousness of the saints.

This supper of God is celebrated upon earth not in heaven. The only reference to this great supper is in the nineteenth chapter of the Apocalypse. Both references are in context with the

Battle of Armageddon and the return of the Messiah. There is no evidence that they should be separate events.

It is called the marriage supper of the Lamb and the supper of the great God. There is only one bride for the Lamb. She is the church of Jesus Christ that has been by this time resurrected. They have been called and they are ready. The wife is described as ready dressed in fine linen and the armies of Christ are also clothed in fine linen. Both refer to the church. The bride accompanies the Lamb to the Battle of Armageddon.

The Battle of Armageddon is compared to a great feast. It is the flesh of the mighty, and the kings of the earth as well as the slave man that are eaten at this great feast. They are the sacrifice. The great Winemaker presses the grapes in the winepress, and they are ready to be served. The blood of the grapes is the blood of wicked men. The birds of the air and the beast of the field feast upon this great feast and become drunk with the blood of sinful man.

The ten nations that join the Antichrist for one hour become the sacrifice. Some of these nations gather from the Euphrates to invade Israel become the victims of Christ's sacrifice. Some of these ten nations are the armies of the east and they become a sacrifice this day. The Apocalypse does not call the slaughter of wicked man a sacrifice but two Old Testament prophets clearly prophesy of a sacrifice made by God on the day of the Lord.

> For this is the day of the Lord God of hosts, A day of vengeance, That He may avenge Himself on His adversaries. The sword shall devour; it shall be satiated and made drunk with their blood; For the Lord God of hosts has a sacrifice in the north country by the River Euphrates (Jeremiah 46:10).

> Be silent in the presence of the Lord God; For the day of the Lord is at hand, For the Lord has prepared a sacrifice; He has invited His guests. And it shall be, in the day of the Lord's sacrifice, That I will punish the princes and the king's children, And all such as are clothed with foreign apparel. In the same day I will punish All those who leap over the threshold, Who fill their masters' houses with violence and deceit (Zephaniah 1:7, 8).

The guests that day are the fowls of the air and the beasts of the field. The guests are partakers of the flesh and blood of this sacrifice. You shall eat fat till you are full, and drink blood till you are drunk, at My sacrificial meal which I am sacrificing for you" (Ezekiel 39:19).

Those who become the sacrifice in that day are not blessed but those who are called to the marriage supper are blessed. But who are blessed and who are called -- the fowls and beast who are guests, or the saints who are dressed in fine linen ready for warfare? Consider this verse.

> Let us be glad and rejoice and give Him glory, for the marriage of the Lamb has come, and His wife has made herself ready. And to her it was granted to be arrayed in fine linen, clean and bright, for the fine linen is the righteous acts of the saints. Then he said to me, Write: 'Blessed are those who are called to the marriage supper of the Lamb!'" And he said to me, "These are the true sayings of God" (Rev. 19:9)

If you can call beasts and fowls blessed, they are surely blessed that day. They are also called by the angel to attend the feast.

However, the saints are blessed because they are able to participate in this great battle. They wore the garment of righteousness that permits the saints to participate in this great war. They are called because they have been found worthy. Their armors are of linen like the garment of the Lamb. They wear the righteousness of the Lamb and are ready for battle. The righteous ones aid in the death of the unrighteous. Victory is won in the name of righteousness. In this sense does the church participate in this great supper?

Further Study

1. What are the victories of Jerusalem according to Zechariah 12?

2. Would you like to fight in the Battle of Armageddon on the Lord's side? Why?

3. Describe the fall of Babylon from Isaiah 13:19-22.

PART F:

ALL THINGS NEW:
THE REWARDS OF JUSTICE

16. The Covenants of God are Fulfilled to Israel

The Millennium

Read Rev. 20: 1-10

Awake from the dust of the earth and from the fire of Christ's judgment. The vials of Christ's wrath are completed. Christ, upon the white horse, has conquered the earth from the clutches of the Antichrist and Satan in the Battle of Armageddon. Armies that surround Jerusalem are smoldering from the judgment of Christ. Israel, for centuries, has declared a coming King of kings and Lord of lords. For centuries the church has praised Christ as King of kings and Lord of lords. John declared Christ to be King of kings and Lord of lords. (Rev.17:14, 19:16) Now during the millennium, Christ is King of kings and Lord of lords. Praise His name! He shall reign forever and ever! Amen.

Babylon, the city of sin and evil is left in ruins forever. The enemies of Christ's land and Christ's people have been destroyed. The commerce of all that is evil has terminated. Sin has been defeated. Witchcraft, idolatry and sorcery are buried with the ashes of the city. (Rev.18:21-24).

The harlot woman, who represents the apostate church and all false religions, has been silenced forever. The truth of righteousness reigns without the interference of any deception.

The Antichrist, the False Prophet, and the Devil have been bound for a thousand years. For one thousand years, the Devil shall not tempt one person on the earth to do evil, nor will he be able to deceive anyone. Christ's reign upon earth has begun. We have now entered a new millennium.

A. God's Promise

This millennium shall take place after the vials of Christ's wrath and after the battle of Armageddon. Christ shall reign upon this earth for a thousand years.

And I saw an angel come down from heaven, having the key of the bottomless pit and a great chain in his hand. And he laid hold on the dragon, that old serpent, which is the

Devil, and Satan, and bound him a thousand years, And cast him into the bottomless pit, and shut him up, and set a seal upon him, that he should deceive the nations no more, till the thousand years should be fulfilled: and after that he must be loosed a little season. And I saw thrones, and they sat upon them, and judgment was given unto them: and I saw the souls of them that were beheaded for the witness of Jesus, and for the word of God, and which had not worshipped the beast, neither his image, neither had received his mark upon their foreheads, or in their hands; and they lived and reigned with Christ a thousand years. But the rest of the dead lived not again until the thousand years were finished. This is the first resurrection (Rev 20:1-5).

John says very little about the millennium, but more is understood from the writings of other prophets, such as Isaiah, Jeremiah, and Zechariah. With divine purpose, the book of Revelation does not tell us much about the millennium for the millennium is about fulfilling Christ's promises and covenants to the Jewish nation, Israel --the land of Israel, and the temple. These are prophesied in the Old Testament for the millennium is many promises fulfilled to Israel.

God promised in the Old Testament to bring them in from the east and from the west and deliver them. The first half of the promise has been fulfilled in part, although many Jews are still spread abroad the earth. In the millennium, God will save Israel, bring justice to the poor, destroy the efforts of the oppressor, deliver the needy, and rule the dominion of the earth (Psalm 72:4).

God will also keep his promise to Abraham and David. God promised both Abraham the patriarch and David the King of Israel everlasting possession of the land of Israel (Genesis 17:7, II Samuel 7:12-16). All nations were to be blessed through Israel. The Savior of Calvary has brought blessings to people of every nation, but in the millennium, every nation shall be ruled and blessed by the King of kings especially Israel.

When your days are fulfilled and you rest with your fathers, I will set up your seed after you, who will come from your body, and I will establish his kingdom. He shall build a house for My name, and I will establish the throne of his kingdom forever. I will be his Father, and he shall be My son. If he commits iniquity, I will chasten him with the rod of men and with the blows of the sons of men. But My mercy shall not depart from him, as I took it from Saul, whom I removed from before you. And your house and your kingdom shall be established forever before you. Your throne shall be established forever (2 Samuel 7:12-16)

Christ was a descendant of King David and God promised that Messiah shall establish the kingdom of Israel forever. The promise was unconditional. God promised to punish them for their sin, but never take the kingdom away permanently. For thousands of years Israel has been ruled by strange nations. What a glory it will be when Christ fulfills His promise to reign upon the throne of David!

B. The Land

The whole earth shall be purged and shaken just before the millennium. The Land of Israel in that day shall be restructured. When the feet of Jesus touch the Mount of Olives, living waters shall flow out from Jerusalem to the western sea, the Mediterranean, and to the eastern sea - the Gulf of Aqaba. We know that in that day Jesus shall be Lord and king over all the earth.

All the land from Geba to Rimmon shall be a flat plain (Zechariah 14:10). Both these cities are Levitical cities. Geba, meaning hill, is about six miles north of Jerusalem and Rimmon, which is a high plateau that can seen from Jerusalem, is about 30 miles south of Jerusalem. But Jerusalem, in the millennium, shall be higher so that it can be seen from the north to the south.

The land of Israel as promised to Abraham and David will be given to Israel, never to be snatched from them again. This promise can only be fulfilled in completeness after the Battle of Armageddon at which the time of the Gentiles comes to an end. Each tribe of Israel shall possess land in that day (Ezekiel 48:30-35).

> And I will plant them upon their land, and they shall no more be pulled up out of their land which I have given them, saith the LORD thy God (Amos 9:15).

The Arab nations shall be swallowed up by the fire of Jacob in that day. None shall remain from the house of Esau. Those in the southern portion of Israel shall possess the Mount of Esau. The Gaza strip, all Samaria, and the Golan Heights will be Israel's claim forever. Every disputable piece of land today shall be the Lord's.

> But upon mount Zion shall be deliverance, and there shall be holiness, and the house of Jacob shall possess their possessions. And the house of Jacob shall be a fire, and the house of Joseph a flame, and the house of Esau for stubble, and they shall kindle in them, and devour them, and there shall not be any remaining of the house of Esau; for the LORD hath spoken it. And they of the south shall possess the mount of Esau; and they of the plain the Philistines: and they shall possess the fields of Ephraim, and the fields of Samaria: and Benjamin shall possess Gilead. And the captivity of this host of the children of Israel shall possess that of the Canaanites, even unto Zarephath; and the captivity of Jerusalem, which is in Sepharad, shall possess the cities of the south. And saviours shall come up on mount Zion to judge the mount of Esau; and the kingdom shall be the LORD'S (Obadiah 1:17-21).

C. Jerusalem

Jesus, the King of Zion, as promised, shall dwell in the Holy City of Jerusalem (Zechariah 8:3). With great mercy He returns, and with prosperity, He reigns. The city shall be called the City of Truth and truth shall reign with divine justice to all nations. Jesus who is the Truth shall dwell in the city. Truth shall be spoken by its inhabitants, for God shall have it no other way. Justice shall be administered with truth. Love, peace, justice, and joy shall prevail (Zechariah 8:16-19). Jerusalem shall be the capital city of the whole world. There will be no need for a wall around the city for the Lord himself shall protect her (Zechariah 2:1-5). The remnant of Israel shall be saved. Every inhabitant of Jerusalem that survives the tribulation, the vials of Christ's wrath, and the Battle of Armageddon shall be holy. Above the city, God will establish his cloud and fire of guidance and protection (Isaiah 4:4-6). The kingdom of David shall be established forever (II Samuel 7:12).

David My servant shall be king over them, and they shall all have one shepherd; they shall also walk in My judgments and observe My statutes, and do them. Then they shall dwell in the land that I have given to Jacob My servant, where your fathers dwelt; and they shall dwell there, they, their children, and their children's children, forever; and My servant David shall be their prince forever (Ezekiel 37:24,25).

The Temple

Read Ezekiel Chapters 40-47

Messiah, the Branch, shall build the temple, as promised, and shall rule from the throne of His temple. Others from afar will help to build the temple (Zechariah 6:12-15). People from all nations shall come to Jerusalem to worship the Messiah. The promise of a temple was an eternal covenant promise of peace

In that day shall there be upon the bells of the horses, HOLINESS UNTO THE LORD; and the pots in the LORD'S house shall be like the bowls before the altar. Yea, every pot in Jerusalem and in Judah shall be holiness unto the LORD of hosts: and all they that sacrifice shall come and take of them, and seethe therein: and in that day there shall be no more the Canaanite in the house of the LORD of hosts (Zechariah 14:16-21).

> *Moreover I will make a covenant of peace with them, and it shall be an everlasting covenant with them; I will establish them and multiply them, and I will set My sanctuary in their midst forevermore. My tabernacle also shall be with them; indeed I will be their God, and they shall be My people. The nations also will know that I, the Lord, sanctify Israel, when My sanctuary is in their midst forevermore (Zechariah 8:1-16).*

Ezekiel's temple as described in Ezekiel 40-47, is believed to be the Messianic temple of the millennium and the glory of the millennial temple shall be greater than any previous temple. The sons of Zadok will have charge of the altar and sacrifices. The same sacrifices made in the Old Testament will be offered in the millennium – the grain offering, trespass offering, and sin offering. Passover shall be celebrated. The Sabbath shall be observed. Why would they revert to practices that followed the law only? Christ shows them through the millennial temple the perfection of the law and all his promises. Temple procedures shall be shaped by a new understanding of Christ's mercy and grace. The law has been perfected by the grace of Christ and the salvation of a new covenant. The glory of this last Temple will be greater than all temples preceding it (Haggai 2:9).

The temple is where God shall dwell in their midst forever (Ezekiel 43:7). Even the Prince (Christ) shall be allotted property in the city of Jerusalem (Ezekiel 45:6). From the temple shall flow rivers of waters causing fruitfulness where there was no fruitfulness and healing for the nations.

D. The People

Citizens of Jerusalem shall live to be old men and old women. Children shall be playing in the streets not hiding in fear and dread. Each citizen shall live in peace and happiness. Israel will no longer be a curse to the nations of the world but Israel shall be honored (Zechariah 3:10). Israel shall not be a nation insubordinate to other peoples. The Jew shall be honored, because of the Prince of Peace. Everyone shall live at peace with one another (Isaiah 65:23-25). Even the animals of the earth shall live at peace with one another

> *Israel shall know that God is in her mist. And I will bring them, and they shall dwell in the midst of Jerusalem: and they shall be my people, and I will be their God, in truth and in righteousness (Zechariah 8:9).*

The nations shall know that Israel is Christ's chosen people (Isaiah 61:9). If God has chosen to graft the church into the promises of God, so God can and will graft again into the olive tree of Israel the natural branches of Israel (Hosea 6:2,3). The Jewish people shall be as jewels in Christ's crown (Zechariah 9:16). They shall never be embarrassed for their faith in God (Ezekiel 36:16-23). Although Israel has in the past profaned the name of the Lord; God restores His name to full respect during the millennium (Ezekiel 36:16-23).

Attitudes towards righteousness shall change. The law that the Jew has honored all these years shall not be upon tablets of stone but shall be written upon the heart of every man.

Peace shall exist until the moon is no more (Psalm 72:5). The moon shall cease to be needed in the New Jerusalem that descends from God out of heaven after the millennium. (Rev. 21:23).

E. The Church

The book of Revelation very briefly addresses the church during the millennium.

> *And I saw thrones, and they sat on them, and judgment was committed to them. Then I saw the souls of those who had been beheaded for their witness to Jesus and for the word of God, who had not worshiped the beast or his image, and had not received his mark on their foreheads or on their hands. And they lived and reigned with Christ for a thousand years. But the rest of the dead did not live again until the thousand years were finished. This is the first resurrection. Blessed and holy is he who has part in the first resurrection. Over such the second death has no power, but they shall be priests of God and of Christ, and shall reign with Him a thousand years (Revelation 20:4-6).*

Six times in Revelation chapter 20, John makes reference to a thousand years and the words *"a thousand years"* is never used in all the remainder of scripture to refer to the millennium. It is very clear that those who have given their lives for the gospel shall be resurrected at the time of the first resurrection and reign with Christ during the millennium. They sit upon thrones. The words "reign *with Christ*" do not appear anywhere else in scripture. All in the church of Thyatira who hold fast until the Lord comes shall have power over the nations. This too must have reference to the millennium (Rev. 2:24-26).

The last words spoken by David were the sharing of divine words concerning the type of man who must rule men. He must be just and rule in the fear of God. Then David uses the singular pronoun *He*. "He shall be like the light of the morning when the sun rises…" Only Christ can rule men justly. David also knew that he was unable to fulfill this kind of rule, but knew that He who did rule evil men must be armed with iron and spear. Then in Revelation we are told that Christ, who comes to sit upon the throne of David, does rule with a rod of iron (Rev. 2:27). See also 2 Samuel 23:11-17)

There is yet another comparison. David said that the ruler of Israel shall be like the light of the morning sun 2 Samuel 23:4), then in Revelation it is written that the ruler with a rod of iron shall be given the morning star (Rev. 2:28).

F. The Nations

All the nations shall be ruled by Christ during the millennium. All shall go up to Jerusalem to worship. The nations shall come to Jerusalem to learn the laws and ways of God. The laws of God, which everybody disdains today, shall rule the nations. Kings of the earth shall bring to Christ presents. They shall go up to Jerusalem with the Jew because the nations will know then who God is. Those of the nations who do not go up to Jerusalem to worship will see no rain (Zechariah 14:17). Christ shall be praised daily and be blessed by all nations.

G. Law and Order

> *For unto us a Child is born, Unto us a Son is given; And the government will be upon His shoulder. And His name will be called Wonderful, Counselor, Mighty God, Everlasting Father, Prince of Peace. Of the increase of His government and peace there will be no end, Upon the throne of David and over His kingdom, To order it and establish it with judgment and justice From that time forward, even forever. The zeal of the Lord of hosts will perform this (Isaiah 9:6, 7).*

Israel shall be a holy people unto God. God shall remove her iniquity (Romans 11:24-27). Christ's mercy unites His chosen people in the millennium. God promised an eternal kingdom and He shall keep his promise (2 Samuel 7:14-16).

War armament shall be replaced with farming implements. One nation shall help another nation. The millennium shall be a reign of righteousness according to the laws of Christ.

> *They shall not defile themselves anymore with their idols, nor with their detestable things, nor with any of their transgressions; but I will deliver them from all their dwelling places in which they have sinned, and will cleanse them. Then they shall be My people, and I will be their God (Ezekiel 37:23).*

There is no war because the millennial kingdom is a kingdom based upon the laws of God --laws that will be understood by Israel and laws that shall be transferred from the tablets of stone to fleshly tablets of the heart. For the majority of Jews, this will not occur until the millennium.

The Gentile nations from afar will be rebuked by the Messiah. The Gentiles will also see justice from the Messiah King.

> *Behold! My Servant whom I uphold, My Elect One in whom My soul delights! I have put My Spirit upon Him; He will bring forth justice to the Gentiles. He will not cry out, nor raise His voice, nor cause His voice to be heard in the street. A bruised reed He will not break, And smoking flax He will not quench; He will bring forth justice for truth (Isaiah 42:1-3).*

Justice shall be executed with true wisdom, and fairness. The saints who do not take the mark of the Beast will rule the earth with Christ at this time. God will punish any evil work. No one will get away with his sin, but the righteous shall prosper. Didn't God promise in the Old Testament that the righteous would prosper and the wicked would be destroyed? This shall be literally and immediately fulfilled as Christ rules the world.

The marvelous aspect of this rule is that Christ will impose righteousness through religious means, not through force. So the schooling in righteousness that will take place will be the sweet exercise of worship and spiritual instruction (Isaiah **11:1-10**) so beautifully pictures life in the millennium; read it.

H. Time

The tribulation period prepares the world for the millennium. Earthquakes shake the earth of all uncleanness. The heavens and the earth shake so that they are purged. The heavens were purged when Satan was cast to the earth at the fifth trumpet. The earth is purged on the day of the Lord. Fire consumes all witchcraft and idolatry in preparation for the reign of Christ. The wrath of God destroys most of earth's population. Now, during the millennium, man is purified by Christ's rule. The will of God is completed on earth as it is in heaven.

Hosea taught the people that in the third day God would raise up His people, His land, and His temple and live with Zion's Deliverer. The third day is considered to be the third millennium after Christ (Hosea 6:2).

However, the exact time of restoration is not known as Jesus informed His disciples just before he ascended into heaven (Matthew 24:39, Matthew 25:11).

I. Shall Eden Be Restored?

Shall the millennial kingdom return to the state of Eden before man had sinned? Eden paradise will be restored in some ways but not completely.

In Genesis the dew was from heaven[39] and again in the millennium the dew shall be from heaven.

For the seed shall be prosperous, The vine shall give its fruit, The ground shall give her increase, And the heavens shall give their dew— I will cause the remnant of this people To possess all these (Zech 8:12).

This heavenly dew coincides with the prosperity of the millennial kingdom. Abundance of all that is good shall be the portion to Israel and to those nations who worship God.

For the Lord will comfort Zion, He will comfort all her waste places; He will make her wilderness like Eden, And her desert like the garden of the Lord; Joy and gladness will be found in it, Thanksgiving and the voice of melody (Isaiah 51:3).

So they will say, 'This land that was desolate has become like the Garden of Eden; and the wasted, desolate, and ruined cities are now fortified and inhabited.' Then the nations which are left all around you shall know that I, the Lord, have rebuilt the ruined places and planted what was desolate. I, the Lord, have spoken it, and I will do it." 'Thus says the Lord God: "I will also let the house of Israel inquire of Me to do this for them: I will increase their men like a flock (Ezekiel 36:35-37).

The millennial kingdom is different than Eden in many ways. These ways are associated with the curse of sin. The Garden of Eden had no weeds; man did not have to work by the sweat of his brow; and there was no sickness and pain. There was no condemnation because sin did not exist for man until Eve and Adam had sinned and then they were cast out of the garden.

Satan existed in the Garden of Eden. Satan was present to tempt Eve to disobey God but during the millennium, Satan will be bound for one thousand years unable to temp man to sin. However man will have to deal with his own sinful nature as a result of the curse of sin and generations of evil that have prevailed upon the earth. Man will have to learn again the commandments of God and learn how to be obedient again.

In the Garden of Eden, man was not ruled by the Ten Commandments; they were not given to man in written form until the days of Moses. There was only one commandment or wish by God. Adam and Eve were told not to eat of the tree of the knowledge of good and evil. There was only one "thou shalt not" but man chose not to obey God's wishes.

A new kingdom ruled by Christ will not atone for sin. There is no remedy for sinfulness except through the blood of Christ. However, we did see that sacrifices would again be made for sin during the millennium.

During the millennium, man shall still be under the curse of sin. The effect of that curse shall be lessened because Christ the Messiah shall reign with righteousness. Hospitals and sickness will exist but not prevail, for man shall live a long life.

The lamb shall again lie down with the lion. The animal world shall live at peace and be vegetarians. Man shall live with the knowledge of world history, world science, and worldly views; but these shall be perfected as man again follows God and obeys his commandments. The commandments of God shall be very important for every nation and every individual, for by them shall Christ rule the nations and every individual.

Israel shall be a people after God and Jehovah shall be their God. Every promise in the Old

Testament to Israel that has not been fulfilled in Christ or before the millennium shall be fulfilled in the millennium. God keeps His promises in His time.

Further Study

1. What does Isaiah 11 tell us about the millennium?
2. What do you learn about the Temple of the millennium from Jeremiah chapters 40 – 47?

17. The Covenants of God with the Church are Fulfilled

The New Heavens & New Earth

Read Rev. 20, 21

There are four events that happen between the millennial kingdom and the New Jerusalem. First, in the battle of Gog and Magog, Christ destroys those nations and the millions of individuals that come up against Him and the saints in the unwalled city of Jerusalem. Secondly, Satan finally shall be cast into the lake of fire and brimstone. Thirdly, the unrighteous and unbeliever shall face the great white throne judgment seat of Christ and fourthly, the unrighteous and the unbeliever shall be cast into the lake of fire (Rev. 20:7-15) We will not discuss these events in this book.

Just as the millennium shall be the eternal promise to Israel, the new heavens and earth shall be the eternal promise to the church. Nothing in history can compare to the wonders of the believer's eternal home. The new heavens and the new earth shall far exceed the glories of Eden, as this chapter will show.

Revelation chapters 21 and 22 describe the eternal home of all righteous believers. Isaiah, also, prophesies concerning the new heavens and the new earth. Note that the heavens are plural and the earth is singular. A New Jerusalem comes down from God out of heaven.

> Now I saw a new heaven and a new earth, for the first heaven and the first earth had passed away. Also there was no more sea. Then I, John, saw the holy city, New Jerusalem, coming down out of heaven from God, prepared as a bride adorned for her husband. And I heard a loud voice from heaven saying, "Behold, the tabernacle of God is with men, and He will dwell with them, and they shall be His people. God Himself will be with them and be their God. And God will wipe away every tear from their eyes; there shall be no more death, nor sorrow, nor crying. There shall be no more pain, for the former things have passed away." Then He who sat on the throne said, "Behold, I make all things new." And He said to me, "Write, for these words are true and faithful." (Rev. 21:1-5)

For behold, I create new heavens and a new earth; and the former shall not be remembered or come to mind. But be glad and rejoice forever in what I create; for behold, I create Jerusalem as a rejoicing, and her people a joy. I will rejoice in Jerusalem, and joy in My people. (Isaiah 65:18, 19).

John writes and says that there is no more *sea*. If this is not referring to literal seas of water, it could be symbolic of that fact that there shall be no more heathen nations of the world. All believers with the Jewish remnant shall be one nation and Jehovah, who shall tabernacle among men, shall be the God of both peoples, Jew and Christian. The same God made eternal promises to both peoples.

The New Jerusalem shall replace the Jerusalem of the millennium. This New Jerusalem is far better than the millennial kingdom. All that causes tears shall vanish. All former happenings that caused tears shall be erased from the hard drive of our memories. For the first time, the promised people shall receive immortality --no more death, --no more pain. Everything is made new.

And He said to me, "It is done! I am the Alpha and the Omega, the Beginning and the End. I will give of the fountain of the water of life freely to him who thirsts. He who overcomes shall inherit all things, and I will be his God and he shall be My son. But the cowardly, unbelieving, abominable, murderers, sexually immoral, sorcerers, idolaters, and all liars shall have their part in the lake which burns with fire and brimstone, which is the second death (21:6-8).

The overcomer in Christ shall inherit all the promises of God without limitation - without the limitation of fleshly desires. The Bible definitely promises a fiery death for every unbeliever and unrighteous person.

Read Rev. 21:9-21.

The eternal inhabitants are engraved with reality. The engraving of the twelve tribes on the gates of the city represents the Jewish population and the engraving of the twelve disciples upon the foundation of the wall represents the Christian population. The millennial city has no walls, but the eternal city has walls. The promise of oneness to the church is fulfilled. No beauty is denied from this city.

But I saw no temple in it, for the Lord God Almighty and the Lamb are its temple. The city had no need of the sun or of the moon to shine in it, for the glory of God illuminated it. The Lamb is its light. And the nations of those who are saved shall walk in its light, and the kings of the earth bring their glory and honor into it. Its gates shall not be shut at all by day (there shall be no night there). And they shall bring the glory and the honor of the nations into it. But there shall by no means enter it anything that defiles, or causes an abomination or a lie, but only those who are written in the Lamb's Book of Life (Rev. 21:22-27).

The New Jerusalem is different from the millennial kingdom, in that there is no temple in the New Jerusalem. There is a dual personal temple – the Lamb and the Almighty are the temple.

Again we see that there is no sun or moon because of the divine dual illumination of the Lamb and of the Almighty. The gates are never closed because there is no fear of an enemy approach for all eternity. Nothing or no person that would cause sin shall enter its gates. Only those who have kept His commandments shall enter its gates (Rev. 22:14).

> *And he showed me a pure river of water of life, clear as crystal, proceeding from the throne of God and of the Lamb. In the middle of its street, and on either side of the river, was the tree of life, which bore twelve fruits, each tree yielding its fruit every month. The leaves of the tree were for the healing of the nations. And there shall be no more curses, but the throne of God and of the Lamb shall be in it, and His servants shall serve Him. They shall see His face, and His name shall be on their foreheads. There shall be no night there: They need no lamp nor light of the sun, for the Lord God gives them light. (Rev. 22:1-5)*

Everything about the city speaks of life and healing. The curse that was put upon man in the Garden of Eden because of sin is forever annulled. The name of Christ shall prevail over the name and mark of the Beast. Righteousness and perfect holiness shall be reflected in every inhabitant and every believer shall be a son of God who inherits all things (Rev. 21:7) because Christ is the Alpha and the Omega, the Beginning and the End, the giver of life, and He is the one who was, and is, and is to come -- the Almighty.

> *Beloved, now we are children of God; and it has not yet been revealed what we shall be, but we know that when He is revealed, we shall be like Him, for we shall see Him as He is (1 John 3:2).*

We cannot change the word of the Almighty. The philosophies of men cannot change the truth of eternal and unchanging realities. Denying the gospel or creating your own gospel, will not change the prophetic outcome of the book of Revelation. This same Jesus, who was the Lamb slain for our sins, is the same Lamb of God who shall give life and happiness in the New Jerusalem. No other prophet is the way to eternal life. As the gospels have spoken: *"Repent, for the kingdom of heaven is at hand"* (Matthew 3:2). And Jesus said:

> *Let not your heart be troubled; you believe in God, believe also in Me. In My Father's house are many mansions; if it were not so, I would have told you. I go to prepare a place for you. And if I go and prepare a place for you, I will come again and receive you to Myself; that where I am, there you may be also" (John 14:1-3).*

PART G:

THE RAPTURE

---

18. The Marriage Bonds

Love to embrace you, a ring to cherish, and a friend to hold your hand; these are the joys of every bride and groom. In biblical days when a groom was ready to marry, his father confronted the bride's father with a marriage proposal. The groom proposed and the bride either accepted or rejected the proposal. The two fathers sealed the proposal with a toast of wine. Sometimes a ring was presented to the bride as a seal of the engagement. A written contract and the terms of the marriage were recorded and witnessed by two people. The dowry terms were transcribed in a document called the *ketubah* which remained as the bride's possession until the consummation of the marriage. The engagement was called "Shiddukhin," and only a bill of divorcement could break this engagement. During the engagement period of a year, a new home, which was an addition onto his father's house was prepared for the bride.

After the ketubah was the wedding. The marriage festival continued for a week. By celebrating for a full week, the bride was "fulfilling her week.[1]" But the "days of the marriage" were thirty days.[2] The Wedding occurred at night. Torches signaled the groom's nearness. The groom was dressed like a king as much as his wealth permitted. The bride came forth ready to meet the groom draped with her wedding garments. Both usually wore a crown. A wealthy groom wore a golden crown. The groom returned to His Father's house with his bride for the marriage ceremony (Genesis 29:27).

Jewish matrimony etches the prophetical panorama of the betrothal and consummation of the church, the bride of Christ. The Father of our Lord Jesus Christ has designed in the archives of His eternal plans an agreement with anyone who will believe. The groom has sealed the betrothal of marriage by his own blood. The betrothal agreement has been written in the books of the New Covenant and these have been sealed by the Spirit of truth and by the sacrifice of the Groom. The Word of God prevails as the church's precious possession until the consummation. When we believe in Christ, the marriage vows are sealed and cannot be broken except by a bill of apostasy - a complete turning away from the Saviour.[3] During the church's betrothal which is now, Christ is preparing a home in heaven for His bride. "I go to prepare a place for you, and if I go and prepare a place for you, I will come again and receive you to Myself; that where I am, there you may be also" (John 14:2-3). When the clock of time ceases to tick, when the harvest is ripe (Rev. 14:15,18, Joel 3:13) and when sin has blackened the souls of men with the charcoal of hate, unholiness, and deception; Christ, as King, shall return to "snatch away" the church homeward to His Father's home. What a day of rejoicing and hope and love

John concluded his Revelation with the motto, "Come quickly Lord Jesus." May we initiate this search through the Revelation of John with victorious shouts of the same entreaty, "Come quickly Lord Jesus!" The nearer we approach His coming, the louder we shall shout, "Come!" With this shout is a hope for there will be a day of rapture for the church.

The Harvest Rapture of the church is an emotional state of intense joy, love, and excitement, but it is far more than this. The Harvest Rapture takes place at the same time as the resurrection of the righteous.

> *Behold, I tell you a mystery: We shall not all sleep, but we shall all be changed— in a moment, in the twinkling of an eye, at the last trumpet. For the trumpet will sound, and the dead will be raised incorruptible, and we shall be changed. For this corruptible must put on incorruption, and this mortal must put on immortality. So when this corruptible has put on incorruption, and this mortal has put on immortality, then shall be brought to pass the saying that is written: "Death is swallowed up in victory (1 Corinthians 15:51).*

MEANING OF RAPTURE

The word *rapture* is not a precise word to describe the coming of Christ for His bride. The church shall be caught away in the clouds. The word for *'caught away'* is the greek word *harpagesometha* from the root *harpadzo*.[4] The early church fathers did not use the word *rapture* in any prophetical sense but to refer to an ecstatic trance, but they only used the term, *The Second Coming* to refer to the rapture. The Greek word *harpadzo* means to steal, carry off, snatch away, or seize.[5]

There is no single English word to precisely illustrate the *'snatching away.'* The meaning of the word suggests swiftness and an act that is done so quickly that it happens unobserved. I shall refer to the 'catching away' as the *'harpadzo.'* With the Greek word, there is reference to speed. The angels who reap the harvest in chapter 14 do so with a quick action or the wheat would not cut.

The Greek word to describe Jesus' ascension was not 'harpadzo' but *'analambano'* meaning he was taken up or received. The apostles witnessed the ascension, but the 'harpadzo' will happen in a twinkling of an eye so that no man will witness the disappearing.

Harpadzo implies a rescue from threatening danger. Jude applies the word to the souls of men that need to be rescued from the fires of judgment. "But others save with fear, pulling (snatching, seizing) them out of the fire, hating even the garment defiled by the flesh (Jude 23).

The Harvest Rapture of the church is not the Second Coming of Christ to the world as King and Judge. The Rapture is only one part of the return of the Lord when Christ returns to the clouds to meet the saints in the air. The Rapture occurs but a short time before the second coming of Christ during which time Christ returns to earth as King over all the earth. This is explained in later chapters under the day of the Lord.

The Rapture of the church, which is the catching away of those believers who are alive, must occur simultaneously to the resurrection of the dead in Christ.

> *For this we say to you by the word of the Lord, that we who are alive and remain until the coming of the Lord will by no means precede those who are asleep. For the Lord Himself will descend from heaven with a shout, with the voice of an archangel, and with the trumpet of God. And the dead in Christ will rise first. Then we who are alive and remain shall be caught up together with them in the clouds to meet the Lord in the air. And thus we shall always be with the Lord. Therefore comfort one another with these words (1 Thessalonians 4:15-18).*

Both the dead in Christ and those who are alive at Christ's coming are gathered into the clouds to meet the Lord in the air. But all inferences to a rapture and a resurrection in the book of Revelation do not simultaneously happen. The "Harvest Rapture" is the only incident and place in the book of Revelation that fits both the harpadzo and a resurrection. This Harvest Rapture unites and blends biblical facts pertaining to the harpadzo and the resurrection most accurately.

19. False Glimpses of a Rapture

A. Come up Hither (pre-tribulation view)

Read Rev 4.

"After these things I looked, and behold, a door standing open in heaven. And the first voice which I heard was like a trumpet speaking with me, saying, "Come up here, and I will show you things which must take place after this. "Immediately I was in the Spirit; and behold, a throne set in heaven, and One sat on the throne" (Revelation 4:1-2).

There are scholars like Lehman Strauss[1] who claim that this verse is the clearest statement within scripture proving that the rapture precedes the tribulation (I Thessalonians 4:16). This view states that the word *come* is an invitation for the believers to arise in a pre-tribulation rapture to the marriage supper of the lamb. But, what bride needs an invitation to her own wedding celebration? According to the meaning of the word "*harpadzo*," there is no invitation but a snatching away without warning as a thief in the night (Rev. 19:15).

The summons in this verse is to John, not the church. This summons to *come and enter* through the open door is an invitation to *"come and see"* not *"come and stay"*. John received here a revelation by the Spirit of God concerning the future and the judgment of the world. John did not rapture into a new home in glory.

The word *come* is used fifty-six times in the book of Revelation. Each of the four beasts of the seal period says to John, *'come and see.'* Each *'come '*is not an invitation to participate in the rapture.

However, there is one 'come' in the Apocalypse that intimates a rapture. The two witnesses, who are slain, arise from death when the angel says, *"Come up hither."* They ascended up to heaven in a cloud, and their enemies beheld them" (Rev.11:12). The word *'harpadzo'* is not used here and this ascension into heaven was witnessed by all their enemies who stood about Jerusalem. But the harpadzo (rapture) remember transpires in a twinkling of an eye and no man shall attest the harpadzo.

Again, John is given the invitation, "Come, I will show you the judgment of the great harlot who sits on many waters, with whom the kings of the earth committed fornication, and the inhabitants of the earth were made drunk with the wine of her fornication." (Rev. 17:1–2) If we incorrectly use this invitation as many symbolize the pre-tribulation summons of Revelation 4:1, 2; then have John and the believers lost their soul to the evils of Babylon? Yes. We cannot use the word *come* to justify a belief in the rapture or resurrection unless clearly stated. All the *comes* are proof that we cannot define the rapture in Revelation chapter 4.

Is Coming Still

Seven verses later, in Revelation chapter four, the four beasts sing, "Holy, holy, holy, Lord God Almighty, He who was, He who is now, and He who is coming" The same is repeated in the eleventh chapter of the Apocalypse. "We give You thanks, O Lord God Almighty, The One who is and who was and who is to come, Because You have taken Your great power and reigned" (Rev.11:17). If Christ is still *the coming one* seven verses later and again in chapter eleven, then how can the rapture precede the tribulation in chapter four?

There are seven throne scenes in the book of Revelation. John perceives in the first throne scene, twenty-four elders, four beasts, and numerous angels encircling the throne (Rev. 4:4). This heavenly scene eventuates at the beginning of the seal period. If the rapture transpires before the tribulation, why is there not a host of people from every nation around the throne before the tribulation period begins?

In the Spirit

John was *in the spirit* when he envisioned the future. Some contend that this is symbolic of the catching away of the church. Some assert that John fell into a trance. Both are dangerous assumptions. We use the word trance today to refer to mediums, channelers, and witches who get caught up into the imaginations of the mind and communicate with the evil spirit world. God has forbidden such activity. John is not conveying any such state of mind when he said that he was *in the Spirit*.

Beck translates this verse more correctly: "I came under the Spirit's power."[2] Trances are self-induced visions like the false visions of the false prophets, but the visions of John were not self-induced, but were received from God supernaturally. We must not be deceived as to what it means to be and to live *in the Spirit*. When the Rapture breaks forth, we will not be *in the Spirit*, but rather this mortal flesh shall put on immortality. We shall arise, spirit and body. The phrase *in the Spirit* has no reference to the Rapture because both the body and soul shall see their redemption in that day. It is unscriptural and insulting to the glory of the Rapture and resurrection to suggest a "spirit rapture" only. The first resurrection is concurrent with the Rapture—a bodily resurrection. We don't see any resurrection in the fourth chapter of Revelation. We shall be reunited with the body and both are clothed with immortality. Praise God!

B. Tribulation Martyrs

> *And when he had opened the fifth seal, I saw under the altar the souls of them that were slain for the word of God, and for the testimony which they held: And they cried with a loud voice, saying, How long, O Lord, holy and true, dost thou not judge and avenge our blood on them that dwell on the earth? And white robes were given unto every one of them; and it was said unto them, that they should rest yet for a little season, until their fellow servants also and their brethren, that should be killed as they were, should be fulfilled (Rev. 6:9-11).*

There are innumerable tribulation martyrs during the fifth seal period. The apostasy increases as men's hearts disregard God. Sin expands in the hearts of man like cancer cells that swell in a human victim who is fed estrogen. As a result of this apostasy, many valiant believers in Christ's' word are killed by wicked hands, slaughtered like sheep for a sacrifice, and dismissed by society as pests.

These martyrs are tossed under an altar just as sacrificial blood was cast beneath the altars as unwanted dregs in Old Testament times. The believer will be hated of all nations. This is not the golden altar that is seen before the throne during the sixth seal. This is a different altar. This altar is heathen not holy. Saints are slain by the hands of occult worshippers and apostate worshippers. Martyrs, that shall be considered holy from every nation, are sacrificed for the advancement of Satanism and evil (Rev. 6:9). These martyrs at the end of the seal period comprehend that God has not yet judged wicked men because they cry out: "How long, O Lord, holy and true dost thou not judge and avenge our blood on them that dwell on the earth?" (Rev. 6:10). We see here that God, during the seal period, had not yet served judgment upon evil men for persecuting the righteous. The martyrs are told to rest for a season until other fellow servants of the gospel are martyred as well. During the hour of apostasy, the prospects of salvation will be slim. I do not believe these martyrs that are slain upon evil altars are new Christians who will have just received salvation during the tribulation period, but only faithful and mature saints who will have the strength to suffer persecution.

These martyrs are beheld under the altar, and then they are detected before the throne, clothed in white and with palms in their hands because they died and went to heaven.

> *These are they who came out of great tribulation: and have washed their robes and made them white in the blood of the Lamb: therefore, they are before the throne of God: and serve him day and night in his temple (Rev. 7:14-16).*

Have these martyrs been resurrected, or are they absent from the body and present with the Lord, having not yet received their resurrected bodies? There is no evidence that these martyrs are raptured because they died.

The following verses in Revelation 4:15-17) are prophetic. God shall in the future dwell among them. In the future, they shall hunger no more. In the future there shall be no need of the sun. In the future God shall wipe away all tears from their eyes. These promises are not fulfilled in chapter four but later—after the real Harvest Rapture and resurrection.

C. Two Witnesses Raised

> *Now after the three-and-a-half days the breath of life from God entered them, and they stood on their feet, and great fear fell on those who saw them. And they heard a loud voice from heaven saying to them, "Come up here." And they ascended to heaven in a cloud, and their enemies saw them. In the same hour there was a great earthquake, and a tenth of the city fell. In the earthquake seven thousand people were killed, and the rest were afraid and gave glory to the God of heaven. The second woe is past. Behold, the third woe is coming quickly (Rev. 11:11-14).*

The Beast from the bottomless pit (Antichrist) smites the two prophets of the Lord causing them to die. For 3½ days their bodies lie in the street of Jerusalem. The people of the earth rejoice over their death. "Come up hither" is the unique command. Is the resurrection of these two prophets symbolic of the rapture? No! The Spirit of God descends upon them and they ascend to heaven in a cloud. Their enemies behold the resurrection of the two witnesses; but remember, the Rapture is not visible to the world. Christ's own resurrection was not visible. There is no resemblance of the rapture here because the two witnesses are dead and only the two witnesses are invited to *come*.

The 3½ days of their death, reflect back to the death of Jesus Christ. Jesus said, that even if one were raised from the dead they would not believe (Luke 16:31).

Here, two prophets are raised after the likeness of Jesus' resurrection and the nations repent not. The prophets arise as a witness against the power of the Antichrist who claims to be the Christ. The 3½ days is also prophetic. They announced that for 3½ years the Antichrist will rule with terror, then according to the Harvest Rapture view, the resurrection will take place. In the same hour of their resurrection, a great earthquake shakes the earth. One tenth of the city falls and seven thousand are killed (Rev.11:11-14). A tenth is Christ's tithe. Was this Christ's revenge upon a city that killed His two prophets?

D. Rapture of 144,000

> *And I looked, and, lo, a Lamb stood on the mount Sion, and with him an hundred forty and four thousand, having his Father's name written in their foreheads. And I heard a voice from heaven, as the voice of many waters, and as the voice of a great thunder: and I heard the voice of harpers harping with their harps: And they sung as it were a new song before the throne, and before the four beasts, and the elders: and no man could learn that song but the hundred and forty and four thousand, which were redeemed from the earth. These are they which were not defiled with women; for they are virgins.*

These are they which follow the Lamb whithersoever he goeth. These were redeemed from among men, being the firstfruits unto God and to the Lamb. And in their mouth was found no guile: for they are without fault before the throne of God (Revelation 14:1-5).

Nearing the end of the seventh trumpet, John saw in his vision the Lamb on Mount Zion with the one hundred forty-four thousand. Immediately the one hundred forty-four thousand are singing about the throne. Because they are standing on mount Zion, I conclude that they are alive not dead. This suggests a rapture but not a resurrection.

These 144,000 are very unique among men. Their song is unique only to the 144,000. No one can chant their song. They are redeemed from the earth and redeemed from among men. They are designated as the firstfruits unto God and the Lamb. They are named the *firstfruits* because they are, firstly, redeemed from the earth. The Jewish nation was required to give the firstfruits of her land as an offering unto God. Israel thus becomes the firstfruits having been redeemed from the land. They are taken up from the land unto God.

They are also called the firstfruits because they are redeemed from among men. The nation of Israel was appraised and chosen as the firstfruits of His harvest, not any Gentile nation. Israel was holiness to the Lord, the firstfruits of His harvest. Disaster was promised to all who devour these first-fruits. Disaster was promised to anyone who would come against His chosen people Israel (Jeremiah 2, 3).

The firstfruits of the Levitical offerings were without blemish—the best of the land. These offerings were presented to God without being burnt upon the altar (Leviticus 2:12). The one hundred forty-four thousand are sealed from the fire and plagues of the earth and they are raptured without death into glory. These are raptured first, as the firstfruits unto God and the Lamb. They qualify as firstfruits because they are holy. They are not defiled with women. They are virgins. No guile is found in their mouth. They are without fault before the throne of God. They follow the Lamb.

Are the firstfruits of the resurrection, Jewish or Christian believers? God named Israel His firstfruits (Jeremiah 2:3). James earmarked the believers of his day "a kind of firstfruits" (James 1:18). When you weigh the evidence of scripture, the firstfruits more likely refer to Israel. The 144,000 are clearly identified with the twelve tribes of Israel. Whether they are Jew or Gentile believers, Jude comforts the church with the knowledge that God is able to keep us faultless. "Now to Him who is able to keep you from stumbling and to present you faultless before the presence of His glory with exceeding joy" (Jude 24). This is the goal of every believer whether Jew or Gentile.

E. The Spirit Departure

The pre-tribulation view believes that the Spirit of God departs from the world with the believer. How could this be? The so called tribulation martyrs face more difficulty than any Christian with the help of the Holy Spirit in previous history. No way could a believer find overcoming victory during the tribulation of the Antichrist without the presence of the Holy Spirit in his life. When one is saved, the Holy Spirit comes to indwell the believer.

The Holy Spirit is the divine power that convicts the sinner and calls him to repentance. If the Holy Spirit has been removed in a pre-tribulation rapture then no one will be given a chance to repent during the tribulation. We are told that "no man repents but the opportunity for man to repent is possible during the tribulation until the time of the Harvest Rapture or else the choice to "repent or not repent" would not exist.

20. Day of the Lord or the Day of Christ

A. Day of Christ

> *"For God did not appoint us to wrath, but to obtain salvation through our Lord Jesus Christ, who died for us, that whether we wake or sleep, we should live together with Him. Therefore comfort each other and edify one another, just as you also are doing"* (1 Thessalonians 5:9–11).

"We have not been appointed unto wrath." What does that mean? Christ's purpose for all men is that they might repent and be saved and know the truth. Man has been appointed to eternal life not unto eternal wrath. Christ's' plan was to redeem all. This verse shows Christ's' eternal redemptive provision for all mankind.

The context of 1 Thessalonians 5:9 is in reference to the wrath of God as it pertains to the judgment in the day of the Lord not the total tribulation period. The day of judgment by Christ Himself occurs after the church is raptured. The day of the Lord is a day of destruction and pain (v.3). The day of the Lord is a day of darkness, and a day of destruction (v5.). The day of the Lord is not the total duration of the tribulation but the wrath of God and more particularly, the very final day. The climax of all is the day of the Lord, when the King of kings returns to demolish the kingdoms of this world. He, Himself, will enact this judgment (Rev. 19:15).

The Rapture, on the other hand, is a day of rejoicing; therefore, the context of 1 Thessalonians 5:9 does not apply to the Rapture. "For God did not appoint us to wrath, but to obtain salvation through our Lord Jesus Christ." Those who are not sleeping, those who are wearing the breastplate of faith and love, and those who are wearing the helmet of salvation, are those who have not been appointed to wrath. They will be raptured or resurrected. "Who died for us, that whether we wake or sleep, we should live together with him." Raptured or resurrected and the promise of everlasting life is the redemptive destiny compared to an appointment with the wrath of God.

Let us examine the following verses as we discover that the day of Jesus Christ is not the day of the Lord. Every Greek text translates this verse as the day of Christ.

That you may approve the things that are excellent, that you may be sincere and without offense till the day of Christ (Philippians 1:10).

...holding fast the word of life, so that I may rejoice in the day of Christ that I have not run in vain or labored in vain (Philippians 2:16).

That you may not to be soon shaken in mind or troubled, either by spirit or by word or by letter, as if from us, as though the day of Christ had come (2 Thessalonians 2:2).

Who will also confirm you to the end, that you may be blameless in the day of our Lord Jesus Christ (1 Corinthians 1:8).

Deliver such a one to Satan for the destruction of the flesh that his spirit may be saved in the day of the Lord Jesus (1 Corinthians 5:5).

...you have understood us in part, that we are your boast as you also are ours, in the day of the Lord Jesus (2Corinthians 1:14).

Being confident of this very thing, that he which hath begun a good work in you will perform it until the day of Jesus Christ" (Philippians 1:6).

"And this I pray, that your love may abound still more and more in knowledge and all discernment, that you may approve the things that are excellent, that you may be sincere and without offense till the day of Christ, being filled with the fruits of righteousness which are by Jesus Christ, to the glory and praise of God. " (Philippians 1:9–11).

Each verse uses the term *the day of Christ* or *the day of our Lord Jesus,* but not *the day of the Lord.* The *day of the Lord* is a judgment day for the unbeliever, but the *day of Christ* is our victory day of Rapture and resurrection. The *day of the Lord Jesus Christ* is the day of salvation not destruction. This is the day in which to rejoice and is not a day of darkness. With joy, this is the day the church is waiting for.

The *day of Christ* is the climatic day for the Christian according to Philippians 1:10. Until this day the believer is to be found without fault and sincere before God and the world. There is no concern to be without offense after the day of Christ because this refers to the Rapture. If the *day of Christ* was the *day of the Lord* then the church would see no Rapture before the dreadful *day of the Lord* and the battle of Armageddon. But we know that the church is raptured before the *day of the Lord* because she returns as an army from heaven with Christ to fight in that great day of God.

Paul is able to rejoice in the *day of Christ,* if His followers have held fast to the word of life. The church can rejoice in the Rapture because our labor and life will be proven to be worth all the trials and tribulations of life.

B. Day of the Lord

> *"But concerning the times and the seasons, brethren, you have no need that I should write to you. For you yourselves know perfectly that the <u>day of the Lord</u> so comes as a thief in the night. For when they say, "Peace and safety!" then sudden destruction comes upon them, as labor pains upon a pregnant woman. And they shall not escape. But you, brethren, are not in darkness, so that this Day should overtake you as a thief. You are all sons of light and sons of the day. We are not of the night nor of darkness. Therefore let us not sleep, as others do, but let us watch and be sober. For those who sleep, sleep at night, and those who get drunk are drunk at night. But let us who are of the day be sober, putting on the breastplate of faith and love, and as a helmet the hope of salvation. For God did not appoint us to wrath, but to obtain salvation through our Lord Jesus Christ, who died for us, that whether we wake or sleep, we should live together with Him. Therefore comfort each other and edify one another, just as you also are doing"* (1 Thessalonians 5:1–11).

Notice first that Thessalonians 5 says the day of the Lord comes as a thief in the night, not the day of Christ comes as a thief in the night.

The following verses also refer to the day of the Lord or the day of God. The day of the Lord follows the Old Testament theme of darkness and destruction by the hand of Almighty God.

> *The sun shall be turned into darkness, and the moon into blood, Before the coming of the great and awesome day of the Lord (Acts 2:20).*

> *For you yourselves know perfectly that the day of the Lord so comes as a thief in the night. For when they say, "Peace and safety!" Then sudden destruction comes upon them, as labor pains upon a pregnant woman. And they shall not escape (1 Thessalonians 5:2, 3).*

> *For you yourselves know perfectly that the day of the Lord so comes as a thief in the night. But the day of the Lord will come as a thief in the night, in which the heavens will pass away with a great noise, and the elements will melt with fervent heat; both the earth and the works that are in it will be burned up (2 Peter 3:10).*

> *…Looking for and hastening the coming of the day of God, because of which the heavens will be dissolved, being on fire, and the elements will melt with fervent heat? (2 Peter 3:12).*

> *For they are spirits of demons, performing signs, which go out to the kings of the earth and of the whole world, to gather them to the battle of that great day of God Almighty. (Rev. 16:14)*

In that day the heavens shall melt, the sun and moon shall not shine and in that day the armies of Satan shall be defeated in the battle of the Almighty God.

We also observe that this day shall sneak in upon man as a thief in the night. Paul said that the day of the Lord cometh as a thief in the night (1Thessalonians 5:1). Referring to this same day Paul said "God has not appointed us to wrath" (1 Thessalonians 5:9). Indeed, the church will not face the judgment of God on that day because the day of Christ precedes the destructive day of the Lord. Believers are men of the day not the night. The day of the Lord is only a day of darkness with no hope. The book of Revelation refers to the day of the Lord arriving as a thief, but the believer in Christ shall not be taken by surprise in that hour for the Rapture will have already occurred.

> Behold, I am coming as a thief. Blessed is he who watches, and keeps his garments, lest he walk naked and they see his shame." And they gathered them together to the place called in Hebrew, Armageddon (Rev.16:15-16).

This verse clearly shows us that Christ comes as a thief in the day of the Lord because at that day the nations are gathered for Armageddon.

Cosmic Catastrophes

Read Rev. 16:18-21

In that day, the day of the Lord, there is a mighty and great earthquake. No earthquake in all history will compare to its greatness (Rev.16:18). Cities of the nations fall from the trembling. The earthquake divides the great city of Jerusalem into three parts, but Babylon is destroyed by fire because of the earthquake. Every island disappears into the seas and mountains are flattened. The Mount of Olives is split in two as Christ descends upon it. The earthquake creates a valley in the midst of the Mount of Olives. All the land from Geba to Rimmon south of Jerusalem is turned into a plain (Zechariah 14:10).

There is complete darkness. The sun and moon are darkened and the stars do not shine (Joel 2:10). God showers hail stones weighing one hundred pounds each. Judgment falls in one hour. "Put in the sickle, for the harvest is ripe. Come, go down; for the winepress is full, the vats overflow--for their wickedness is great" (Joel 3:13).

Melt with Fervent Heat

The earth shall melt with fervent heat. Babylon is purged with fire. A destructive fire shall devour the land. The apostle John does not describe the earth as melting but the idea of melting is important as the earth is purged with fire. Fire burns, purges, destroys and melts. The word 'fire' is used twenty five times in the Apocalypse. God purges and judges with fire. Joel said:

> A fire devours before them, And behind them a flame burns; The land is like the Garden of Eden before them, And behind them a desolate wilderness; Surely nothing shall escape them (Joel 2:3).

The word *melt* reflects the justice and judgment of God in the day of the Lord. Spiritually the judgment of God melts the wicked as silver and brass are melted in a furnace. The desires of the wicked shall be destroyed (Psalm 112:10). The inhabitants of Canaan and those who follow the ways of the pagan Canaanites are destroyed. The heart of the wicked shall melt. With pain, faces appear as flames (Isaiah 13:9.20). God destroys sinners. It is the kingdom of the sinful that is destroyed (Amos 9).

Peter describes the elements melting with fervent heat in the day of the Lord.

> *But the day of the Lord will come as a thief in the night, in which the heavens will pass away with a great noise, and the elements will melt with fervent heat; both the earth and the works that are in it will be burned up. Therefore, since all these things will be dissolved, what manner of persons ought you to be in holy conduct and godliness, looking for and hastening the coming of the day of God, because of which the heavens will be dissolved, being on fire, and the elements will melt with fervent heat? (2 Peter 3:10-12).*

All these things shall be dissolved. What things are dissolved? —the heavens, the earth, and the works of man in the earth. These works of man embrace his accomplishments, his deeds, and his acts. All things become new in the kingdom of God. That which does not comply with the character of Christ's kingdom is dissolved. The elements of this world melt with fervent heat. Elements are the rudiments, the principles of first things, and the primary and fundamental principles. The word *element* implies the fundamentals of those things and ideas that belong to this sinful life.

Upon Whom

John inscribes in the apocalypse of Jesus Christ the fate of the men that affix to their forehead or their hand the mark of the Beast. These who worshipped the image of the Beast shall endure the wrath of Almighty God. Those who have shed the blood of saints and prophets shall experience the wrath of God (Rev.16:6). These are given blood to drink for shedding blood. Complete darkness and despair falls upon the seat of the Beast and upon the kingdom of the Beast. They gnaw their tongues for pain (Rev.17:2). The Kingly Christ tramples the grapes of Christ's wrath as He establishes His throne of righteousness upon the earth. The great whore, that great Babylon, falls into the pit of Christ's wrath. The kings of the earth that committed fornication with the great whore are dethroned and their kingdoms are destroyed.

The battle is with the Antichrist. According to Lactantius, the Antichrist will win three battles but for the fourth battle, Christ brings the victory.[1] The Antichrist and false prophets are thrust into hell fire. Satan is cast into the bottomless pit for one thousand years.

God performs a universal triumph; therefore, there is a universal destruction. The wrath of God is indignation upon ALL nations from one end of the earth to the other.

> *For the day of the Lord upon all the nations is near; As you have done, it shall be done to you; Your reprisal shall return upon your own head (Obadiah 1:15).*

> *"For the indignation of the LORD is against all nations, And His fury against all*

their armies; He has utterly destroyed them, He has given them over to the slaughter"
(Isaiah 34:2).

I will utterly consume everything from the face of the land, Says the Lord
(Zephaniah 1:2)

A noise will come to the ends of the earth --For the Lord has a controversy with the
nations; He will plead His case with all flesh. He will give those who are wicked to the
sword, says the Lord (Jeremiah 25:31).

Thus says the Lord of hosts: Behold, disaster shall go forth from nation to nation,
and a great whirlwind shall be raised up from the farthest parts of the earth (Jeremiah
25:32).

Therefore wait for Me, says the Lord, Until the day I rise up for plunder; My
determination is to gather the nations to My assembly of kingdoms, to pour on them
My indignation, all my fierce anger; all the earth shall be devoured with the fire of My
jealousy (Zephaniah 3:9).

Sin is universal and more so by the end of history. There is no repentance in the hearts of men. God, therefore, punishes all unrighteousness upon the earth. Not only will the idolatrous person be punished or destroyed, but God will erase all idolatry from the face of the earth. No more will men worship Baal or any other god. The Battle of Armageddon is the final confrontation with the thunderings of Baal. Never again will man build an altar to the gods or goddesses. God will bring vengeance against violence, deceit, pride, and disbelief. God will finally shock the man that thinks God will not recompense evil.

I will cut off every trace of Baal from this place, The names of the idolatrous priests
with the pagan priests. Those who worship the host of heaven on the housetops; Those
who worship and swear oaths by the Lord, But who also swear by Milcom; Those who
have turned back from following the Lord, And have not sought the Lord, nor inquired
of Him (Zephaniah 1:4-6).

And it shall be, In the day of the Lord's sacrifice, That I will punish the princes and
the king's children, and all such as are clothed with foreign apparel (Zephaniah 1:8).

In the same day I will punish all those who leap over the threshold, Who fill their
masters' houses with violence and deceit. And it shall come to pass at that time That I
will search Jerusalem with lamps, And punish the men Who are settled in complacency,
Who say in their heart, The Lord will not do good, Nor will He do evil (Zephaniah
1:11-12).

Israel has seen her day of the Lord. Babylon destroyed Israel in that day. Now at the end of time, God seeks vengeance upon the Gentile nations not Israel. The wrath of God is the time of judgment for the Gentiles.

Son of man, prophesy and say, 'Thus says the Lord God: "Wail, 'Woe to the day!'
For the day is near, even the day of the Lord is near. It will be a day of clouds, the time
of the Gentiles (Ezekiel 30:2-3).

Proclaim this among the nations: "Prepare for war! Wake up the mighty men, Let
all the men of war draw near, Let them come up. Beat your ploughshares into swords and
your pruning hooks into spears; Let the weak say, 'I am strong.'" Assemble and come, all
you nations, and gather together all around. Cause your mighty ones to go down there,
O Lord. "Let the nations be wakened, and come up to the Valley of Jehoshaphat; For
there I will sit to judge all the surrounding nations. Put in the sickle, for the harvest is
ripe. Come, go down; For the winepress is full, The vats overflow—For their wickedness
is great." Multitudes, in the valley of decision! For the day of the Lord is near in the
valley of decision. The sun and moon will grow dark, and the stars will diminish their
brightness. The Lord also will roar from Zion, And utter His voice from Jerusalem;
The heavens and earth will shake; but the Lord will be a shelter for His people, and the
strength of the children of Israel (Joel 3:9-16).

In that day, God shall destroy all the nations that come against Jerusalem. God will seek
vengeance upon those nations that follow the desires of the Antichrist to annihilate the nation of
Israel. God protects a remnant of His people the Jews. God will avenge Himself on all the nations
about Jerusalem that have risen up against His people and have divided His land. Notice that the
day of the Lord is a day of battle, the Battle of Armageddon.

I will also gather all nations and will bring them down into the valley of Jehoshaphat,
and will plead with them there for my people and for my heritage Israel, whom they have
scattered among the nations, and parted my land (Joel 3:1).

It shall be in that day [that] I will seek to destroy all the nations that come against
Jerusalem (Zechariah 12:9).

Behold, at that time I will deal with all who afflict you; I will save the lame, And
gather those who were driven out (Zephaniah 3:19).

For thus says the Lord of hosts: He sent me after glory, to the nations, which plunder
you; for he who touches you touches the apple of His eye. For surely I will shake my hand
against them, and they shall become spoil for their servants. Then you will know that the
Lord of hosts has sent me (Zechariah 2:8-9).

In that day the wealth of the world will be worth the weight of a dirty rag. Matthew warned
us that it is difficult for a rich man to enter the kingdom of heaven. Now the rich man sees his
ultimate doom.

Wail you inhabitants of Maktesh! for all the merchant people are cut down; all those
who handle money are cut off. "And it shall come to pass at that time that I will search

Jerusalem with lamps, and punish the men who are settled in complacency, who say in their heart, 'the Lord will not do good, nor will He do evil (Zephaniah 1:11-12)

C. The Second Coming

Read Rev. 19:1-21

Jesus returns as the true witness of His justice. He that sits upon the white horse is called Faithful and True (Rev. 19:11). This is the testimony of Jesus; He is true and He is righteous. The testimony of Jesus is the spirit of prophecy (v10). His witness upon the earth at His first coming was true and righteous, and His works completely fulfilled the will of God. So will all prophecy concerning the end time be in accordance with this same spirit. This spirit of prophecy is true and righteous for in righteousness Jesus returns to judge and make war.

His eyes are as a flame of fire; the eyes of the Son of Man see the hearts of men. The wisdom of His sight can judge truthfully, for He is both divine and human. The wisdom of Jesus can blaze the flame of judgment and justice. He can pronounce eternal death, for He provided life for man. He has the right to condemn man for He has saved mankind. He gives sight to the blind, but now he awards darkness to those who thought they could see.

Jesus returns as the judge of the earth and Christ treads the winepress himself (Rev. 19:15). Again Christ comes to do the will of the Father. His vesture is dipped in blood. This gives possible reference to His own blood and the blood that is shed in that day. Upon the cross He shed His blood and bore the sins of mankind. Judgment now descends because man refused the blood of the cross. Whereas the blood of the cross had saved man, now the bloodstained vesture causes blood to flow in the greatest battle of history.

Jesus is given a new secret name. He is called *the Word of God* for He is the fulfillment of all scripture, and He is the complete embodiment of the Deity. His salvation and kingship are greater than human comprehension. Yet, we see Christ at His Second Coming, in a new glorious fashion like never before.

Jesus returns as King. Upon His head are many crowns. As King, He returns with the purpose to establish His kingdom upon earth. He comes to make war with Satan and the Antichrist. The usurpers of His throne are destroyed. The sword of His mouth smites the nations (Rev.19:15). The power of His two-edged sword slashes the nations. At His word the nations fall. And just as in the beginning, His word creates all that is.

> *And I will pour on the house of David and on the inhabitants of Jerusalem the Spirit of grace and supplication; then they will look on Me whom they pierced. Yes, they will mourn for Him as one mourns for His only son, and grieve for Him as one grieves for a firstborn (Zechariah 12:10).*

In that day He shall stand upon the Mount of Olives causing it to split in two.

> *And in that day His feet will stand on the Mount of Olives, which faces Jerusalem*

on the east. And the Mount of Olives shall be split in two, from east to west, making a very large valley. Half of the mountain shall move toward the north and half of it toward the south (Zechariah 14:4).

As King of kings, Christ leads the armies of heaven against the armies of this world. He rides upon a white horse that denotes the victory of righteousness.

The Second Coming is divided into two events: the Rapture and the day of the Lord. The Rapture occurs before the wrath of God; for believers are not appointed unto the wrath of God. The Rapture is a day of victory, but the day of the Lord is a day of wrathful darkness.

Both times Christ came; He came to do the Will of the Father but each coming had a different purpose. We see this in the following chart.

Contrast between Christ's	
First Coming and	**His Second Coming**
Came to see and to save the lost.	Came to condemn the lost.
Laid aside His glory and became meek and mild	Returns with full power to rule with a rod of iron
Came as a servant to man	Comes as King of kings and Lord of lords.
Comes for the Saints	Comes with the Saints
Called Savior	Called faithful and True
Came in swaddling clothes	Clothed in a robe dipped in blood
Voice of a baby	Sound of many waters
As a lamb	As the Lion of Judah

FURTHER STUDY

1. Add to the chart above.

2. Make a Chart comparing the day of Christ and the Day of the Lord

Comparing when, character, happenings

I Thessalonians 2:3

Let no one deceive you by any means for the Day of Christ will not come

Seals Unless the falling away comes first,

Trumpets And the Man of sin is revealed

Day of Christ, the rapture

Whom the Lord will destroy with the brightness of His coming.

Day of the Lord

21. Why the Church Must Go through Tribulation

A. Persecution And Revenge

This brings us to a very important question: Why must the church go through the tribulation? In the Old Testament, incense was brought within the veil to make atonement (Leviticus 16:12, 46), but incense in the Apocalypse proceeds from within the veil in Revelation chapter 8 and is cast to the earth to bring judgment upon evil men. Let's revert to the beginning of the trumpet period. "And the Angel took the censer, and filled it with fire of the altar, and cast it into the earth and there were voices, and thunderings, and lightnings and an earthquake" (Rev. 8:5). The fire of Christ's judgment was scattered throughout the world just as the fire from the Korah rebellion was scattered some distance away (Numbers 16:36). There is a connection between the incense and judgment. The prayers of the martyrs are linked with the judgment upon evil men.

The angel with the censer and incense stands before the heavenly veil or the throne of God. A censer contained hot coals, and incense is sprinkled upon it. The angel then fills the censer with fire from the altar of incense and casts it to the earth. The fire of God creates lightening, voices, thunderings, and an earthquake. The trumpet judgments begin, but it is a result of the prayers of the saints that God pours forth his judgments. Because of the faithfulness of the saints, God can punish the unjust man that stands without excuse. Because of the holiness of the saints, the angel proceeds to cast fire upon the earth. The prayers of the saints are answered as the incense is accepted before God and the trumpets sound forth judgment. The martyr's divine calling to bring forth judgment is the role of the faithful church not the role of lucky believers who are saved during the tribulation.

B. Testimony to God's Righteousness

Paul gives us the answer to why the church must go through the tribulation.

> *…So that we ourselves boast of you among the churches of God for your patience and faith in all your persecutions and tribulations that you endure which is manifest evidence of the righteous judgment of God, that you may be counted worthy of the kingdom of God, for which you also suffer; since it is a righteous thing with God to repay with tribulation those who trouble you (2 Thessalonians 1:4-6).*

First, the faith and patience of the saints provides evidence, proof confirmation, and testimony that God is righteous. The saints having endured tribulation, both in Paul's day as well as during great tribulation at the end-time, are proof of His faithfulness to keep man during the hour of tribulation and proof of the saint's faithfulness to endure until the end and be victorious. The power of the cross is manifested and approved true in the lives of the martyrs. Christ's word is proven to be true and faithful. God can and will preserve us faultless before His throne. God can now judge the world because there is a faithful remnant who can witness to the holiness and justice of God.

Similar justice is found in the redemption of the second Adam. The first Adam failed because of sin, but Jesus, the second Adam, was victorious over sin. Being sinless He was able to procure salvation for all mankind. The saints open the door to the eternal kingdom of God because they shall overcome sin and the devil by the endued power of the indwelling Christ.

Religious and political advances shall not win the millennial kingdom. Not all become righteous because of the faithfulness of the church. Contrariwise, sin shall overcome and kill the righteous. But at the resurrection eternal life shall be realized in every believer, and only by the light of the King's coming shall the millennial kingdom be established.

Second, the saints endorse or sanction the righteousness of God when Christ eventually destroys and recompenses tribulation to those that have troubled the saints. God is righteous to seek vengeance against the enemies of the church. God does this when the angel casts to the earth the fire from the censer that was sprinkled with the incensed prayer of all the saints. The trumpet plagues begin as revenge for the blood of thousands of martyrs. Blood is shed for blood spilled.

The offering of the incense in Numbers is similar to the prayers of the saints in Revelation 8:3. Wrath goes forth from the Lord and a plague begins. Moses said unto Aaron:

> *Take a censer and put fire in it from the altar, put incense on it, and take it quickly to the congregation and make atonement for them; for wrath has gone out from the Lord. The plague has begun (Numbers 16:46).*

Even after the two hundred and fifty men were swallowed up by the fire of the Lord, the rebellion continued until 14,700 were killed. The fire was scattered from the censer as far as possible (Numbers 16:37).

In Ezekiel's vision a man clothed with linen went among the cherubim, or the four beasts. He took coals of fire from among the beasts and scattered them over the city in judgment (Ezekiel 10:2). Similarly, in the Apocalypse, the censer that is filled with fire from the altar was cast to the earth. The plague begins. Unless the days of the tribulation are shortened there would be no survivors.

C. The Purging of A Persecuted Church

NEED FOR HOLINESS

Third, the church shall be counted worthy of the kingdom of God (2 Thessalonians 1:5). The role of purging is vitally important to an understanding of tribulation and the Apocalypse. The incense from the prayers of the saints, as it is cast to the earth, has the power to bring forth judgment. The holiness of the church stands as a necessary testimony to the righteous judgments of God

In the Korah uprising, they had gathered to declare that not only the priests were holy, but, that everyone, that the whole congregation was holy. Moses said, "God will show you tomorrow who is holy." Today, the world is repeating the sins of Korah. All is holy, the people claim. Every man is righteous. The world today considers Christians no holier than they are. The true righteous person is ignored and mocked. Righteousness is now clothed with a new interpretation. Righteousness in man's New Age constitutes a right treatment of Mother Earth. Righteousness has become a subjective opinion of each individual. Every man has become right in his own eyes. But God will in that day show to the whole world who is righteous and God will deliver his holy people in those last days.

The Bible says that the door of the kingdom of God is paved with tribulation. Paul said, "Strengthening the souls of the disciples, exhorting them to continue in the faith, and saying, 'we must through many tribulations enter the kingdom of God'" (Acts 14:21). Has the gospel changed since the early church days? Who is preaching this gospel today?

Persecution moulds a saint. Fellow laborers said of Ignatius: "He inwardly reflected, that the confession which is made by martyrdom, would bring him into a yet more intimate relation to the Lord."[1] The apostles of Acts 5 rejoiced that they were counted worthy to suffer for Christ's name."

Why should we look to escape tribulation, but whereas with victory, we can find ourselves worthy to enter the Kingdom of Heaven and desire that utmost intimate relationship with the Lord? This desire for perfection is not a righteousness that denies the efficacy of the cross, but a righteousness that results from having been imputed with the righteousness of God. Righteousness produces the fruit of righteousness.

The Old Testament priest, Eleazar, had a brazen censer; but in the Apocalypse we see a golden censer because the tribulations of the saints bring forth gold. Their prayers and incense are as pure gold before the throne. They have been tried. They have prevailed. The church of Laodicea was encouraged to find gold tried in the fire. God wants a pure church, and if necessary, she shall be purified by fire. How can the saints judge the world and the angels, if they cannot endure persecution? (Acts 14:21).

Nadab and Abihu in the days of Moses were honorable priests who accompanied Moses to the summit of Sinai. They fell into apostasy and offered profane fire in their censer before the Lord. The Lord consumed them by His fire (Leviticus 10:2). The fire was considered profane because they did not regard the holiness of God and did not give God the glory.

This is what the Lord spoke, saying:

> *By those who come near Me*
> *I must be regarded as holy;*
> *And before all the people I must be glorified (Leviticus 10:3).*

God demands to be treated as holy, not by man's standards and definitions of holiness, but by His laws of holiness. God says:

> *"And I will bring him to judgment with pestilence and bloodshed; I will rain down*
> *on him, on his troops, and on the many peoples who are with him, flooding rain, great*
> *hailstones, fire, and brimstone. Thus I will magnify Myself and sanctify Myself, and I*
> *will be known in the eyes of many nations. Then they shall know that I am the* Lord."
> (Ezekiel 38:22–23).

And if God is not glorified by the worshipper then judgment follows. Nadab and Abihu died by fire, the very instrument by which they worshipped God. Similarly, during the tribulation, "unauthorized fire" (Rev. 8:1-5) shall be consumed by the fiery wrath of God. All unholiness shall be burned by fire from the world, from the nations, and from the church.

The incense of our lives will excite the nostrils of God. Shortly, all incense will bring honor to God as Malachi prophesied.

> *For from the rising of the sun, even to its going down,*
> *My name shall be great among the Gentiles;*
> *In every place incense shall be offered to My name,*
> *And a pure offering;*
> *For My name shall be great among the nations,"*
> *Says the Lord of hosts (Malachi 1:11).*

The Number Seven

The number *seven* is used 391 times in scripture. *Seven* identifies the handiwork and sovereignty of God. Times and days and years are bound by Christ's number seven. Seven days of offerings were made for a holy convocation (Leviticus 23:36). Seven days of rejoicing was the duration of the feast of tabernacles (Deuteronomy 16:13).

We also discover that seven signifies a purging role in scripture for any uncleanness. For seven days the altar was sanctified as holy (Exodus 29:37). The priest sanctified objects and people by dipping his finger in blood and sprinkling it seven times (Leviticus 4:17). Even on the Day of Atonement, the blood was dipped and sprinkled before the veil seven times. The blood of a bird was sprinkled seven times on a leper for cleansing (Leviticus 14:7). Often seven lambs were used as a burnt offering unto the Lord for cleansing of sin (Leviticus 23:28). The offerings of Passover were for a seven day period (Numbers 28:24, 25). A seven day period of reclusive purging was determined for any man with leprosy, for anyone who had killed another person, for touching death, for a child-bearing woman, and for women having an issue of blood. Even David applied seven to the act of purification. "The words of the Lord are pure words, like silver tried in a furnace of earth, purified seven times" (Psalms 12:6).

Scripture also recounts a punishment of 'seven' days or years for the purging of sin. "I will punish you seven times more for your sins" (Leviticus 26:21). Israel served Midian seven years and Babylon seventy years because they had forsaken the Lord (Leviticus 26:21, 24).

The number "*seven*" occurs thirty-one times in the book of Revelation. The Apocalypse records seven spirits, churches, candlesticks, stars, seals, lamps, trumpets, thunders, crowns, angels, plagues, golden vials, mountains, and kings. We cannot deny the purging role prophetically portrayed by the number seven. Christ's judgments are in repeated sevens. There are seven seals of judgment, seven trumpet judgments, and seven vials of wrath. "I will punish you seven times more." There is a purging of sin from the earth during the tribulation period. The kingdom of God cannot unfold in millennial hope if sin if not purged. Purging is necessary from the mere appearance of evil. The church can apply this personally also if sin exists within.

D. The Glory of Tribulation

Tribulation itself produces hope. Paul realized this mammoth truth when he said:

> *And not only that, but we also glory in tribulations, knowing that tribulation produces perseverance; and perseverance, character; and character, hope. Now hope does not disappoint, because the love of God has been poured out in our hearts by the Holy Spirit who was given to us (Romans 5:3-5).*

End time tribulation will fertilize hope in the believer as he witnesses the flowering of prophetic truths and realizes that Christ's return is more eminent than ever. Before our very eyes we shall witness the dramatic events of the Apocalypse. We will not be disappointed by the hope that is planted within us by the Holy Spirit, for tribulation is only for a brief moment. Hope will be motivated by a new outlook on life and death. Our vision of hope will narrow in upon the future and eternal promises of life. The things of this world will no longer provide hope, security and peace. Tribulation has an invisible power to twist our earthly desires until they are focused upon Christ with a love that prevails over the foe. The Church will glory in tribulation as that day approaches.

We will glory in tribulation when we see the character of our lives mature and mold a perseverance, patience, and love that will imitate and glorify our Savior Jesus Christ. We shall transform into His likeness. Christ's likeness will be perfected in human weakness. Ignatius, a martyr prayed, "I thank thee, O Lord, that Thou hast vouchsafed to honor me with a perfect love towards thee, and hast made me to be bound with iron chains, like Thy Apostle Paul.[1] The glory of tribulation reflects the glory of the cross and our Savior who suffered. The deathly shadow of the martyr's fire is surrounded and permeated by the presence of God. This is our hope.

We shall glory in tribulation because tribulation produces fruitfulness. The early church grew through persecution. Lives changed because of the testimony of the faithful. Polycarp, a great martyr firmly stated before his persecutors, "Eighty-and six years have I served Him, and He never did me any injury: how then can I blaspheme my King and my Savior?"[2] The testimony of early martyrs should inspire us to rejoice also in tribulation. When we learn to rejoice, fear is vanquished. "Who shall separate us from the love of Christ, shall tribulation, or distress, or persecution or famine, or nakedness, or peril, or sword? (Romans 8:35) No, Ten Thousand Times No!

Jeremiah knew the fruitfulness of tribulation. Although he was cast into prison and miry pits where he was left to die, he saw deliverance at the hand of Babylon. The king of Babylon granted him freedom in his empire. Although his own people mocked him, and they refused to heed his word, he lived to see the fulfillment of his own prophetic words. In the midst of tribulation, Jeremiah's life abounded with fruitfulness. His words of hope for us today are:

> Blessed is the man, who trusts in the Lord, And whose hope is the Lord.
> For he shall be like a tree planted by the waters,
> Which spreads out its roots by the river,
> And will not fear when heat comes;
> But its leaf will be green,
> And will not be anxious in the year of drought,
> Nor will cease from yielding fruit (Jeremiah 17:8).

Persecution of Christians today has escalated. More Christians are being persecuted now than any other time in history. Churches are being burned. Many American Christians pray in their churches weekly, oblivious to the fact that Christians in many parts of the world suffer brutal torture, arrest, imprisonment and even death — their homes and communities laid waste — for no other reason than they are Christians. The shocking, untold story of our time is that more Christians have died this century simply for being Christians than in the first nineteen centuries after the birth of Christ. They have been persecuted and martyred before an unknowing, indifferent world and a largely silent Christian community.

The glory of martyrdom shall penetrate the darkness. The hope of a persecuted church will be pregnant with immortality. Perhaps, the church is presently too earthly minded to aspire to the glories of tribulation, but one day she shall glory in the hope of immortality. This hope will dispel the darkness of death.

Although hope will comfort the desperate times of tribulation and may we yet heed the wisdom of Cyprian when he wrote:

> It behooves the soldiers of Christ in the divine camp; that no allurements may deceive the incorruptible steadfastness of your faith, no threats terrify you, no sufferings or tortures overcome you because greater is he that is in us, than he that is in the world; nor is the earthly punishment able to do more towards casting down, than is the divine protection towards lifting up.[3]

CHAPTER 22: FURTHER EVIDENCE THAT THE CHURCH WILL GO THROUGH THE TRIBULATION

But the saints of the Most High shall receive the kingdom and possess the kingdom forever, even forever and ever.... I was watching and the same horn was making war against the saints, and prevailing against them, until the Ancient of Days came, and a judgment was made in favor of the saints of the Most High and the time came for the saints to possess the kingdom... then the saints shall be given into his (Antichrist's) hand for a time and times and half a time ... Then the kingdom, shall be given to the people, the saints of the Most High (Daniel 7:18:20-22).

A. Evidence From Daniel

There are three factors in the above verses that identify the saints in the book of Daniel. They possess the kingdom; they are given dominion, and they are persecuted by the Antichrist. According to Daniel the prophet, the Beast -- the Antichrist loses his kingdom and is cast into the flames of hell, but the saints of the Most High receive the kingdom forever.

The pre-tribulation view argues that 'saints' refer to Jewish believers only during the tribulation. However, we can argue that the saints spoken of here refer to the church whether Jew or Gentile because the church is a recipient of the kingdom promises as well as Old Testament believers? Three verses later, Daniel speaks concerning the saints again. This time the Antichrist is making war against them, and wearing them out for 3 ½ years (Daniel 9:16, 19). If the church or the saints encounter war with the Antichrist, then the church must go through the tribulation.

When the Ancient of Days returns, judgment and the kingdom are given to the saints. Has the kingdom ever been promised to the Jews? Kingdom is the inheritance of the church. The New Testament scriptures confirm the prophetic voice of Daniel and identify the saints here as

Christians who are not only given the kingdom but they judge the world. (1 Corinthians 6:2). Examine the following scriptures

> Strengthening the souls of the disciples, exhorting them to continue in the faith, and saying, "We must through many tribulations enter the kingdom of God" (Acts 14:22).

> That you would walk worthy of God who calls you into His own kingdom and glory (1 Thessalonians 2:12).

> Therefore, since we are receiving a kingdom which cannot be shaken, let us have grace, by which we may serve God acceptably with reverence and godly fear. For our God is a consuming fire (Hebrews 12:28-29).

We are not afraid to identify the church with the other times when the word *saints* is used in scripture. Why should we isolate the use of *saints* in Daniel and in the Revelation to refer to the Jews only or to tribulation saints?

Many scholars are convinced that the saints in the book of Daniel refer to the Jews only, but consider this. God in the book of Daniel uses the term *your people* five times when referring to the people of Israel.

> "For the iniquities of our fathers, Jerusalem and Your people have become a reproach to all who are around us. …. "O Lord, hear! O Lord, forgive! O Lord, listen and act! Do not delay for Your own sake, my God, for Your city and Your people are called by Your name" (Daniel 9:16, 19).

This, however, without doubt refers to Israel. The expression, *your people* is an expression delineating the Jewish nation. "Seventy weeks are determined for *your people* and for your holy city" (Daniel 9:24). This again refers to the Jewish nation. "Now I have come to make you understand what will happen to your people in the latter days, for the vision refers to many days yet to come" (Daniel 10:14). Why does Daniel use the term *your people* rather than the word *saints* unless there is a difference of people?

Seventy weeks are determined for Israel but this does not exclude the possibility of the church being involved in persecution during Israel's last week. Remember, the seven thunders have not been given.

B. Evidence from Matthew

Jesus was instructing His disciples concerning the end of the age when He said, "Then they will deliver you up to tribulation and kill you, and you will be hated by all nations for My name's sake" (Matthew 24:9). Whom does the "you" refer to? Are these tribulation saints Jews or Christians? The disciples to whom Jesus was talking were both Jewish men and followers of Christ. Christ may have been addressing Jewish men of Israel, but He was also conversing with His believers and followers.

Jesus warned the disciples, in this same discourse, to be careful that false christs did not deceive them just before the tribulation and during the tribulation period (Matthew 24:24). Jesus would have been speaking to them as believer's not Jewish men because it was the believers who could be deceived in thinking that another was Jesus the Messiah. Other Jews of that day never considered Jesus as the Messiah. The unbelieving Jews of Jesus day were already deceived. However, many Christian Jews and non-Christian Jews in the last days will be deceived at first and accept the Antichrist as the Messiah.

Jesus said that many would be hated for *My name's sake* (Matthew 10:22). This directs our attention to Christian believers not Jews because non-believing Jews do not recognize the name of Jesus.

If the church is raptured prior to the tribulation and Christ has already returned for His bride; then why do Matthew and John warn of Antichrists and false christs that deceive during the tribulation? Why worry about a false christ when Jesus has already returned? There is a warning to beware of false christs during the tribulation because the Rapture has not yet occurred and the believers are possible targets of deception as well.

C. Evidence from Thessalonians

> *Now, brethren, concerning the coming of our Lord Jesus Christ and our gathering together to Him, we ask you, not to be soon shaken in mind or troubled, either by spirit or by word or by letter, as if from us, as though the <u>day of Christ</u> had come. Let no one deceive you by any means; for that day will not come unless the <u>falling away</u> comes first, and the man of sin is revealed, the son of perdition, who opposes and exalts himself above all that is called God or that is worshipped, so that he sits as God in the temple of God, showing himself that he is God (2 Thessalonians 2:1-4).*

FALLING AWAY

A falling away must occur first. The Greek word for a falling away is apostasia. The word apostasia (αποστασια) means apostasy, a falling away, not a taking away. In writing a bill of divorcement, or a bill of apostasy (Βιβλιον τουφ αποστασιου) the word apostasia was used, not because the wife was taken away, but because there was found between the marriage couple a falling away, a falling out, or a rebellion. A bill of divorcement was given because the bride or the groom was found unfaithful, and had committed adultery. This qualifies the word apostasy as a falling away not a taking away.

Pre-tribulationalists distort the meaning of apostasia in the above verse when they translate it to mean *the taking away* instead of *falling away* and apply the *taking away* to the Rapture of the church. Their misinterpretation must be for the sole purpose of placing the rapture of the church before the tribulation. With a pre-tribulation interpretation the verse above would read:

Concerning the coming of our Lord Jesus Christ and our gathering unto him, be not shaken in mind or troubled. For the rapture (day of Christ) shall not come until there be a rapture (apostasia) first.

In other words, the pre-tribulationalists are saying that a taking away will come first before our gathering unto him. This does not make sense and contradicts the pre-tribulation view.

It also contradicts the consolation that Paul is providing for the church. If *apostasia* means *taking away*, as in a rapture, then the fears that Paul was endeavouring to disarm are nullified. The Thessalonian church was afraid that they had already missed the rapture. It makes no sense to tell them that the *taking away* will occur before *our gathering unto him*. It gives no comfort.

WAY OF ESCAPE

God does provide a way of escape, but the escape is not a pre-tribulation rapture. There is a "rest" to the people of God, but this "rest" is not fulfilled until the foe has been destroyed on the day of the Lord. That same day, Christ shall be glorified in the saints at the second coming (2 Thessalonians 1:7).

And to you who are troubled rest with us: when the Lord Jesus shall be revealed from heaven with his mighty angels: In flaming fire taking vengeance on them that know not God; and that obey not the gospel of our Lord Jesus Christ; who shall be punished: with everlasting destruction from the presence of the Lord: and when he shall come to be glorified in his saints..." (2 Thessalonians 1:6-10).

IMMANENCE

The core defence of the pre-tribulation is *immanence*. The word means, *about to happen*. The word *immanence* is not used in scripture, but is further defined by pre-tribulationalists to mean that there is nothing more to be fulfilled in scripture before his coming. This view, according to pre-tribulationists, denies the signs in the heaven and in the earth that we are to look for as Christians, as having no application. The pre-tribulation rapture occurs first while ignoring Biblical prophecy concerning these many signs in the heavens.

One sign is the appearance of Antichrist before the day of Christ. Notice that 1 Thessalonians 2 uses the phrase *day of Christ* and does not use the phrase *day of the Lord*.

IN PAUL'S DAY

Some seemingly make a strong case for a pre-tribulation rapture by saying that Paul expected the Lord to come even in his day. The following verses are used to verify this erroneous point of view.

In a moment, in the twinkling of an eye, at the last trumpet, for the trumpet will sound and the dead will be raised incorruptible, and we shall be changed (1 Corinthians 15:52).

For this we say to you by the word of the Lord, that we who are alive and remain until the coming of the Lord will by no means precede those who are asleep (1 Thessalonians 4:15).

Yes, Paul seems to identify himself and the people of that day by the words "we shall be changed" and "we who are alive". But you cannot take a prophetical statement and interpret it so narrowly. Take the prophecies of Isaiah.

He is despised and rejected by men, a Man of sorrows and acquainted with grief. And we hid, as it were, our faces from Him. He was despised, and we did not esteem Him. Surely He has borne our griefs and carried our sorrows; yet we esteemed Him stricken, smitten by God, and afflicted. But He was wounded for our transgressions. He was bruised for our iniquities. The chastisement for our peace was upon Him, and by His stripes we are healed (Isaiah 53:3-5).

I gave My back to those who struck Me, And My cheeks to those who plucked out the beard; I did not hide My face from shame and spitting (Isaiah 50:6).

The pronouns "we" in Isaiah do not refer to Isaiah and the people of that day. Isaiah did not give his back and cheeks to the scorners, but Christ did. Even the past tense of the verbs is really future incidents. Prophetical statements must be interpreted carefully. In this light, Paul was not necessarily saying that the Lord was coming in their lifetime. Paul knew that he would go to Rome and die for the cause of Christ. Paul also gave credence to the signs that were to happen before the Harvest Rapture.

23. Why I Don't Believe in a Pre-wrath Rapture But the Harvest Rapture

The Harvest Rapture Summary

1. There is no scripture that proves, beyond a doubt, that the rapture shall happen before the tribulation.

2. The saints have been persecuted and they cry out for God's vengeance at the end of the seal period. God had not yet avenged the evil man by the end of the seal period: therefore, the church must go through the seal period. See chapter three.

3. If men today have not the strength to believe and live a strong Christian life, they will not be able to endure persecution and find faith during the tribulation. At the end time, Christ will not be able to find faith. Nevertheless, when the Son of Man comes, will He really find faith on the earth? (Luke 18:8).

4. Tribulation is a biblical word that applies to the church and the people of God throughout the New Testament (see chapter 2).

5. Why does Matthew warn of false christ's during tribulation days, if Christ has already come before the tribulation?

6. The early church fathers believed that the church would go through the tribulation of the Antichrist.

7. Daniel makes a distinction between *my people*, referring to the Jews, and the *saints* (see chapter 22).

8. "Then they will deliver you up to tribulation and kill you, and you will be hated by all nations for My name's sake" (Matthew 24:9). Matthew promises that you will face tribulation and persecution for My name sake, for the sake of Jesus' name. These must be believers.

9. The day of Christ is the Rapture, and the day of the Lord is Armageddon (chapter 20). The day of Christ or the Rapture shall not come until there be a falling away and the man of sin is revealed (see chapter 20, 22).

10. The wheat and chaff shall grow together until the end. A pre-tribulation rapture is not the end.

11. The rainbow at the end of the seals is a sign to the believer not the unbeliever.

12. If no one repents during the trumpets and vials of God's wrath, then how could there be new saints during the tribulation under the Antichrist? If the Spirit of God is taken away from the earth in a pre-tribulation rapture, then how could anyone find repentance? This would make God unjust. The Spirit shall still strive with men during the tribulation but they refuse mercy.

13. Some of the seven churches of Revelation did experience tribulation.

14. The Harvest Rapture (Rev. 14:14) satisfies the demands of Scripture (see Chapter 13).

15. The pre-tribulation view of Revelation 4:1-2, is based upon a false method of interpretation (see chapter 19).

16. The Rapture and resurrection must take place at the same time. This discredits the pre-tribulation view.

17. Why was the Revelation written if the tribulation wasn't written for the benefit of the church? John was told to give his writings to the seven churches of Asia Minor. The unsaved world doesn't heed Bible prophecy.

18. Just before the 3½ years of the abomination, the 144,000 are raptured as the firstfruits. We know that from the Bible. How can these be the firstfruits of the rapture if there is a pre-tribulation rapture? (See chapter 19.)

19. We are told that Christ is still coming after the tenth chapter of Revelation. (See chapter 19).

20. The so-called rapture of Revelation four is only *in spirit*. The real Rapture is a bodily Rapture.

24. A Conclusion: What Must We Do?

The Judge of all the earth shall work divine justice. Trust Him. Tribulation, remember, does not include the wrath of God. Tribulation can refer to the seal period and the seven years of the trumpet period. Tribulation does not deny men the justice of God, but promotes justice. Tribulation martyrs die at the hand of the enemy, but are resurrected to reign with Christ. Death is not the end of life but the beginning. Justice at the end of time becomes righteous and good at the hand of the Almighty God.

Christ is faithful, as judge of all. Christ is faithful to warn of evil and false ways. When we stop blaming Christ for the injustices of tribulation, we shall rejoice in the great victories ahead for every believer. Rejoice in the resurrection and Rapture of the church. Rejoice in the promises of eternal life.

The appointed time is at hand; we must never fear, but look up, for our redemption draws near. Tribulation is a time of victory, justice, and eternal deliverance from our corrupt society today. The cry for justice shall be silenced by the rule of Jesus Christ. The injustices of this world shall burn in hell. Satan and the Antichrist shall finally be bound in hell.

The church's great hope is the day of Christ, but the great dread of the heathen is the dreadful day of the Lord. Both are the result of divine justice.

What must we do when we find ourselves in tribulation?

1. Our duty to Christ demands faithfulness in a fallen world, trust even during times of tribulation, patience as we await the redemption of our bodies, and steadfastness in keeping the faith until we are called into glory. Our reward shall be worth every trial and tribulation when we see Jesus.

2. It is the patience of the saints that is honored in Revelation. God knows what He is doing. Patience is a great secret to survival.

3. We must never allow apostasy to shake our foundation and belief in the word of God.

4. We must continue to look upward for our redemption is very close.

5. We must never forget that God is on the side of the believer and righteous man.

6. We must never stop praying that God will manifest victory in our life and in the lives of others. We must constantly witness that others may see the truth in Christ.

7. The earth shall shake and tremor more and more. Men will repent and believe, or they will curse God. But we must encourage one another, and comfort one another in difficult times.

8. Remember that our warfare in not in the flesh with carnal weapons like the enemy. We must be always clothed with the armor of a Christian soldier -- with righteousness, faith, the word which is the sword of the Spirit, prayer, with the breastplate of truth, and with the helmet of salvation.

9. Never forget that God is enthroned above all kings and kingdoms and He is in control.

10. When you see the temple being rebuilt, store up food for 3 ½ years, and pay bills for the same duration. You can't buy or sell without the mark.

11. Look up, for your redemption is near.

He is the Alpha and Omega, the beginning and the end. Amen. Come quickly Lord Jesus.
For more charts and Graphs go to http:www.apocalyptictremors.com.
If you would like some charts in colour email me:
carolyn@apocalyptictremors.com

Appendix 1:

The Early Church Fathers Speak

A. *The Early Church Fathers Speak on the Time of the End*

Irenaeus: "For in as many days as this world was made, in so many thousand; years shall it be concluded....and in six days created things were completed; it is evident, therefore, that they will come to an end at the sixth thousand year."[1]

Lactantius: "the six thousandth year is not yet completed, and that when this number is completed the consummation must take place, and the condition of human affairs be remodeled for the better, the proof of which must first be related that the matter itself may be plain.....Therefore, since all the words of God were completed in six days, the world must continue in its present state through six ages. That is six thousand years. For the great day of God is limited by a circle of a thousand years, ...and at the end of the six thousandth year all wickedness must be abolished from the earth, and righteousness reign for a thousand years...." "Because the Roman name, by which the world is now ruled, will be taken away from the earth, and the government return to Asia; and East will again bear rule, and West be reduced to servitude." [2]

B. *The Early Church Fathers and the Church in the Tribulation*

Athenasius: "The people of Athenasius' day thought that Constantius may have been the Antichrist because he took the lead of Bishops and presided in Ecclesiastical cause, laid waste the Churches and transgressed Canons. He said that the horror of the persecution might be only excelled by the son of lawlessness, meaning the antichrist. He not only places the church at the hands of the antichrist; but also associates the abomination of desolation with the church." [3]

Cyprian: "...therefore are they before the throne of God and serve Him day and night in His temple. But if the assembly of the Christian martyrs is shown and proved to be so great, let no one think it a hard or a difficult thing to become a martyr, when he sees that the crowd of martyrs cannot be numbered." [4]

Hippolytus: "..and how he shall work error among the people, gathering them from the ends of the earth; and he shall stir up tribulation and persecution against the saints" [5]

Hippolytus: "...shall be sent through every city and country to destroy the faithful; and the saints shall travel from the west to the east, and shall be driven in persecution from the east to the south, while others shall conceal themselves in the mountains and caves; and the abomination shall war against them everywhere, and shall cut them off by the sea and by land by his decree, and shall endeavor by every means to destroy them out of the world; and they shall not be able any longer to sell their own property, nor to buy from strangers, unless one keeps and carries with him the name of the Beast, or bears its mark upon his forehead. For then they shall all be driven out from place to place, and dragged from their own homes and haled into prison, and punished with all manner of punishment, and cast out from the whole world." These shall awake to everlasting life." [6]

Irenaeus: "...as stubble conduces towards the growth of the wheat, and its straw, by means of combustion, serve for working gold. And therefore, when in the end the Church shall be suddenly caught up from this, it is said, ... For this is the last contest of the righteous, in which when they overcome, they are crowned with incorruption." [7]

Barnabus: "Thus, He saith, they that desire to see me, and to attain unto my Kingdom, must lay hold on me through tribulation and affliction." [8]

Shepherd of Hermas: "Blessed are ye as many as endure patently the great tribulation that cometh, and as many as shall not deny them life." [9]

Augustine: "Truly Jesus Himself shall extinguish by his presence that last persecution which is to be made by Antichrist. But on the other hand, it is no less rash to affirm that there will be some persecutions by kings besides that last one, about which no Christian is in doubt....Truly Jesus Himself shall extinguish by His presence that last persecution which is to be made by antichrist." [10]

Victorinus: "He speaks of Elias the prophet, who is the precursor of the times of

Antichrist, for the restoration and establishment of the churches from the great and intolerable persecution."[11]

Turtulian: "...and that the Beast Antichrist with his false prophet may wage war on the Church of God;"[12]

C. Early Church Fathers on the Antichrist

Hippolytus: "...on account of his tyranny and violence. For the deceiver seeks to liken himself in all things to the Son of God. Christ is a lion, so Antichrist is also a lion; Christ is a king, so Antichrist is also a king. The Savior was manifested as a lamb; so he too in like manner, will appear as a lamb, though within he is a wolf. The Savior came into the world in the circumcision, and he will come in the same manner. The Lord sent apostles among all the nations, and he in like manner will send false apostles. The Savior gathered together the sheep that were scattered abroad, and he in like manner will bring together a people that is scattered abroad. The Lord gave a seal to those who believed on Him; and he will give one in like manner. The Savior appeared in the form of man, and he too will come in the form of a man. The Savior raised up and showed His holy flesh like a temple, and he will raise a temple of stone in Jerusalem." [13]

Lactantius: "He shall harass the word with an intolerable rule; shall mingle things divine and human; shall contrive things impious to relate, and detestable; shall meditate new designs in his breast, that he may establish the government for himself; he will change the laws, and appoint his own; he will contaminate, plunder, spoil, and put to death." [14]

Hippolytus: "He will be harsh, severe, passionate, wrathful, terrible, inconstant, dread, morose, hateful, abominable, savage, vengeful, iniquitous. And, bent on casting the whole race of men into the pit of perdition, he will multiply false signs." [15]

Irenaeus: "For he being endued with all the power of the devil, shall come, not as a righteous king, nor as a legitimate king, in subjection to God, but an impious, unjust, and lawless one; as an apostate, iniquitous and murderous; as a robber, concentrating in himself all satanic apostasy, and setting aside idols to persuade men that he himself is God, raising up himself as the only idol, having in himself the multifarious errors of the other idols."

"an apostate and a robber, is anxious to be adored as God; and that, although a mere slave, he wishes himself to be proclaimed as a king. For he being endued with all the power of the devil, shall come, not as a righteous king, nor a legitimate king in subjection to God, but an impious, unjust, and lawless one; as an apostate, iniquitous, and murderous, as a robber, concentrating in himself satanic apostasy, and seeking aside idols to persuade that he himself is God raising up himself as the only idol, having in himself the multifarious errors of the other idols. This he does, in order that they who do worship the devil by means of many abominations, may serve himself by this one idol, of whom the apostle thus speaks in the second Epistle to the Thessalonians."

"And there is therefore in this beast, when he comes, a recapitulation made of all sorts of iniquity and of every deceit, in order that all apostate power, flowing into and being shut up in him, may be sent into the furnace of fire...since he sums up in his own person all the commixture of wickedness which took place previous to the deluge, due to the apostasy of the angels And Antichrist also sums up every error of devised idols since the flood, together with the slaying of the prophets and the cutting off of the just." [16]

D. Early church Fathers on the Mark of the Beast

Irenaeus: "And therefore, when in the end the church shall be suddenly caught up from this, it is said, 'There shall be tribulation such as has not been since the beginning, neither shall be." For this is the last contest of the righteous, in which, when they overcome, they are crowned with incorruption. But when this antichrist shall have devastated all things in this world, he will reign for three years and six months, and sit in the temple at Jerusalem; and then the Lord will come from heaven in the clouds, in the glory of the Father, sending this man and those who follow him into the lake of fire: but bringing in for the righteous the times of the kingdom, that is, the rest the hallowed seventh day They shall lay Babylon waste, and burn her with fire, and shall give their kingdom to the Beast, and put the Church to flight.." [17]

Hippolytus: "And the churches, too, will wail with a mighty lamentation, because neither 'oblation nor incense' is attended to, nor a service acceptable to God; but the sanctuaries of the churches will become like a garden-watcher's hut, and the holy body and blood of Christ will not be shown in those days. The public service of God shall be extinguished, psalmody shall cease, the reading of the Scriptures shall not be heard: but for men there shall be darkness, and lamentation on lamentation, and woe on woe and the whole world, in fine, comes to the consummation, what remains but the manifestation of our Lord and Savior Jesus Christ, the Son of God, from heaven, for whom we have hoped." [18]

"And by reason of the scarcity of food, all will go to him and worship him; and he will put his mark on their right hand and on their forehead, that no one may put the sign of the honorable cross upon his forehead with his right hand; but his hand is bound. And from that time he shall not have power to seal anyone of his members, but he shall be attached to the deceiver, and shall serve him: and in him there is no repentance. But such an one is lost at once to God and to men, and the deceiver will give them scanty food by reason of his abominable seal." [19]

"Then will he send the cohorts of the demons among mountains and caves and dens of the earth, to track out those who have been concealed from his eyes, and to bring them forward to worship him. And those who yield to him he will seal with his seal; but those who refuse to submit to him he will consume with incomparable pains and bitterest torments and machination, such as never have been, nor have reached the ear of man, nor have been seen by the eye of mortals." [20]

"He will also enwrap righteous men with the books of the prophets, and thus burn them and power will be given him to desolate the whole earth for 42 months. When these things shall so happen, then the righteous and the followers of truth shall separate themselves from the wicked, and flee into solitude's." [21]

Lactantius: "As many as shall believe him and unite themselves to him, shall be marked by him as sheep; but they who shall refuse his mark will either flee to the mountains, or being seized, will be slain with studied tortures. He will also enwrap righteous men with the books of the prophets, and thus burn them; and power will be given him to desolate the whole earth for forty two months...then the righteous and the followers of truth shall separate themselves from the wicked, and flee into solitude's." [22]

Victorianus: "He shall cause also that a golden image of Antichrist shall be placed in the temple at Jerusalem, and that the apostate angel should enter, and thence utter voices and oracles."[23]

E. Early Church Fathers and the Tribe of Dan

Thus did the Scriptures preach before-time of this lion and lion's whelp? And in like manner also we find it written regarding Antichrist. For Moses speaks thus: "Dan is a lion's whelp, and he shall leap from Bashan." But that no one may err by supposing that this is said of the Saviour, let him attend carefully to the matter. "Dan," he says, "is a lion's whelp" and in naming the tribe of Dan, he declared clearly the tribe from which the Antichrist is destined to spring. For as Christ springs from the tribe of Judah, so the Antichrist is to spring from the tribe of Dan. And that the case stands thus, we see also from the words of Jacob: "Let Dan be a serpent, lying upon the ground, biting the horse's heel." What then is meant by the serpent but Antichrist, that deceiver who is mentioned in Genesis who deceived Eve and

217

supplanted Adam (bruised Adam's heel)? But since it is necessary to prove this assertion by sufficient testimony, we shall not shrink from the task. Victorianus interprets Jeremiah as indicating that he is from the tribe of Dan. [24]

"The snorting of his horses was heard from Dan. The whole land trembled at the sound of the neighing of His strong ones; for they have come and devoured the land and all that is in it, the city and those who dwell in it" Jeremiah 8:16).

That it is in reality out of the tribe of Dan, then, that that tyrant and king, that dread judge, that son of the devil, is destined to spring and arise, the prophet testifies when he says, "Dan shall judge his people, as he is also one tribe in Israel." But someone may say that this refers to Samson, who sprang from the tribe of Dan, and judged the people twenty years. Well, the prophecy had its partial fulfillment in Samson, but its complete fulfillment is reserved for Antichrist. For Jeremiah also speaks to this effect: "From Dan we are to hear the sound of the swiftness of his horses: the whole land trembled at the sound of the neighing, of the driving of his horses." And another prophet says: "He shall gather together all his strength, from the east even to the west. They whom he calls, and they whom he calls not, shall go with him. He shall make the sea white with the sails of his ships, and the plain black with the shields of his armaments. And whosoever shall oppose him in war shall fall by the sword." That these things, then, are said of no one else but that tyrant, and shameless one, and adversary of God, we shall show in what follows. [25]

Appendix 2:

Extra Charts

Chapter 18
Fall of Babylon
Come out from among

Chapter 14
angel warnings
1. fear God
2. Babylon is fallen
3. Don't take the mark
Patience of saints

Chapter 17
Scarlett woman
Antichrist on scarlet beast
fornication, abominations
drunk with blood of saints
make war with lamb

Abomination of Desolation: Continues

Wrath of Satan Kingdom of Satan

Fulfilling God's Purposes

Trumpets 5,6,7

Harvest Rapture

**Chapter 14
144,000 Raptured**

Reaping the Grapes
All who take the mark thrown
into the wrath of God

**Rapture and Resurrection
Saints, Church,
Reaping of harvest**

1. Loathsome Sores
2. Seas turn to blood
3. Rivers, strings became
blood
4. Sun scorches men
5. Darkness
6. Euphrates dries up,
demonic frogs deception
7.It is done, War with the
lamb
45 days?

Christ on White Horse
Supper of the great God
10 kings under Antichrist
defeated
Antichrist and false
prophet cast into lake of
fire.

1, 2, 3, 4, 5, 6, 7

Vials of God's Wraths

Day of the Lord

Vials of God's Wrath

Armageddon

King of Kings and Lord of Lords

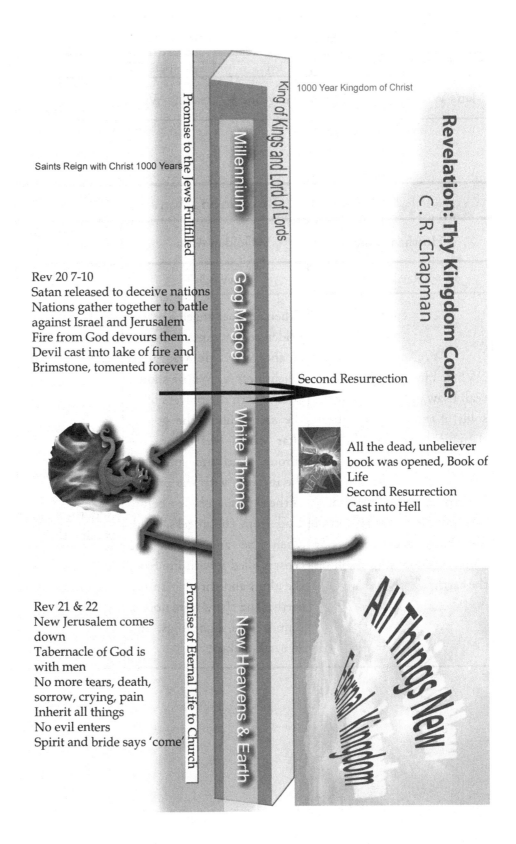

Revelation: Thy Kingdom Come
C. R. Chapman

1000 Year Kingdom of Christ

King of Kings and Lord of Lords

Promise to the Jews Fulfilled

Saints Reign with Christ 1000 Years

Millennium

Gog Magog

White Throne

New Heavens & Earth

Promise of Eternal Life to Church

Rev 20 7-10
Satan released to deceive nations
Nations gather together to battle
against Israel and Jerusalem
Fire from God devours them.
Devil cast into lake of fire and
Brimstone, tomented forever

Second Resurrection

All the dead, unbeliever
book was opened, Book of
Life
Second Resurrection
Cast into Hell

Rev 21 & 22
New Jerusalem comes
down
Tabernacle of God is
with men
No more tears, death,
sorrow, crying, pain
Inherit all things
No evil enters
Spirit and bride says 'come'

All Things New
Eternal Kingdom

Separating Vengeance from Wrath			
7 Seals	Trumpets 1-4	Trumpets 5-7	Vials of Wrath
Man's Wrath	Christ's Vengeance	Satan's Wrath	God's Wrath of Christ's Wrath

Revelation Altars		
Heathen Altar	Golden Altar	Altar in Temple in Jerusalem
Rev. 6:9	Rev 8:3-5	Rev 11:1
"When He opened the fifth seal, I saw under the altar the souls of those who had been slain for the word of God and for the testimony which they held. And they cried with a loud voice, saying, "How long, O Lord, holy and true, until You judge and avenge our blood on those who dwell on the earth?" "	"Then another angel, having a golden censer, came and stood at the altar. He was given much incense, that he should offer it with the prayers of all the saints upon the golden altar which was before the throne. And the smoke of the incense, with the prayers of the saints, ascended before God from the angel's hand. Then the angel took the censer, filled it with fire from the altar, and threw it to the earth. And there were noises, thunderings, lightnings, and an earthquake."	"Then I was given a reed like a measuring rod. And the angel stood, saying, "Rise and measure the temple of God, the altar, and those who worship there."

Trumpets 1-4	Trumpet 5	Trumpet 6	Trumpet 7
Vengeance of Christ	1st Woe Demonic Locust	2nd Woe Demonic Horsemen	3rd Woe Abomination of Desolation
2 years	5 months	1 year, 1 month, one day, one hour	3 1/2 years

Trumpet Agenda			
During Trumpets 1-4			**During Trumpet 7**
Christ's Vengeance			Wrath of Satan
Two Witnesses warn of coming judgment.	Trumpets 5,6	Breaking of Treaty	The Antichrist and false prophet empowered by Satan to rule the world.
Temple is rebuilt			Temple is desecrated.
Time of peace to the Jews.			Great persecution under the Antichrist and great injustices.

	Seals	Trumpets	Vials	Heaven
SUN	Black as sackcloth of hair	1/3 smitten, Shone for 2/3's of the day (8:12). Smoke from the abyss darkened the sun (9:12).	Scorched men with fire (16:8).	Shall not light upon man. (7:16) No sun
MOON	Became as blood	1/3 smitten Shone 2/3's of the day		No moon (21:23).
STARS	Fell to earth (6:1)	1/3 smitten, Shone for 1/2's of the day. Star wormwood fell (8:10). Star falls and abyss opens (9:1). Satan threw 1/3 of stars to the earth.		No night. Christ is the bright and morning star (22:16).

The Rapture	Jewish Harvest
144,000 raptured	Firstfruits
The Harvest Rapture	Feast of Ingathering
7 wraths of God, 7 weeks or 49 days	Offerings for Seven Days

The Beast from the Sea Rev. 13:1-10	The Beast from the Earth Rev 13:11-18
The Antichrist	The False Prophet
From the Sea. (From Gentile nations or from the abyss.)	From the earth (From the Jewish Nation.)
Leopard like, feet of a bear, mouth of a lion, (world empires of Daniel – Babylon, Persia, Greece, Rome	Two horns like a lamb (religious deception).
Empowered by the dragon (Satan)	Authority of the first beast (the Antichrist).
Seven heads and ten horns (the seventh kingdom, Roman Empire possibly).	
Ten crowns on his head (Ten kingdoms that rule for one hour with the Beast	
Blasphemous name (the Antichrist)	Spoke like a dragon
One head was wounded and was healed.	Performs great signs and wonders, makes fire come down from heaven, deceives men.
Men worshiped the dragon and Beast	Causes all to worship the beast and make an image to him. All that don't worship the Beast he causes to be killed.
	All to receive mark of the Beast on the hand or forehead if they want to buy or sell.

Comparison of Firstfruits	
Firstfruits of the Old Testament	**Firstfruits of Rapture: 144,000**
Celebrate the feast of weeks.	
Firstfruits of wheat harvest at year's end (Exodus 23:22)	144,000 are the Firstfruits gathered at the end, at the end of the 7th trumpet.
Firstfruits brought to temple (Ex. 23:22).	144,000 raptured into heaven
No grain offering was to be made with leaven that represented sin.	144,000 as the Firstfruits were without blame, virgins.
Firstfruits not burned for a sweet aroma (Lev. 2:12).	They were raptured. They did not die.
Grain offering seasoned with salt (Lev. 2:13).	
They were to give grain- green heads beaten from full heads.	144,000 tried and tested
Offering of firstfuits was to be made on the day after the 7th Sabbath (Lev. 23:15).	144,000 redeemed from the earth at the end of the 7th trumpet at harvest-time (Rev. 14)

Antichrist	Christ
Antichrist receives great authority from Satan (Rev. 13:2).	All authority from God the Father, (Matthew 28:18, John 5:27, John 12:49).
Brings false peace	Peace is eternal and internal in the heart. (John. 14:27, 16:33, Rom. 5:1, Eph. 2:14).
Rules over every tribe, tongue, and nation.	TRIBE: Break down tribal warfare as in Africa, TONGUE: dissolve ethnic fighting as in Europe, Asia NATION: Cause all wars to cease between nations.
Worker of miracles by the power of Satan	Works miracles by the power of God
Sits where Christ shall sit and desecrates the temple	Sits upon the throne of David in the city of Jerusalem Taught in the temple and cast out money changers.

He will sit in the temple of Yahweh and declare that He is Yahweh (2 Thess. 2:4). Profane temple (Matt. 24:15).	He is Yahweh Taught in the temple and cast out money changers.
Full of pride	Full of humility
The Antichrist exalts himself above all the gods of the earth. He regards not the god of his fathers, or the goddesses of nature, nor any god (Dan. 11:37). He exalts himself above everything that is called god (2 Thess. 2:4, Dan. 11:36–37; 2 Thess. 2:4, 11; 3:51). Today, everything is called god. He exalts himself above the God of gods. Dan 11:36	Let this mind be in you which was also in Christ Jesus, who, being in the form of God, did not consider it robbery to be equal with God, but made Himself of no reputation, taking the form of a bondservant, and coming in the likeness of men. And being found in appearance as a man, He humbled Himself and became obedient to the point of death, even the death of the cross (Phil. 2:5-8).
Promoter of evil Antichrist will be the embodiment of all evil. Destroyer, a murderer, a liar and full of deceit.	Righteousness is the scepter of His kingdom. Christ was the incarnation of all righteousness and love. God does not lie.
Hater of Women, not the desire of women (Dan 11:37).	All made one in Christ Jesus, Jews, Gentiles, rich and poor, male and female, slave and free (Gal 3:28).
He will do everything according to his own selfish will (Dan. 11:36).	Came to do the Father's Will (John 6:38).
Master of deceit. (2 Thess. 2:10).	Speaks only truth. (John 14:6).
He will not regard the God of his fathers. (Dan. 11:37).	Recognized the God of the Old Testament as the God of the New
He will be an intellectual genius (Dan. 8:23).He will be an oratorical genius (Dan. 11:36).	Matthew 7:28-29 And so it was, when Jesus had ended these sayings, that the people were astonished at His teaching, for He taught them as one having authority, and not as the scribes (Mark 1:22).
He will be a political genius (Rev. 17:11–12).	He will be King of kings.
He will be a commercial genius (Dan. 11:43; Rev. 13:16–17).	My God shall supply all your needs according to His riches in glory.

He will be a military genius (Rev. 6:2; 13:2).	The Antichrist will be utterly crushed by the Lord Jesus Christ at the Battle of Armageddon (Rev.19).
He will make a seven-year covenant with Israel but will break it (Dan. 9:27).	God makes everlasting covenants.
He will be a religious genius (2 Thess. 2:4; Rev. 13:8).	He is omnipotent and omniscient.
He will attempt to destroy all of Israel (Rev. 12).	God saves Israel and the believer.
He will briefly rule over all nations (Ps. 2; Dan. 11:36; Rev. 13:16).	King of kings and Lord of lords.
He will be the first creature thrown into the lake of fire (Rev. 19:20)	God created hell for the devil and his angels.
Speaks blasphemy (Rev 13:5) With pride he blasphemes God, robs all worship, and makes war against the King of kings.	Jesus honors the Father (John 8:49).

Eden	Millennium	New Heaven
Adam and Eve walked with God.	Christ will rule on earth from Jerusalem. We shall reign with Him.	We will be with Christ and God.
Sun, moon, and stars	Sun, Moon, Stars	No sun, moon or stars
Man is made in the image of God but disobeys.		
Satan tempts man	Man will be ruled by Iron rod of Christ.	
Satan can't tempt Man. He is bound.	Satan has been cast into hell forever.	
Life span of man decreases with time.	Live to be old	Live forever
Dirt streets	Dirt streets	Streets of gold
Marriage	Marriage	No marriage
Man works by the sweat of his brow.	Ruled by the righteous who took not the mark.	Glorify God, praise Him

Tree of knowledge of good and evil		Tree of life that bears fruit always and leaves for the healing of the nations.
Curse of sin	Sin exists	No more curse. No more sin in the New Jerusalem.
Man becomes a living soul	Man continues	Man becomes immortal beings.
Results of sin exist - sorrow, death, pain	Sin but without Satan	No sorrow, no death, no crying, no pain
Adam walked with God	Temple of millennium	No temple

Revelation 7 Just before Seventh Seal and Trumpets	Revelation 21-22 New Heavens and Earth
Seal of the servants of God on their foreheads to protect them (v.3).	His name shall be on their foreheads (21:2:4).
Listing of the twelve tribes of Israel (v.5-8).	Names of 12 tribes on gates (v12).
People from all nations standing before the throne of God having come out of tribulation (9).	The leaves of the tree were for the healing of the nations (v.22:2).
And the nations of those who are saved shall walk in its light (v.21:24).	
Many people standing before the throne of God (v.9, 15)	A river proceeds from the throne of God (v1).
Overcomers serve God night and day (v.15).	His servants shall serve Him (v3).
Serve in His temple (v.15).	No temple, the Lord God Almighty and the Lamb are its temple (v.21:22)
Promise that God shall dwell with man (v.15	
The Lamb is in their midst (v.17)	The throne of God and of the Lamb shall be there (v.3)
Promise: Shall not hunger or thirst anymore but be lead to living fountains of water (v16, 17)	God will wipe away every tear from their eyes. (v4)
Promise: Serve Him day and night in His sanctuary (v.15).	Servants shall reign forever and ever (v.5).

The Authority of the LION in Revelation	
First Beast of seals like a Lion	Revelation 4:7 The first living creature was like a lion, the second living creature like a calf, the third living creature had a face like a man, and the fourth living creature was like a flying eagle.
Jesus: Lion of the tribe of Judah.	Revelation 5:5 But one of the elders said to me, "Do not weep. Behold, the Lion of the tribe of Judah, the Root of David, has prevailed to open the scroll and to loose its seven seals."
Demonic locust had teeth like a lion.	Revelation 9:8 They had hair like women's hair, and their teeth were like lions' teeth.
Demonic horse had heads of lions.	Revelation 9:17 A nd thus I saw the horses in the vision: those who sat on them had breastplates of fiery red, hyacinth blue, and sulfur yellow; and the heads of the horses were like the heads of lions; and out of their mouths came fire, smoke, and brimstone.
Angel with the book spoke like a lion.	Revelation 10:3 … and cried with a loud voice, as when a lion roars. When he cried out, seven thunders uttered their voices.
The Antichrist beast had a mouth of a lion	Revelation 13:2 Now the beast which I saw was like a leopard, his feet were like the feet of a bear, and his mouth like the mouth of a lion. The dragon gave him his power, his throne, and great authority.

Is There a Contradiction?	
Matthew 13:30-43	**Rev 14:14-20**
1st Tares gathered	1st Rapture, wheat is reaped
2nd Wheat gathered	2nd Grapes cast into the vials of God's wrath
but	1st Evil men are cast into hell 2nd Heaven, New Jerusalem (Rev 21).
	Second death, (Rev. 20:11-14).

	Rev.Text	Who is Present?	What Happened?	When
			Seven Throne Scenes	
1st	4:1-5:14	24 elders, 4 best, lamb, God, 10,000's of angels	Praising God Proclamation of the ne who is worthy to open the seals.	Before the 1st seal.
2nd	7:9-8:6	The above plus a great multitude no man could number of all nations and kindred clothed in white robes washed in the blood and with palms in their hands. These came out of great tribulation.	Praised God's salvation and recognized the martyrs. Incense and prayers of the saints ascended	After the seal period
3rd	11:15-19	24 elders and great voices	Seven the angel sounded, 'the kingdoms of our Lord, and of his Christ. Elders praised God and prophesied. The temple of God was opened in heaven	After the resurrection of the two witnesses and at the beginning of the seventh trumpet.
4th	14:2-5	24 elders, 4 beasts 144,000	Song of the 144,000 sung	Just after the mark of the beast is given and the rapture of 144,000 and before the everlasting gospel is preached by angels
5th	15:1-5	Those who had victory over the mark of the beast	Song of Moses and the Lamb The temple of the tabernacle was opened in heaven	Just after the Harvest rapture. After the mark of the beast and before the vials of God's
6th	19:1-10	Much people in heaven, four beasts and 24 elders, voices of a great multitude	Praise for God's vengeance. Rejoicing that the marriage of the Lamb is come	Just before the second coming and the battle of Armageddon

Seven Throne Scenes				
	Rev.Text	Who is Present?	What Happened?	When
7th	20:4	Many who sat upon thrones. Martyrs. beheaded . 2. Those who did not take the mark, nor worshipped his image	People sitting upon thrones and judgment was given unto them	After the mark of the beast is given and before the millennium

Antiochus Epiphanes ca. 212–163 BC (Archetype of Antichrist)	Antichrist
Antiochus lived fourteen years in Rome and learned the foundational strategies that finally made the greatest Empire of history	The Antichrist also shall be a man that knows the ways of the world and the ways of Rome.
Durant, the famous historian has said, "Antiochus iv was both the most interesting and the most erratic of his line, a rare mixture of intellect, insanity, and charm." 1. He was a man of deceit. The Maccabees write, "and spake peaceable words unto them, but all was deceit.2 He deceives in the name of peace. Behind his back, he was called "Epimanes," meaning "madman."	He is worshipped, yet cunningly conquers to exalt himself. …and a mouth speaking pompous words (Daniel 7:8)
Antiochus enforced one law and culture. As an ardent Hellenist, he coerced his subjects to embrace Greek ideals and customs. He constrained Jews to participate in games that they regarded as indecent.3	…And shall intend to change times and law (Daniel 7:25).
He taxed Jews for 1/3 of their grain crops and ½ of their fruit.	Mark of the Beast shall be imposed upon all.

Antiochus Epiphanes ca. 212–163 BC (Archetype of Antichrist)	Antichrist
He seized Jerusalem without fighting, and plundered its wealth. Bacchides enforced these outrageous instructions with an innate ruthlessness, subjecting the Jews to many forms of injustice.	
Day after day he tortured distinguished citizens and publicly flaunted the spectacle of a captured city, until his criminal excesses provoked the victims to reprisals.5 They put to death certain women who had caused their children to be circumcised. And they hanged the infants about their necks, and rifled their houses, and slew them that had circumcised them...wherefore they chose rather to die, that they might not be defiled with meals, and that they might not profane the holy covenant: so then they died.6	The Antichrist being empowered by Satan will enact the wrath of Satan with unimaginable cruelty. Early Church Fathers write the following concerning the abomination by the Antichrist. He will enwrap righteous men with the books of the prophets, and thus burn them...” 7
Antiochus forced the worship of foreign deities and the partaking of food which the Jews deemed unclean. He pillaged the Temple treasury and banned the religious practice of daily sacrifices for three years and six months.	Antichrist will do sacrilege in the temple and rule for 3 ½ years.
Antiochus was invited to invade Judea by the sons of Tobias	Let us hope that renegade Jews will not betray Israel to the hand of the Antichrist.
According to Durant, Antiochus loved women.8	...but the Antichrist will hate women. Daniel prophesied that he would give 'no regard' to women, hence many feel that he may be homosexual. "He shall regard neither the God of his fathers nor the desire of women, nor regard any god; for he shall exalt himself above them all." The Antichrist also forces women to aid him in his battles; therefore, they turn against him.9

Antiochus Epiphanes ca. 212–163 BC (Archetype of Antichrist)	Antichrist
	Because they give not glory to him he will order incense pans to be set up by all everywhere, that no man among the saints may be able to buy or sell without first sacrificing; for this is what is meant by the mark.10
He forced the Jews to forsake their ancestral law of circumcision. Upon their altars he sacrificed swine, which was the gift to the vile god Dionysus. The Temple was rededicated to Zeus and used for the worship of Baal-Shamaen. A Greek altar was built over the Jewish altar. Jews who refused to eat pork or who possessed the Book of the Law were jailed or murdered. The Book of Law was burned. Jews were compelled to work on the Sabbath and to sing wild and sensuous songs in homage to Dionysus. He forced Jews to erect shrines to the Greek deities. The Samaritans, who complied with Antiochus, called their temple "The Temple of Jupiter Hellenios." 11	Under the eye of the spectators he will remove mountains from their places, he will walk on the sea with dry feet, he will bring down fire from heaven, he will turn the day into darkness and the night into day, he will turn the sun about where so ever he pleases; and in short, in presence of those who behold him, he will show all the elements of earth and sea to be subject to him in the power of his specious manifestation." 12 According to Hippolytus his passion and wrath is determined to destroy mankind. Hippolytus identifies him as the unrighteous judge of Luke 18. Irenaeus called Satan; "the apostate angel" and the Antichrist as one whom will "bruise" mankind like eggs that are crushed in the hand.13 Irenaeus saw him as the illegitimate king and leader of apostasy
Antiochus Epiphanes the king of Syria... issued a decree in those times, that all should set up shrines before their doors, and sacrifice, and that they should march in procession to the honor of Dionysus, waving chaplets of ivy; and that those who refused obedience should be put to death by strangulation and torture.14	"For when Antichrist is come, and of his own accord concentrates in his own person the apostasy, and accomplishes whatever he shall do according to his own will and choice, sitting also in the temple of God, so that his dupes may adore him as the Christ.15

Antiochus Epiphanes ca. 212–163 BC (Archetype of Antichrist)	Antichrist
Jews were to worship as Greeks or die.	The Antichrist will enforce not the worship of many gods but the worship of one, himself. An image will be erected to himself, the embodiment of Satan. The Antichrist will exalt himself to the position of the only God. Daily Sacrifices will be removed. The temple will be desolated with abominations.
Antiochus allured his whole kingdom to be "one people." 16	Antichrist, in order to establish worldwide power will follow the present day directives toward a one-world government and a one-world religion. His one faith will be the worship of himself, the satanic Antichrist.
Antiochus labelled his coins, "Antiochus Theos Epiphanes" meaning "God Made Manifest." 17 But, he did not dictate the worship of himself as god. Durant says that, "Antiochus thought of establishing and requiring the worship of himself as a god." 18	
	All worship the Antichrist and Satan.
Antiochus does not perform great wonders or miracles	

Antiochus Epiphanes ca. 212–163 BC (Archetype of Antichrist)	Antichrist
Antiochus came to a tragic end. According to Durant, Antiochus died in Persia on the way, of epilepsy, madness, or disease.19 However, according to Hippolytus, Antiochus was eaten up of worms and died. 20 In the histories of the Maccabees we read concerning the death of Antiochus. He proudly proclaimed that he would make Jerusalem the common burial place of the Jews, but the Almighty Lord smote him with pain of the bowels so that the worms rose up out of his body. He pleaded with God and said, "It is meet to be subject unto God, and that a man that is mortal should not proudly think of himself, as if he were God. 21 God did not heed his cries and promises. He died"	Antichrist shall be cast into Hell. The Antichrist also in his attempts to destroy the Jewish people, but will be cut off by the appearing of our Lord and Savoir Jesus Christ. He shall be cast into hell where "the worm dieth not and the fire is not quenched."
Walter K. Price thinks differently. The evidence is strong that Antiochus IV not only encouraged the worship of Zeus, but he encouraged the worship of himself also. On many of the coins that survive from that day can be seen the figure of Zeus whose features closely resemble those of Antiochus IV Epiphanes.	Antichrist performs great deceptive wonders. Irenaeus calls these wonders, magic. Let no one imagine that he performs these wonders by divine power, but by the working of magic ... since the demons and apostate spirits are at his service, he through their means, performs wonders. 22

End Notes for Chart: Antiochus and Antichrist

1. Will Durant, The Story of Civilization, The Like of Greece, New York, Simon & Schuster, 1939, p.573.

2. 1 Maccabees 1:30

3. Durant, The Life of Greece, p.581.

4. Daniel 11:24

5. Josephus, The Jewish War, Ed. Gaalya Cornfeld, Grand Rapids: Zondervan, 1982, pp. 13, 14.

6. 1 Maccabees 1:60-64.

7. Lactantius, Divine Institutes, p. 214.

8. Durant, The Life of Greece, p. 573.

9. Daniel 11:17, 37.

10. Hippolytus, Treatise on Christ and Antichrist,p, 214.

11. Merrill C. Tenney, New Testament Times, Grand Rapids: Eerdmans, c1965, p. 33.

12. Irenaeus, Anti-Nicene Fathers, vol. 1, Irenaeus Against Heresy, 557 bk. 5, chap. 28.

13. Irenaeus, Ante-Nicene Fathers, Irenaeus Against Heresies, 554, bk. 5, chapter 25.

14. Hippolytus, Treatise on Christ and Antichrist, p.214, paragraph 49.

15. 1 Maccabees 1:41

16. Hippolytus, Appendix to the Words of Hippolytus, chap. 26, p.249.

17. Durant, The Life of Greece, p. 574.

18. Ibid. p. 582.
    Communications, #204..

19. Durant, The Story of Civilization, vol. 2, The Life of Greece, p.574.

20. Hippolytus, Treatise on Christ and Antichrist, p. 214

21. 2 Maccabees 9:12.

22. Irenaeus, Irenaeus Against Heresy, p.557.

ENDNOTES

CHAPTER 1: APOCALYPSE OF JESUS CHRIST

1. Elwell, W. A., & Comfort, P. W., *Tyndale Bible Dictionary*, Tyndale reference library. Wheaton, Illinois: Tyndale House Publishers, 2001, p. 68.

2. Mays, J. L., Harper & Row, Society of Biblical Literature. *Harper's Bible Commentary*. San Francisco: Harper & Row, 1996.

3. Swete, H. B. *The Apocalypse of St. John*, Electronic, 2nd Ed.. New York: The Macmillan Company, 1907, p.135. See Appendix 3.

CHAPTER 2: UNDERSTANDING TRIBULATION

1. Shepherd of Hermas 20:3.

2. Shepherd of Hermas 10.

3. Shepherd of Hermas 6:1.

CHAPTER 3: CRY FOR JUSTICE

1. Josephus, F., & Whiston, W., *The Works of Josephus, Complete and Unabridged*. Peabody: Hendrickson. 1996, Book 14, chapter 2, ABS CdRom.

CHAPTER 4: IMAGE OF THE SEAL PERIOD

1. Roberts, Alexander. Ante-Nicene Fathers, Vol. 7, *Commentary on the Apocalypse*, Electronic Ed., Eerdmans: Grand Rapids, Reprint 1986, p.348.

2. Vincent, M. R., *Word Studies in the New Testament*, vol. 2. Bellingham, WA: Logos Research Systems, Inc. 2002: p.478.

3. Marvin R. Vincent. *The Writings of John, Word Studies in the New Testament*, Vol. 2, Peabody: Hendrickson, 476.

4. Vincent, *Word Studies in the New Testament*, p.479.

Chapter 5: The Great Falling Away

1. Zodhiates, S., *The Complete Word Study Dictionary: New Testament*, Electronic Edition. Chattanooga, TN: AMG Publishers, 2000.

Chapter 6: Four Horsemen of the Apocalypse

1. Strauss, Lehman. *The Book of the Revelation*, Electronic Ed., Neptune: Loizeaux Brothers, 1964, p.135.

2. Marvin R. Vincent. *Word Studies in the New Testament*, Electronic Ed., Vol. 2. Grand Rapids: Eerdmans, p. 494.

3. Gowans, Stephen .*California; Truth behind White Horse of Conquering*. http://www.uspoliticsonline.net/showthread.php?p=446773

4. Weilechowski , Aimee. *The 1983 Trial of Alija Izetbegovic in Context*, Institute on East Central Europe: Columbia University, N.Y., March 1996. http://www.ciaonet.org/conf/ieoc03/iec03_04-96.html

5. Alija Izetbegovic, http://www.srpska-mreza.com/library/facts/alija.html From http://freetruth.50webs.org/A7b.htm

6. Ibid. Hanjar means sword

7. Vincent, *Word Studies*, p.496, quoted from Thucy 1, 49.

8. Ibid., quoted from Illiad, X, p. 376.

Chapter 7: Christ's Trumpet Vengeances

1. Lightfoot, J.B., ed. and Translatorc, *Letter of the Smyrneans on the Martyrdom of Polycarp*,The *Apostolic Fathers*, vol. 3, Ignatius and Polycarp. Peabody: Hendrickson, 1989, 1st printed by Macmillan in 1889, p.481.

2. Water, M., *The New Encyclopedia of Christian Martyrs* , Alresford, Hampshire: John Hunt Publishers Ltd., 2001 p.132.

3. Alfred Edersheim, *The Temple*, Grand Rapids: Eerdmans, rep 1975, pp. 313, 314. Incense would have been carried in the right hand while the censer was carried in the left hand. In Herod's temple it was necessary for the high priest to rest the censer on a large "foundation stone" because there was no ark upon which to rest the censer.

4. Ibid.

5. Lightfoot, John, *A Commentary on the New Testament from the Talmud and Hebraica*, vol. 1 Matthew – 1 Corinthians, (Bellingham, WA: Logos Research Systems, Inc.), p. 15.

6. Ibid., p.16.

7. Josephus, F. & Whiston, W., *The Works of Josephus: Complete and Unabridged*, Peabody: Hendrickson, 1996. Ant. 2, p. 305.

CHAPTER 8: CHRIST'S TRUMPET WARNINGS

1. Josephus, F., & Whiston, W. *The Works of Josephus, Complete and Unabridged*, Peabody: Hendrickson, 1996. Ant. 2, p. 305.

2. Scott, B. The Feasts of Israel, Bellmawr, New Jersey: The Friends of Israel Gospel Ministry, Inc. 1997.

3. Mitch and Zhava Glaser, *The Fall Feasts of Israel*, (Chicago: Moody Press, 1987), p.41.

4. John Lightfoot, *Talmud and Hebraica*, Vol. 1: p. 5.

5. Alexander Roberts, Ante-*Nicene Fathers*, Irenaeus, Divine Institutes, Oak Harbor: Logos Research System, vol. 1: p.214.

CHAPTER 9: THE TWO WOES OF IRONIC JUSTICE

1. From: http://en.wikipedia.org/wiki/Thelyphonida

2. I Say this because of my own studies in Mysticism and New Age. See http:/www.apocalyptictremors.com

3. Fred Gettings, *Visions of the Occult*, London: Rider 1987), p. 62.

4. Ibid., p.64.

5. Ibid., p.146.

CHAPTER 10: WRATH OF SATAN

1. Roberts, A., Donaldson, J., & Coxe A. C., *The Ante-Nicene Fathers Vol. V, Translations of the writings of the Fathers down to A.D. 325*, Oak Harbor: Logos Research Systems, 1997, Hippolytus, *Appendix to the Works*, Vol. V: chapters 25-26, p.248.

2. Roberts, A., Donaldson, J., & Coxe, A. C., *The Ante-Nicene Fathers Vol. V*, Oak Harbor: Logos Research Systems, 1997, Hippolytus, Anti-Nicene Fathers, Vol. 5, part 2, *Treatise on Christ or Antichrist*, p. 215

3. Roberts, *Appendix to the Works*, 248.

4. Ibid. Ch. 23.

5. Roberts, Alexander. Ante-Nicene Fathers, Vol. VII, Victorianus, *Commentary on the Apocalypse*, p. 358.

6. Roberts, Treatise on Christ on Christ or Antichrist, 218.

7. Roberts, Alexander. Ante-Nicene Fathers, Vol. VII, Lactantius, *The Divine Institutes*, p.214.

8. Roberts Alexander, Ante-Nicene Fathers, Vol. V, Cyprian, *Epistles of Cyprian*, p.347.

9. Ibid. chapter 30, .250.

10. Roberts, Alexander. Ante-Nicene Fathers, Vol. V, Hippolytus, *Treatise on Christ and Antichrist*, p. 214.

Chapter 11: Reign of Antichrist

1. Abingdon Bible Dictionary, *Asura, and Bell and the Dragon*, ABS American Bible Society Electronic edition.

2. Strong, J. (1996). *The exhaustive concordance of the Bible: Showing every word of the text of the common English version of the canonical books, and every occurrence of each word in regular order.* (electronic ed.). Ontario: Woodside Bible Fellowship. Daniel 8:25, צרמי mirmah means deceit or craftiness.

3. Alexander Roberts, Ante-Nicene Fathers, Vol. I, Irenaeus, *Irenaeus Against Heresies*, book 5, chapter 28, p.557.

4. Alexander Roberts, Ante-Nicene Fathers, Vol. 1. Hippolytus, *Appendix to the Words of Hippolytus*, chapter 26, p. 249.

5. Irenaeus, *Irenaeus Against Heresies*, book 5, chapter 25, p.554.

6. Irenaeus, *Irenaeus Against Heresy*, book 5, chapter 28, p.557.

7. John Lightfoot, *A Commentary on the New Testament from the Talmud and Hebraica*, Matthew – Corinthians, Vol. 1, Place Names in the Gospels, p. 372.

8. *The Apocrypha: King James Version*, 1 Maccabees 8:6 (Bellingham WA: Logos Research Systems, Inc., (London: Oxford 1995).

9. Ibid.

10. Lactantius, Divine *Institutes*, bk. VII, *Of a Happy Life*, Chapter 15, p.212.

11. Flusser, D. (1988). *Judaism and the origins of Christianity.* (Jerusalem: The Magnes Press, p.396.

12. Riskin, Shlomo, *A Light unto the Nations*, Jerusalem Post, International Edition, December 11, 1993, p.23.

13. Lactantius, *The Divine Institutes* by, book 7, chapter 17, p.214.

14. Will Durant, *The Story of Civilization*, The Life of Greece, (New York, Simon & Schuster, 1939, p.573.

15. 1 Maccabees 1:30

16. Strong, J. (1996). #2048. (electronic ed.). Ontario: Woodside Bible Fellowship. Desolation means to make dry, make a desert - Abomination of desolation.

17. Durant, *The Life of Greece*, p.581.

18. Josephus, *The Jewish War*, Ed. Gaalya Cornfeld, Grand Rapids: Zondervan, 1982, pp.13-14.

19. 1 Maccabees 1:60-64.

20. Merrill C. Tenney, *New Testament Times*, Grand Rapids: Eerdmans, c1965, p.33.

21. Hippolytus, *Treatise on Christ and Antichrist*, p.214, paragraph p.49.

22. Roberts, A., Donaldson, J., & Coxe, A. C. *The Ante-Nicene Fathers* Vol. VII : Oak Harbor: Logos Research Systems. Lactantius, Divine *Institutes*, 1997, p. 214.

23. Myers, A. C. *The Eerdmans Bible Dictionary* . Grand Rapids, Mich.: Eerdmans 1089., p. 1089.

24. Hippolytus, Treatise *on Christ and Antichrist*, p.214.

25. 1 Maccabees 1:41

26. Durant, *The Life of Greece*, p. 573.

27. Durant, *The Life of Greece*, p. 574.

28. Ibid. p. 582.

29. Ibid.

30. Tan, P. L. (1996, c1979). *Encyclopedia of 7700 illustrations*, Garland TX: Bible Communications, #204.

31. Irenaeus, Irenaeus Against Heresy, p. 557.

32. Durant, *The Story of Civilization*, vol. 2, The *Life of Greece*, p. 574.

33. Hippolytus, *Treatise on Christ and Antichrist*, According to the Maccabees, p. 214.

34. 2 Maccabees 9:12.

35. Ginzberg, L., Szold, H., & Radin, P., *Legends of the Jews* 2nd Ed., Philadelphia: Jewish Publication Society, 2003, p. 983.

36. Hippolytus, *Appendix to the Works of Hippolytus*, chapter 19, p. 247.

37. Hippolytus, *Treatise on Christ and Antichrist*, Deuteronomy 33:22, v14, p. 207.

38. Irenaeus, *Irenaeus Against Heresies*, p.559.

39. Enc. Judaica, Ed., p.259. BR 98.14 and 99.11; Tan. Wa-Yehi 12; Shitah Hadashah 11, where it is stated that the Messiah was a Danite on his maternal side; this view is very likely related to the one found in early Christian authors about the Danite descent of the anti-Christ; comp. Irenaeus, V, 30, Hippolytus, De Consum. Mundi 19, and Bousset, Antichrist, Index, s. v. "Dan"; Yelammedenu 36 Targumim Gen. 49:16–18. See Chapter 12: Christ's Trumpet Protections

40. Ginzberg, L., Szold, H., & Radin, P. *Legends of the Jews* (2nd Ed.). Philadelphia: Jewish Publication Society, 2003.

41. Yohannes Zeleke, *The Story of the Ethiopian Jews* From: http://www.binacf.org/files/The%20Story%20of%20the%20Ethiopian%20Jews.pdf

Chapter 13: The Harvest Rapture

1. Kasdan, B. (2007). *God's appointed Times* : A practical guide for understanding and celebrating the Biblical holidays ,2nd ed., Clarksville, MD: Messianic Jewish Publishers p.65.

2. D.A. Miller, Forbidden *Knowledge*, SanJuan, Capistrano: Joy Publishing, 1991, p. 84.

Chapter 14: Prelude to the Day of the Lord

1. Kittel, G., Friedrich, G., & Bromiley, G. W. *Theological Dictionary of the New Testament* Grand Rapids, MI: W.B. Eerdmans, Single volume, CD Word Library, Inc. Dallas Theological Seminary, 1995, p. 286-287.

2. Zodhiates, S. (1998). *Sermon Starters: Volumes 1-4.* Chattanooga, TN: AMG Publishers.

3. Kittel, *Theological Dictionary of the New Testament*, vol. 3, p.167.

4. Ibid. p. 168.

5. Kittel, *Theological Dictionary of the N.T. CD Word.*

Chapter 15: The Great Day of God

1. Brickner, D., & Robinson, R., (2008). *Christ in the Feast of Pentecost*, Chicago, IL: Moody Publishers, p.30. Revelation 16:14, see also Zechariah 14:1-2, Ezekiel 13:5, Jeremiah 46:10

2. Ed. Merrill C. Tenney, *The Zondervan Pictorial Encyclopedia of the Bible*, Vol. 3, Hadad-rimmon by S. Barabas, (Grand Rapids: Zondervan, 1975,) p.7.

3. ABS, CD Library *Abingdon Bible Dictionary*, Baal.

4. Wood, D. R. W., & Marshall, I. H., *New Bible Dictionary*, 3rd ed. Leicester, England; Downers Grove, Ill.: Inter Varsity Press 1996, p. 548.

5. Ibid.

6. John Lightfoot, *A Commentary on the New Testament from the Talmud and Hebraica*, Vol. 1, Place Names in the Gospels, Chapter 16, p. 86.

7. Lightfoot, J., *A Commentary on the New Testament from the Talmud and Hebraica*,

Matthew-1 Corinthians: Volume 2, Matthew-Mark, Bellingham, WA: Logos Research Systems, Inc., 2010, p. 110.

8. Millstone Lyrics, http://www.sing365.com/music/lyric.nsf/Jesus-lyrics-Brand-New/0 2084A0E25B494F348257226000FA5D2

9. Babylon from Wikipedia, http://en.wikipedia.org/wiki/Babylon

10. Reported by Richard Owen in Rome, March 11, *2010, Chief exorcist Father Gabriele Amorth says Devil is in the Vatican* The Sunday Times From: http://www.timesonline.co.uk/tol/comment/faith/articel7056689.ece

11. From: http://www.suite101.com/content/cases-of-demonic-possession-soar-a71117, Emily Eppig, Sept 30, 2008.

12. BBC News, Thurs February 17, 2005. From http://news.bbc.co.uk/2/hi/europe/4272689.stm14.

13. From EndTimesSecrets.com. http://www.endtimessecrets.com/I_sit_as_queen_there_is_no_other.htm

14. Things they Don't Tell You About Christianity From: http://freetruth.50webs.org/A7b.htm.

15. Rome The Second Time, Saturday, June 27, 2009. From http://romethesecondtime.blogspot.com/

16. From http://fatherjoe.wordpress.com/instructions/debates/anti-catholicism/pope-john-paul-ii-kisses-the-koran/

CHAPTER 18: MARRIAGE BONDS

1. A bill of divorcement was called a bill of apostasy, Βιβλιϖον αφποστασιου

2. αφρπαφασοϖμεθα from the root harpadzo, αϑρπαϖζω

3. Gerhard Friedri chapter ed., *Theological Dictionary of the New Testament*. 1964-1976. Vols. 5-9, Vol. 10, p. 4. Compiled by Ronald Pitkin. G. Kittel, G. W. Bromiley & G. Friedrich, Ed., Theological Dictionary of the New Testament, (Eerdmans: Grand Rapids, MI, 1986), Vol. I, p. 472.

CHAPTER 19: FALSE GLIMPSES OF A RAPTURE

1. Lehman Strauss, *Revelation*, (Neptune: Loizeaux Brothers, 1964), p.127.

2. Harris, Ralph, Executive Editor, *The Complete Biblical Library*, Springfield: Missouri, volume on Revelation, Rev. 4:2, p.79.

Chapter 20: Day of Lord Vs. Day of Christ

1. Lactantius, Divine *Institutes*, p.215.

2. See also Zephaniah 2:4-6, Jeremiah 46:9, Jeremiah 50:4

Chapter 21: Why the Church goes Through Tribulation

1. Water, M., *The New Encyclopedia of Christian Martyrs*, Alresford, Hampshire: John Hunt Publishers Ltd., 2001, p. 96.

2. Water, M., *The Christian book of records*, Alresford, Hants, UK: John Hunt Pub., 2002, p.178.

3. Water, M., *The New Encyclopedia of Christian Martyrs*, Alresford, Hampshire: John Hunt Publishers Ltd., 2001, pp.231–232.

Footnotes for Appendix 1

1. Irenaeus Against Heresies, Chapter 28, Book 5.

2. The Divine Institutes, Bk. 7, Chapter 14 and 15.

3. Philip Schaff, Henry Wace. Ed., *Nicene and Post-Nicene Fathers of the Church*, vol. 4, *History of the Arians by Athenasius*, (Grand Rapids: Eerdmans, re. 1987) chapter 77, p. 299.

4. Ibid., *Treatises of Cyprian,*, treatise 11, chapter 1, p. 505.

5. Alexander Robert's, James Donaldson eds., *The Ante-Nicene Fathers*, Volume 5, Fathers of the Third Century, *The Extant Works and Fragments of Hippolytus*, by Hippolytus, Grand Rapids: Eerdmans, rep. 1986, part 2, verse 5, p.205.

6. Anti-Nicene Fathers, vol. 5, *The writing of the Fathers down to A.D. 325*, Fragments of Hippolytus, by Hyppolytus, Grand Rapids, Eerdmans, p.190.

7. *The Apostlic Fathers*, Vol. 1, Irenaeus Against Heresies, by Iranaeus, p. 558.

8. Lightfoot, *Apostolic Fathers*, Epistle of Barnabas 7:35.

9. Shepherd of Hermes 6:9.

10. Saint Augustine, *The City of God*, New York: the Modern Library, 1950, Book 18:53, p. 665.

11. Anti-Nicene Fathers, vol. 7, *Fathers of the Third and Fourth Centuries*, Commentary on the Apocalypse of the Blessed John, Chapter 12:2, p. 351.

12. Roberts, A., J. Donaldson, and A. C. Coxe.). *The Ante-Nicene Fathers Vol. III: Translations of the writings of the Fathers down to A.D. 325. Latin Christianity: Its Founder, Tertullian.* Oak Harbor: Logos Research Systems, 1997, p. 563.

13. Hyppolytus, *The Ante-Nicene Fathers*, Vol.5, Treatise on Christ And Antichrist, p. 206.

14. Lactantius, *The Ante-Nicene Fathers*, Vol.7, Divine Institutes, chap. 16, p. 213.

15. Hyppolytus, *The Ante-Nicene Fathers*, Vol. 5, Treatise on Christ and Antichrist, chap. 26, p.249.

16. Iranaeus, *The Anti-Nicene Fathers*, Vol. 1, Irenaeus Against Heresies, pp. 553, 558.

17. Ibid p558.

18. Hippolytus, Appendix *to the Words of Hippo*, chap. 34, p. 251.

19. Ibid. chap. 28., p. 249.

20. Ibid. p. 250.

21. Hippolytus, *Treatise on Christ and Antichrist*, p. 214.

22. Ibid.

23. Lactantius, *Divine Institutes*, Bk. 7, chap. 17, p. 214.

24. Victorianus, *Commentary on the Apocalypse*, chap. 5.13, p. 357, Taken from Daniel 11:45

25. Irenaeus, *Commentary on Apocalypse*, p. 355.

26. Roberts, A., Donaldson, J., & Coxe, A. C., The Ante-Nicene Fathers Vol. V., Oak Harbor: Logos Research Systems. The Extant Works and Fragments of Hippolytus, Part II, Treatise on Christ and the Antichrist, 1997, p. 207.